What's Law Got To Do With It?

What's Law Got To Do With It?

The Law, Specialized Courts
and Domestic Violence in Canada

Edited by
JANE URSEL
LESLIE M. TUTTY
and JANICE LEMAISTRE

RESOLVE

Cormorant Books

Canada Council
for the Arts
Conseil des Arts
du Canada

The publisher gratefully acknowledges the support of the
Canada Council for the Arts and the Ontario Arts Council
for its publishing program. We acknowledge the financial support
of the Government of Canada through the Book Publishing
Industry Development Program (BPIDP) for our publishing activities.

Printed and bound in Canada

LIBRARY AND ARCHIVES CANADA CATALOGUING IN PUBLICATION

What's law got to do with it?: the law, specialized courts and domestic
violence in Canada / edited by Jane Ursel, Leslie M. Tutty and Janice leMaistre.

Includes bibliographical references.
ISBN 978-1-897151-29-7

1. Family violence — Law and legislation — Canada. 2. Family violence — Canada.
I. Ursel, E. Jane II. Tutty, Leslie Maureen III. leMaistre, Janice

KE8925.W53 2008   345.71'02555   C2008-903725-1
KF9320.W43 2008

Cover design: Bryan Jay Ibeas
Cover image: Homefront #8 (encaustic on paper) © Teresa Posyniak.
Text design: Tannice Goddard, Soul Oasis Networking
Printer: Marquis Book Printing

CORMORANT BOOKS INC.
215 SPADINA AVENUE, STUDIO 230, TORONTO, ONTARIO, CANADA M5T 2C7
www.cormorantbooks.com

Contents

Foreword

Holly Johnson

The response of the criminal justice system toward domestic violence began a major transformation in the early 1980s. Starting with a directive from the federal Solicitor General to the RCMP, police forces across the country implemented "mandatory" or "zero tolerance" charging policies in cases of intimate partner violence. This was the first step in a series of policy changes designed to improve the response of the justice system to victims and those accused of domestic violence. Since that time, a succession of changes has taken place, which include specialized court processes, use of risk assessment tools by police and courts, civil legislation, sentencing changes that recognize domestic violence as an aggravating factor, a new law on criminal harassment (stalking) and restricted access to firearms for applicants with a history of domestic violence. Training for police and Crown prosecutors has also been put into place in many jurisdictions, and criminal justice agencies have developed collaborative partnerships with community agencies serving victims and perpetrators.

The initial impetus for these changes and others was the activism and lobbying by grassroots women's organizations who were the first to establish emergency shelters for abused women in the 1970s. Thanks largely to these groups, there is now a better understanding about the realities of domestic violence for victims and their families. For example, it is less common today to hear the question, Why don't abused women just leave? We now know that many victims face a complex reality: they typically have emotional and financial ties to the abuser; they share a home and often children. Custody and access issues are often intertwined with criminal justice issues. The woman may fear retaliation from the abuser if she goes outside the family for help. There may be strong pressure from family or friends to stay together, or religious or cultural reasons for keeping the abuse private. In some cases, abused women are unsure that what has happened to them is a matter for the police. Or, they may fear a negative response from police or the courts, especially if their cultural community has had poor relations with the justice system in the past.

Involving the justice system is one of many options abused women must consider in the aftermath of an assault, and the decision to call the police is not straightforward. It is usually made after many failed attempts to end the violence in other ways. A minority of women report partner violence to the police, even when they fear for their lives and even when the assaults have taken place over an extended period of time. Clearly, there are many dimensions to this decision, and it is not one that is taken lightly. This knowledge has helped inform training for criminal justice professionals and policies designed to encourage victims to report to police. Criminal justice agencies must continue to work to remove barriers to reporting and to develop appropriate responses to ensure the safety of women and their children.

It is now recognized that the justice system does not operate in isolation but is an important component in an effective societal response to domestic violence. First of all, the justice system is in a position to make a strong statement condemning domestic violence and reinforcing anti-violence norms. But the effectiveness of the justice system depends on many factors, some of which are outside its own mandate. For example, an effective justice system response depends on cases being taken seriously, adequate training for criminal justice officials, protection for victims, appropriate supports to enable victims to continue through the court process and holding perpetrators accountable through appropriate sentencing and treatment programs. Laws alone are not enough, nor can the criminal justice system alone meet the complex needs of victims for safety and justice.

The gains made by Canadian courts over the past decade in instituting specialized processes to better respond to the needs of victims and accused persons have been impressive. In addition, risk assessments tools are increasingly common and treatment programs for violent partners are growing. It is essential that these innovations go hand-in-hand with research and evaluation of their effectiveness. Evaluations to date show promising results with respect to expediting court appearances, expanding sentencing options, connecting victims to support services and reducing recidivism. An important research finding is that the justice system is more effective in responding to domestic violence if it is actively involved in strong interagency collaboration within the community. The experience of violent victimization by an intimate partner can be highly traumatizing: victims often feel bewildered and betrayed by what has happened to them and conflicted about the decisions confronting them. When victims are connected to specialized support services, they are less likely to withdraw and refuse to testify, factors which very often jeopardize the case against the accused.

Despite these impressive gains, legitimate concerns are also being raised about the potential for aggressive charging and prosecution policies to fail to serve the needs of victims in some cases. Once a call is made to the police, there is a danger that the abused woman will lose control over important decisions that affect her future. Research has shown that when abused women call the police for help, their motive is usually to receive protection and stop the violence. They are much less likely to call police because they want their partner to be arrested and, in fact, may recant when their decision to discontinue the case is overridden by inflexible justice system policies. Throughout the criminal justice process, the needs of victims and the objectives of the justice system often come into conflict: police and prosecutors tend to focus on arrest, conviction and sentencing — in other words, the outcome of the case — while victims are often more concerned about protection and procedural issues. In addition, victims' needs may change over time while the criminal justice system with its rigid goals and procedures may not be able to adapt to these changing needs. This often leads to frustration and loss of confidence on both sides.

Intimate partner violence continues to be a severely underreported crime and it is difficult to know the extent to which this reflects a lack of confidence in the justice system. In order to strive to improve the response to domestic violence, the justice system collectively must continue to critically examine its own processes and policies. This is essential so that victims who wish to see abusers charged and tried in criminal court will meet with professionals and protocols that take their case seriously and at the same time offer flexibility to arrive at the best possible outcome for them and their children. This means questioning whether evaluations are asking the right questions, such as: What do women need and want when they report to the police? Do their needs vary under different circumstances? Do existing policies and procedures make women safer and, if not, how can they be improved? Are women deterred from reporting because of concerns about criminal justice processes? Women encounter many barriers to reporting to the police and the justice system has a responsibility to ensure that fear of revictimization is not one of them. They must not be deterred from reporting by a fear of poor treatment or lack of input into decisions taken on their behalf.

An important objective of reform of the justice system with respect to domestic violence must be to develop structures and policies that respond to the different needs of victims. This is especially salient in Canada where police and court practices vary widely across jurisdictions. Rigorous evaluations are needed to identify best practices as well as to build on these to ensure that the justice system across Canada contributes to reducing domestic violence and that responses are based on sound evidence of what makes women's lives safer. This volume pulls together a fine collection of articles that shows Canadian governments and researchers have embarked on this important journey.

CHAPTER ONE

The Justice System Response to Domestic Violence: *Debates, Discussions and Dialogues*

Jane Ursel, Leslie M. Tutty and Janice leMaistre

> Josif Fekete ... had been separated from his wife, Betty, for about a year. They had an ongoing custody dispute over their three-year-old, Alex. Josif Fekete had the boy for a court-ordered visit Sunday, and brought him home about 6:30 p.m. When Betty Fekete came down from her third-floor apartment to pick him up, her husband pulled out a shotgun and killed her, his son and himself, police say.
>
> CBC News (September 29, 2003)

Josif Fekete's murders of Betty and Alex Fekete, and his subsequent suicide, happened in the context of a long-documented history of serious intimate partner violence in the city of Red Deer, Alberta. The family was well-known to the police, staff in the local transition house for abused women and representatives from the Child and Family Authority (child protection services). Yet, tragically, the interventions from these first-line response systems did not prevent their deaths.

The public outcry in response to such homicides is often the impetus to develop changes to the systems in the hope of better addressing the needs of victims and their children. The police and justice system response to domestic violence are central in providing safety not only through intervening but by holding offenders accountable for their criminal behaviour through the courts, correctional system and other judicial tools such as peace bonds. What do we know of the justice system response to domestic violence? How effectively do these responses protect victims and their families? What do we know of the efficacy of the new specialized domestic violence courts and revisions to the family court process to address custody and access in the context of domestic violence? These questions are the central focus of our book.

The first section of this chapter provides background about the Canadian context of intimate partner violence and its consequences. The major institutional responses and innovations to domestic violence are briefly outlined, followed by a more detailed description of the justice system response. The chapter concludes by providing an overview of the chapters presented in this volume, written by some of Canada's leading experts and researchers in domestic violence.

Domestic Violence in Canada

The serious nature of intimate partner violence and the harm to women and their children must be acknowledged (Statistics Canada, 2005a; Tutty & Goard, 2002). The costs to society for charging abusive partners and providing treatment in the hope of stopping domestic violence are substantial (Bowlus, McKenna, Day & Wright, 2003; Hankivsky & Greaves, 1995; Healey, Smith, & O'Sullivan, 1998).

The 2004 General Social Survey on Victimization (Statistics Canada, 2005a) estimated that 7% of Canadian women and 6% of men are the victims of an act of violence from an intimate partner over a five-year period. While the self-reported rates of abuse appear to be equal, abuse against women by male partners occurs more often and tends to result in more serious consequences, such as fear of death. In this national study, 44% of women reported being injured, compared to 19% of men: 13% versus 2% sought medical help. Women were almost twice as likely as men to report having been beaten (27% versus 15%), and three times more likely to report having been choked (25% versus 8%). Perhaps most informative is that women fear their partners' violence to a significantly greater extent: 34% of women compared to 10% of men admitted being afraid for their lives (Statistics Canada, 2005a). Nevertheless, while men are the primary perpetrators of serious violence against women partners (Johnson, 2006), women can both physically and emotionally abuse male partners and about 10% of arrests for spousal assault are against women as the sole perpetrator.

Further, lesbians and gay men can be assaulted by their intimate partners. The Canadian 2004 General Social Survey on Victimization reported that the rate of spousal violence among gays and lesbians was twice that of heterosexuals (15% as compared to 7%). Notably, however, while the rates of violence were committed against individuals who self-identified as gay or lesbian, the gender of the perpetrator was not clarified (Statistics Canada, 2005a).

The ultimate act of violence for abused women is the risk of them being murdered by their partners. The spousal homicide rates for Aboriginal women are eight times the rate for non-Aboriginal women (Statistics Canada Homicide Survey, cited in Johnson, 2006).

While spousal murders like the Fekete case are rare, they typically occur in the context of domestic violence. According to Beattie's (2005) analysis of 30 years of data from Canada's Homicide Survey, one in five solved homicides involve one partner murdering the other, whether married, common-law or boyfriends, current or ex-partners. Furthermore, over the past 30 years, Canadian women are four to five times more likely to be the victims of a spousal homicide than are men. When considering the pattern of spousal homicides-suicides, as in the Fekete case, over half (57%) of Canada's familial homicide-suicides involved spouses, the majority of which were committed by males (97%) (Aston & Pottie-Bunge, 2005).

Forms of Intimate Partner Violence

Domestic violence takes many forms and typically extends throughout the relationship. Intimate partner abuse is different from the marital disagreements that all couples experience. While the context of some initial violent acts may start as a couple's quarrel, it is typically about control or jealousy. Partner abuse is not about anger in reaction to a dispute but the intentional and instrumental use of power to control the woman's actions (Kimmel, 2002). The term "coercive control" (Stark, 2007) perhaps says it best.

The physical abuse of women by their partners often results in serious injuries and, for some, lifelong disabilities. Psychological abuse is always a factor when women are physically assaulted. The control and degradation of being emotionally abused by an intimate partner may have as strong or a stronger effect on a woman's self-esteem and thus on her ability to protect herself and her children (Dutton & Goodman, 2005). Psychological abuse entails making degrading comments and sexual slurs that target the most private and personal aspects of a woman's life. Further, partners often isolate and or alienate women from friends and family, acts that keep victims from accessing these supports that might allow them to escape the violence. Psychological abuse commonly includes threats to murder the woman, and sometimes her children, or for the man to commit suicide: threats that elevate the risk of harm to a new level and that must be taken seriously, especially if the partner possesses a weapon such as a firearm (Campbell, 1995; Tutty, 1999).

Some abusive intimate partners, mostly men, stalk or criminally harass their partners (AuCoin, 2005), typically, but not always, after they have ended the relationship. Stalking is persistent, malicious, unwanted surveillance and invasion of privacy that may include following, making numerous and unwanted phone calls and spreading false allegations. Estimates of the percentage of women victims of intimate partner violence that have been stalked are as high as 50% (Beattie, 2003; Mechanic, Weaver & Resick, 2000).

Pregnant women are abused to a disturbing extent, with estimates suggesting that one out of five pregnant women suffer abuse by their partners (Gazmararian, et al., 1996). Some women identify their first pregnancy as the beginning of the violence (Burch & Gallup, 2004) and abuse during pregnancy is often more serious than before (Martin et al., 2004). Chang, et al. (2005) recently identified abused women who were pregnant or in postpartum as especially vulnerable to injury-related deaths.

Women are commonly raped and/or sexually coerced by abusive partners (Bergen, 2004; Campbell & Soeken, 1999). Sexual assault may result in serious physical injuries. In the context of being in an ongoing intimate partner relationship, the assaults are likely repeated, rather than being a one-time traumatic event, as is more often the case in stranger or acquaintance rape.

In summary, intimate partner violence takes many forms and has the potential to injure and cause significant and long-lasting physical and emotional trauma. While not all of the above forms of abuse constitute criminal acts, the majority do, highlighting the necessity of a responsive justice system.

The Institutional Response to Intimate Partner Violence

Since Canadian society acknowledged that domestic violence is a serious social issue, a number of institutions have created policies or special services to more adequately address the problem. This section describes common institutional responses, including the development of shelters for abused women and making it easier to access health, and child welfare services.

Emergency shelters or transition houses are the one institutional response that developed exclusively to address the safety needs of abused women. A little over 30 years ago, Canada had no shelters specific to woman abuse. Today, the latest Transition House Survey, conducted in 2005–06 by Statistics Canada (Taylor-Butts, 2007), was sent to 553 shelters known to provide residential services for abused women. Canada's shelters are well used. In the year ending March 31, 2004, 105,700 women and children were admitted to these shelters. While a minority of these simply needed housing, most (over 74%) were leaving abusive homes. That so many women would need such services was inconceivable a mere quarter century ago.

Not all women leaving abusive relationships require shelter services. The 2004 General Social Survey (Statistics Canada, 2005a) reported that while 11% of women who had experienced spousal violence in the past five years had contacted a shelter, only about 6% to 8% actually used the residential service, still a large number of women as indicated by the Transition House Survey results noted previously. Emergency shelters not only provide refuge to abused women and their children for periods ranging from three to six weeks, but many offer crisis telephone lines, outreach (to women who may never need to reside in a shelter) and follow-up (to previous shelters residents) to address the ongoing challenges entailed in leaving abusive partners (Tutty, 2006).

Since physical injuries are a frequent result of intimate partner abuse, health initiatives include training physicians, nurses and dentists to screen patients for domestic violence, whether in the emergency room or clinic (Gutmanis et al., 2007; Thurston et al., in press). Public health nurses, who conduct home visits as part of their jobs, similarly often screen for abuse.

In 1998, Conti estimated that although fewer than 15% of abused women ever seek medical care, about three-quarters of women that do need medical attention use hospital emergency departments, often presenting with complaints that do not indicate abuse. Varcoe (2001) suggests that only 2% to 8% of trauma patients in emergency rooms are identified as abuse victims, even though research strategies and identification protocols identify abuse in approximately 30% of the same population. Further, women using emergency departments are unlikely to disclose abuse unless asked directly (Ramsden & Bonner, 2002), reinforcing the importance of universal screening.

Concern about children exposed to domestic violence has emerged as the significant problem of women being abused by intimate partners and has gained societal recognition (Weaver-Dunlop et al., 2006). The recent *Canadian Incidence Study of Reported Child Abuse and Neglect* noted that child welfare workers reported that the most common risk factor affecting mothers or other female caregivers in cases of substantiated child maltreatment was domestic violence: for 51% of victims, their mother or female caregiver was a victim of domestic violence (Trocmé et al., 2005).

Substantial differences are apparent in the child welfare response to children exposed to domestic violence across developed countries. In some provinces and countries, narrowly defined approaches have been adopted such that child protection services only become involved when children have been directly (physically) abused or when emotional harm to the children has been demonstrated. At the other end of the continuum are broad-based approaches in which any child exposed to domestic violence is deemed to be in need of protection (Jaffe, Crooks & Wolfe, 2003; Nixon et al., 2007).

In summary, the community response to intimate partner violence in Canada has created a substantial number of programs and services to assist victims of domestic violence to remain safe and, if possible, to decide to leave relationships in which they and their children have been abused. However, these agencies and services are but one aspect of Canada's response to such violence. Over the past 30 years, the justice system has evolved substantially in its approach to both prosecuting the accused and assisting victims.

The Justice System Response to Domestic Violence

Two major components of the justice system are involved in domestic violence cases. The first, and perhaps the best known, is the criminal justice system (CJS) that enforces and administers the Criminal Code of Canada. There is no separate domestic violence offence: abusers are subject to a variety of charges, from common assault to uttering threats to murder, that would apply to anyone regardless of the relationship between the victim and the perpetrator. Domestic violence cases are identified by the nature of the relationship between the victim and the accused and not by a particular charge. While the Criminal Code is under federal jurisdiction, its administration is a provincial/territorial responsibility, which is why different models of court specialization have evolved in different provinces.

One factor that makes domestic violence cases so challenging for the justice system is that when a person is charged with assault against his/her partner, the victim is usually needed as a witness. However, the victim is often ambivalent about providing evidence against her/his partner in court for a number of reasons, including his/her own safety (Ursel, 2002). The last important distinction with respect to the criminal justice system is that the burden of proof to determine a person's guilt is very high, "beyond a reasonable doubt." This means that without strong evidence, usually provided by the victim/witness, it is extremely difficult to obtain a conviction.

The second component of the justice system is "civil justice," which operates under a lower burden of proof "on the balance of probabilities" that sometimes makes it a more accessible system. Two aspects of the civil justice system that are involved in domestic violence cases are protection orders, granted by magistrates or judicial justices of the peace, and Family Courts, which may rule on divorce, custody and access cases in which domestic violence was a feature of the dissolving relationship. Each of these three areas of the justice system — criminal justice, protection orders and Family Court — will be explored in subsequent book sections. As an introduction, we briefly review the discussions and debates in the literature around the relative merits of these three areas of justice system intervention.

The Criminal Justice System

Intervention in domestic violence cases by the criminal justice system has generated a large volume of literature concerning its potential benefits and limitations. The debate is largely fuelled by two major groups: critics of the justice system who argue that criminalizing domestic violence does more harm than good, and reform advocates who maintain that the CJS has an important role to play in domestic violence but requires substantial reform to do so effectively. The one point about which the two perspectives converge is that the traditional justice system was not well equipped to respond fairly or effectively to domestic violence cases. Beyond this point, there is little consensus between the two groups.

The advocates of reform, who present analyses of four different models of court specialization in this book, maintain that meaningful changes in the justice system can make it more effective and that a more responsive system for adjudicating family violence matters. Advocates of reform acknowledge that the justice system cannot adequately address domestic violence cases on its own: a number of the CJS reforms are predicated on significant co-operation with and referrals to social services for victims and perpetrators. In contrast, the critics argue that no amount of tampering with the system can overcome its inherent patriarchal, race and class biases to make it an effective response to domestic violence cases. To consider this long-standing debate, let's begin at the point of consensus — what was wrong with the traditional justice response — and then venture into the points of dispute within the literature.

Problems with the Traditional Justice Response

As previously noted, critics and reform advocates alike agree that the traditional paradigm of criminal justice is ill equipped to respond to domestic violence cases for a number of reasons. First, the CJS "is organized around discrete incidents and official investment in incidents is shaped by their legal seriousness and probabilities of conviction ... but domestic violence typically involves multiple incidents, sometimes of escalating seriousness, with little physical evidence and few witnesses" (Worden, 2000, p. 233). Second, because of the adversarial nature of the criminal justice process, it is assumed that "both sides" are committed to winning "their case," that is the victim has the same interest as the Crown attorney in public conviction, punishment and rehabilitation. However, victims of domestic violence have diverse motivations for seeking CJS intervention (Ford & Regoli; 1993; Ursel, 1998b, 2002).

In addition, many victims face collateral legal issues such as divorce, custody and child support proceedings. In short, domestic violence cases typically involve a process rather than a discrete incident. They are complex and messy rather than being straightforward evidentiary matters. Third, there is a paradox within the CJS that is at once very powerful (at times a matter of life or death) and profoundly limited. At one point in time, a quick police response, a denied bail request or a jail sentence may be critical for preventing a domestic homicide; however, such outcomes cannot, in and of themselves, prevent the cycle of abuse.

Historically, measures of success within the CJS have been one-dimensional, focusing on "outcome" rather than "process," and mired within "single incident" frameworks. This approach encourages police officers, Crown attorneys and judges to view their roles as single, decisive interventions, much like a surgeon who quickly invades the body, cuts out the cancer and sews up the incision. This approach neglects the needs of family violence victims. For many, the roots of their victimization lie deep within their personal histories, their family histories and, certainly, our culture of violence. Survival and recovery are seldom "single-event" propositions. A single police response, court appearance and stay in a woman's shelter do not miraculously change the complex web of love, fear, dependency and intimidation that compose the fabric of abused women's lives.

In short, definitions of success and the culture of work within the CJS must change in order to provide justice for these women. If reform can change the goals of intervention from conviction (a one-dimensional outcome) to redressing dangerous power imbalances (a complex process of empowerment), then the CJS could possibly offer meaningful interventions to women at risk. The authors in Part 2 of this book explore whether the shift to specialized domestic violence courts in Manitoba, Ontario, Alberta and the Yukon are introducing reforms that address these concerns.

Debates on the Criminal Justice Response to Domestic Violence

We will briefly review the major criticism of the CJS, with an emphasis on the Canadian literature, as well as the three aspects of the CJS most usually held up to criticism: policing, courts and corrections. Since the early 1980s, police departments across North America have adopted more rigorous arrest policies for domestic violence cases (Buzawa & Buzawa, 2003). These pro-arrest policies limit police discretion, giving clear direction to their officers that if there are "reasonable and probable grounds" that a crime occurred, that they should lay criminal charges. This move was in response to concerns expressed by women's organizations that police were not taking women's calls for help seriously and were not making arrests when there was evidence that a crime had occurred (Pedlar, 1991; McGillivray & Comaskey, 1999; Bonnycastle & Rigakos, 1998).

Critics of the CJS raise the concern that mandatory arrest policies overcriminalize certain categories of the population, as a result of class and ethnic biases within police services. Canadian sociologist Laureen Snider (1998) states, "Lower income, visible minority and Aboriginal women have paid a heavy price for mandatory criminalization. It is primarily their communities ... that are targeted for enhanced surveillance" (p. 146). Other Canadian criminologists maintain that involving police and the justice system makes the problem worse rather than better, as women then become subject to a large "patriarchal" justice system (Currie, 1990). Finally, Comack and Balfour (2004) suggest that mandatory arrest policies lead to widespread dual arrests, whereby the victim who calls for help ends up being charged because of false allegations from her abusive partner.

These are serious criticisms and must be considered in assessing the ramifications of domestic violence policies within the justice system. First, the evidence that low-income and Aboriginal people are overrepresented in arrest statistics is clear in the chapters in this book that report on class and ethnicity. However, before we conclude that this overrepresentation is a product of bias we must consider who makes the calls to the police and why they do so. In chapters 4 and 5, the authors report that it is the victim herself who calls the police in the overwhelming majority of cases. The violence against women survey concluded that a woman's "decision to involve police is related to the severity of the violence and whether children were involved ... A woman is three times as likely to call the police if she had children who witnessed the violence, four times as likely if she is injured and five times as likely if she fears her life is in danger" (Johnson, 1996, p. 142–143).

If it is the victim that calls the police, how do we explain the over-representation in arrests of persons of lower income or particular ethnicity? The police data in Winnipeg consistently show that the two districts in the city that receive the most number of "domestic" calls are characterized as low-income districts with a high proportion of Aboriginal residents. Two factors may explain this pattern. First, national victimization studies in Canada have consistently revealed that Aboriginal women are three times more likely to suffer abuse than non-Aboriginal women. Further, according to the 2004 Canadian General Social Survey, Aboriginal women are more likely to call the police than non-Aboriginal women (Johnson, 2006). Thus, their overrepresentation in calls to police may reflect the very real risks they face in their lives, rather than arbitrary oversurveillance as Snider argues.

Secondly, women with low incomes are also overrepresented in calls to the police (Ursel, 2006). This fact may reflect the reality that poorer women often do not have a range of options to protect themselves. Women from more affluent neighbourhoods conceivably have more resources to protect themselves than women with little income. This pattern is also evident in the socio-economic characteristics of individuals who use shelters for abused women. National studies (Tutty, 2006) and local statistics reveal that low-income women disproportionately use shelters and other "free" services provided by the community. Police are a free service, one that operates 24 hours a day. Thus it may not be surprising that a disproportionate number of individuals at high risk and who have limited resources may call the police when they fear for their lives or the lives of their children. Given that the police are often their only resource for protection, limiting or removing that support would result in placing the lives of many more women at risk, particularly low-income or Aboriginal women. The statistics on prior arrest for crimes of violence among the accused who appear before specialized family violence courts (Ursel & Hagyard, chapter 5; Tutty, McNichol & Christensen, chapter 7, both in this volume) suggest that the women who called the police had substantive reasons to fear for their safety.

The other concern about mandatory arrest policies articulated by Comack, Chopyk and Wood (2000) is that they lead to a high number of dual arrests. "A persistent problem with zero-tolerance protocols has been counter-charges or double charging of women who have turned to the criminal justice system for protection from an abusive partner" (Comack & Balfour, 2004, p. 156). While this is of great concern to all women's advocates, little research has focused on this issue. Ursel and Hagyard's chapter on the Winnipeg specialized court presents "before and after" data on the impact of mandatory charging that indicates an initial small increase in dual arrests following the charge policy. However, the incidence of dual arrests is low relative to the total number of arrests, data which are supported by the Calgary study as well (Tutty, McNichol & Christensen, chapter 7 in this volume). Overall, before mandatory arrest policies were introduced in Winnipeg, police arrested a single accused in 94% of the households to which they had been called, with 6% resulting in a dual arrest. After mandatory arrest polices in 1993, the number of dual arrests rose to 9% over several years and then dropped to 7% in 2003. Women's advocates supporting CJS intervention have lobbied police services to introduce training for the officers to determine who is the primary or dominant aggressor in order to decrease the number of inappropriate dual arrests. This training appears to have led to a decline in dual arrests in Winnipeg.

The critics of the CJS have tended to focus on the policing component; however, some express concerns about how courts and corrections influence cases of domestic violence. The nature of these criticisms are threefold: first, the legal system is patriarchal and, therefore, offers no real opportunities to empower women; second, sentencing is punitive and will only result in eventually releasing offenders who are even angrier and more likely to reoffend; and third, involvement of the criminal justice system redirects public expenditure into the courts and prisons and away from social services that could be of real benefit to victims and their children and to the perpetrators (Currie, 1990; Snider, 1998).

The first two criticisms are concerns that the creation of specialized courts are designed to address. Advocates of reform and critics both share the concern that traditional courts were neither effective at considering victims' needs and interests, nor at holding offenders accountable and providing substantive opportunities to change their behaviour. To address the first two concerns, the chapters on specialized criminal courts in Ontario, Manitoba, Alberta and the Yukon consider the extent to which these courts respect the circumstances of the victims and provide effective intervention programs for offenders. We present these studies and leave it to the reader to decide.

The final concern, regarding redirecting social expenditures to the justice system from the social service system, does not appear to be borne out in the jurisdictions that have specialized courts. One of the first consequences of specialization is the expansion of victim services both within the government and among non-governmental agencies to respond to the support needs of victims and the treatment needs of offenders. A Manitoba study indicates that from 1983 to 1990, the period in which CJS involvement was introduced in Manitoba (see chapter 5), funding to women's agencies increased from $0.50 per capita to $4 per capita (Ursel, 1991, p. 282). Since 1990, the funds for women's agencies have increased to over $10 per capita. Thus, engaging the CJS in better addressing domestic violence cases has effectively raised the profile of spousal abuse in Manitoba and resulted in steady increases in funding to community agencies responding to the issue.

While there are differing perspectives on the costs and benefits of CJS intervention, everyone engaged in the debate agrees that domestic violence cases are serious and must receive a serious response. Our chapters on specialized courts add to this debate and discuss the extent to which CJS specialization can be an effective component in a broad range of necessary institutional and informal social responses to domestic violence.

The Civil Justice System

The two components of the civil justice system that directly address domestic violence matters are protection order legislation, available in some provinces and territories, and Family Court, which operates in all jurisdictions in Canada. The introduction of protection order legislation, which enables individuals at risk to apply for protection from an abusive partner, has generally been received by the community as a positive development. Unlike the issue of mandatory arrest, there is no body of literature that singles out the existence of a protection order option as a flawed initiative. Canadian studies indicate that applications for protection orders vary substantially across jurisdictions (Busby, Koshan & Wiegers, chapter 9 in this volume). In Canada the 2004 General Social Survey reported that 8% of female victims of violence and 12% of female victims of stalking sought restraining or protection orders (Johnson, 2006). However, studies in the United States indicate widespread use (Holt et al., 2002, 2003). The results of a national U.S. telephone survey indicated that 16% of sexual assault victims, 17% of physical assault victims and 37% of stalking victims obtained a temporary protective order against their abuser (Tjaden & Thoennes, 2000).

There is, however, a lively debate in the literature about how effective these orders are. Studies of re-abuse after receiving a protection order have indicated a range of re-offense rates from 12% (Carlson, Harris & Holden, 1999) to 23% (Holt et al., 2002) to 48% in a two-year follow-up study (Klein, 1996). In Canada, 25% of women with orders against a violent partner reported breaches, and 50% of women with orders against a stalker reported breaches (Johnson, 2006).

Others are concerned about how accessible these orders are. One U.S. study indicated that only 35% of the women who applied for protection orders were granted them. Laurie's (2006) study in Winnipeg identified that the rates for granting protection orders varied from year to year with a high of 65% and a low of 43%. Interestingly, studies on victim satisfaction with protection orders tend to report quite high levels (Kaci, 1994; Keilitz, Hannaford & Efkeman, 1997). Ptacek (1999) found that 62% of women with protection orders reported that their partners did violate the order; however, only 9% indicated that the breach resulted in physical assault. Women interviewed in Winnipeg indicated that if the violation was a phone call or a letter they often didn't bother contacting police. They seemed to expect some low-level violations until their partners "got the message" that they were serious; they were most likely to report to the police if the violation included a physical assault.

Because protection orders fall within provincial jurisdiction, the legislation differs from province to province. Six provinces and two territories in Canada have such legislation.[1] Busby, Koshan and Wiegers (chapter 9) and

Laurie (chapter 10) in this volume identify both the various protections offered under the legislation as available in Manitoba, Saskatchewan and Alberta and the decision-making process involved in determining eligibility for protection orders. Because the introduction of protection orders is relatively new in Canada, the research in this field is limited and the above chapters will make a substantial contribution to the field.

The final area of legal intervention to be discussed is Family Court. What factors must be considered in decisions about child access and custody in cases of divorce involving families with a history of domestic violence? The tragic murder of Alex and Betty Fekete and subsequent suicide of Josif Fekete cited at the beginning of this chapter underlines how critical decisions in Family Court are to the safety and well-being of women and children victims of domestic violence. Despite the fact that Betty's history of abuse was well-known to police, shelter staff and child welfare authorities, a Family Court judge ordered unsupervised visits for the father, Josif Fekete. It was in the exercise of this court-ordered right to visitation that the murder/suicide occurred.

There is growing concern that the emphasis on joint custody and the importance of children maintaining contact with both parents has overshadowed awareness of cases in which ongoing contact is dangerous (Tutty, Barlow & Weaver-Dunlop, 2007). In addition, until recently, so much attention has been paid to the criminal justice system and its impact on domestic violence that important decisions in Family Court have not received sufficient attention. There is, however, a growing literature in Canada addressing this issue (Neilson, 2004; Bala, 2004; Jaffe & Crooks, 2006). We are pleased to include the work of several of these Canadian researchers in our book.

Overview of the Book

The law is always controversial and in no area more so than domestic violence. To inform our understanding of "What's Law Got To Do With It?" we have compiled a number of very recent studies of the justice system's response to domestic violence in Canada. The book is divided into three sections. Part 1 presents the personal experience of the justice system from two very different perspectives. In chapter 2 we hear the voices and opinions of women whose partners were arrested for abusing them. Seventy-two women were interviewed about their experiences as wives and witnesses in the CJS. Chapter 3 recounts the unique experience of a woman who worked in a woman's shelter for 11 years and then became a Crown prosecutor in the Winnipeg Family Violence Court. She compares her experiences as a counsellor in the shelter with her experiences as a prosecutor and addresses the rewards and challenges of both jobs.

Part 2 focuses on the criminal court process and begins with an introduction to the criminal justice system, a discussion of different models of court specialization, and presents a comparative analysis of four courts in Western Canada. This comparative court study examines three specialized courts in Winnipeg, Calgary and Edmonton and the non-specialized court process in Regina. The authors identify the different choices made in each city about the administration of their courts and present the findings from these different models of justice.

The next four chapters in Part 2 present recent studies of court specialization in Manitoba, Ontario, Alberta and the Yukon. Each of the four chapters identifies the characteristics of the accused, the nature of the court process and the sentencing outcomes. The authors reflect on the unique approach of the specialized court in their jurisdiction and some of the outcomes that result from the different strategies of implementation.

Part 3 focuses on the civil justice system. In chapter 9, Busby, Koshan and Wiegers present an analysis of the different protection order legislation in Manitoba, Saskatchewan and Alberta, and the different remedies they provide. Chapter 10 examines the protection offered by the Manitoba legislation in cases of stalking. The author identifies the criteria for eligibility in circumstances of stalking, the challenges related to these criteria and the factors associated with an applicant's success in being granted a protection order. The final chapter on civil legislation, "Domestic Violence and Child Custody Disputes," raises some critical issues that arise in Family Courts across Canada. The authors call for a paradigm shift in the way in which Canadian courts currently respond to custody disputes involving allegations or histories of domestic violence.

Finally, chapter 12 summarizes the learnings gleaned from and the interconnections among the research studies, perspectives and experiences presented in each chapter. The authors conclude by identifying current challenges and offering practical suggestions about further reform within the justice system to better address the needs and problems faced by victims of domestic violence.

Notes

1   The Canadian jurisdictions that currently have "protection order legislation" are Saskatchewan (1995), Prince Edward Island (1996), Yukon (1999), Alberta (1999), Manitoba (1999), Nova Scotia (2003), the Northwest Territories (2005), Newfoundland and Labrador (2006).

PART I

The Experience
of Justice

CHAPTER TWO

Women's Views of Programs to Assist Them with the Justice System

Leslie M. Tutty, Deb George, Kendra Nixon and Carmen Gill

Women constitute the majority of victims of serious intimate partner violence (Johnson, 2006) and are most likely to call the police for assistance. Despite being the largest "consumers" of the criminal justice system with respect to intimate partner violence, the justice response to domestic violence has been of long-standing concern to those who work closely with abused women (Bennett, Goodman & Dutton, 1999; Crocker, 2005; Eraz & Belknap, 1998; Jordan, 2003; Tutty et al., 2001). While specialized domestic violence courts and other justice initiatives have been developed in Canada and across North America with the common goal of assisting victims' safety, what do we know of women's opinions of the efficacy of these innovations?

Women who have been assaulted by intimate partners have relatively little control once the justice system process has begun. They may call the police or not; decide to co-operate with the prosecution or recant or refuse to testify; submit a victim impact statement (which the judge might use or not) and attend court preparation programs or receive court advocacy, if available. They cannot, as many believe, lay charges against their abuser: this is at the discretion of the police if the evidence warrants charges. Once charges have been laid, victims typically become merely witnesses: decisions about whether to proceed to trial are the mandate of the Crown prosecutor's office. Finally, the disposition of any contested charges that go to trial is the responsibility of a judge or, less commonly, a jury.

Police services are typically the first justice system response to domestic assaults. In recent 2004 research that collected data on 24,000 spousal violence incidents reported to the police from many Canadian jurisdictions, 84% involved women victims (Ogrodnik, 2006). Appropriately, Canadian women who suffer severe violence from a partner are more likely to report such incidents to the police than those not as seriously affected by their partner's abuse. However, the majority of abused women do not contact the police for assistance. In a random sample of over 25,000 homes across Canada, the Statistics Canada General Social Survey of 2004 estimated that only 36% of women victims reported domestic violence to the police (Johnson, 2006, p. 55). A relatively high proportion of severely assaulted women choose not to involve the police: 62% of women who feared for their lives and 57% of women who were injured.

Some researchers have asked women for their impressions of police intervention. In several Canadian studies, women were generally satisfied with the actions of the police. In Grasely et al.'s 1999 research, almost one-third of the 74 victims who had police contact commented that the most helpful police actions were removing or charging their abusers. More than half (129) of 201 women who had contact with the police in Prairie Research Associate's 1996 Manitoba study were pleased both with the fact that charges had been laid and with the type of charges. Notably though, a minority (39 women) were not satisfied. Finally, and not surprisingly, Russell's 2002 British Columbia study concluded that victim satisfaction with police action was greater when the police acted according to victims' wishes: arresting the abuser when wished or not arresting when they simply wanted the offender talked to or removed. However, even if women initially opposed the arrest, many later conceded the benefits of the arrest process.

With respect to women's perceptions of the courts, a comprehensive British study by Dobash, Dobash, Cavanagh and Lewis (2000) concluded that victims had diverse wishes with respect to prosecution, which could change over time and according to the woman's circumstances. In several studies, what women most wanted from the court system was to prevent further violence (Ford, 1991; Holder & Mayo, 2003; Lewis et al., 2000).

Victims generally looked to the police for short-term protection and to the courts for a more long-term solution (Lewis et al., 2000).

Victims interviewed in several studies did not wish their partners prosecuted (40% of 74 victims) in Plecas et al.'s study in Abbotsford, BC (2000, cited in Brown, 2001; Hoyle & Sanders, 2001). In both MacLeod's 1987 Canadian research and Hoyle and Sanders' British research, most women preferred not to have long-term involvement with the legal system; they simply wished the violence to cease or to have their partner removed. In Roberts' 1996 Yukon study, many women victims did not believe that prosecution would not meet their needs; they wanted to be heard and to have the criminal justice system acknowledge the abuse.

In addition to the above research on victims' satisfaction with aspects of the justice process, involvement in the court system often presents multiple challenges to abused women. It is not uncommon for partners to attempt to coerce or persuade women to drop charges or to not co-operate with police (Ursel, 2002). Many cases do not proceed to court and, when they do, defence lawyers and others may treat women witnesses poorly. If women refuse to testify, sometimes because of threats from the abusers, they may be held in contempt of court and even jailed until they co-operate. Court preparation programs are one example of programs that have been developed to prepare and support women through the difficult court process, but research has not established whether these are helpful.

As noted above, a number of studies have focused on the effectiveness of the police and court system response to intimate partner violence. However, less is known about victims' perceptions and experiences with the justice system. In evaluating programs and approaches to domestic violence, an increasing emphasis on better outcomes for the victims is becoming apparent (Worden, 2000). As Lewis and colleagues noted in 2000, this is coupled with a growing belief that the justice system must respond to women's needs if it is to be effective in reducing domestic violence. As well, the justice system needs the active involvement of women in contacting the police and providing evidence. To be effective, the justice system must understand victims' experiences, including their motivations and the difficulties they face.

This chapter focuses on research with respect to women's perspectives about two programs developed to assist women after the police have laid charges against their spouses for intimate partner violence: Calgary's Home-Front domestic court caseworkers and the Domestic Violence Program offered through Family Service Regina.

Calgary's HomeFront specialized Domestic Violence Court (Tutty, McNichol & Christensen, chapter 7 in this volume) is a first-appearance court in which the accused appear shortly after having been charged by police. The HomeFront court caseworkers support victims with safety planning, understanding the court process and making referrals to legal and community resources. Victims are contacted by the court caseworkers within 24 hours of charges being laid, prior to the accused's first court appearance or as soon after as possible, to provide them updates and information about the accused person's case.

Family Service Regina's Domestic Violence Program assists victims of intimate partner violence with counselling and court preparation. It is a non-government, non-profit agency serving over 6,000 individuals and families every year. For victims of partner abuse, the agency offers safety planning, information, support and advocacy, referrals for practical and emotional needs, and help in dealing with the criminal justice system

The Research Participants

Overall, this research project entailed interviews with over 175 women from Calgary, Regina, Winnipeg, Saskatoon and Edmonton. The interviews inquired about the participants' responses to a broad range of issues connected with the justice and community response to domestic violence, including the police, the courts and other formal and informal services[1] (Tutty, Ursel et al., forthcoming). Included in the analysis for this chapter is a subset of 72 women whose partners had been involved with the criminal justice system and who received services from the HomeFront court caseworkers or staff from Family Service Regina's Domestic Violence Program: 42 from Calgary and 30 from Regina.

This section documents the demographic characteristics of participants and identifies any significant differences between women from the two cities. With respect to age, almost 60% of the women in Calgary and over 80% of the women in Regina were between 26 and 45 years old when interviewed (see Table 2.1).

Table 2.1: Age of Respondents

Age	Regina N = 30		Calgary N = 42		Total N = 72	
25 and less	2	6.7%	7	16.7%	9	12.5%
26 to 35	13	43.3%	14	33.3%	27	37.5%
36 to 45	12	40.0%	11	26.2%	23	31.9%
46 and above	3	10.0%	10	23.8%	13	18.1%

In both cities the women were primarily of Caucasian background with a small number from Aboriginal and other visible minority groups, including two women from Central or South America, one woman of Asian descent and three women from other visible minority groups (Table 2.2).

Table 2.2: Racial Background of Respondents

Racial Background	Regina N = 30		Calgary N = 42		Total N = 72	
Caucasian	22	73.3%	35	83.3%	57	79.2%
Aboriginal	5	16.7%	4	9.5%	9	12.5%
Other visible minority	3	10.0%	3	7.1%	6	8.3%

As shown in Table 2.3, there was a significant difference in the education levels of the respondents such that the women interviewed in Calgary had less formal education than those from Regina (chi-square = 16.0, p = .001, phi coefficient = .48, indicating a moderate to strong effect). However, no differences were found in employment status (Table 2.4).

Information with respect to the nature of the relationship when the couple was together is displayed in Table 2.5. There was a significant difference in the marital relationships such that women in Calgary were more likely to be living in common-law and boyfriend relationships than women in Regina, most of whom were married (chi-square = 9.5, p = .009, phi coefficient = .36, indicating a moderate relationship). The relationships were an average length of 6.9 years with a range of six months to 33 years.

Table 2.3: Education Levels of Respondents

Education	Regina N = 28		Calgary N = 41		Total N = 69	
Not completed high school	1	3.6%	17	41.5%	18	26.1%
Completed high school	9	32.1%	4	9.8%	13	18.8%
Some post-secondary (university or technical)	11	39.3%	8	19.5%	19	27.5%
Completed post-secondary (university or technical)	7	25.0%	12	29.3%	19	27.5%

Table 2.4: Employment Status of Respondents

Employment Status	Regina N = 27		Calgary N = 39		Total N = 66	
Full-time	15	55.6%	16	41.0%	31	47.0%
Part-time/Casual	4	14.8%	5	12.8%	9	13.6%
Not employed	5	18.5%	11	28.2%	16	24.2%
Sick leave/Disability	1	3.7%	7	17.9%	8	12.1%
Student	2	7.4%	0	0%	2	3.0%

Table 2.5: Relationship Status when with Abusive Partner

Maritial Status	Regina N = 30		Calgary N = 42		Total N = 72	
Married	23	76.7%	17	40.5%	40	55.6%
Common law	2	6.7%	10	23.8%	12	16.7%
Boyfriend	5	16.7%	15	35.7%	20	27.8%

When the women were interviewed, the majority (53 of 62 women or 85.5%) were no longer involved with their partners since the incident in which the police had laid charges. The fact that the majority of women willing to be interviewed were no longer in a relationship with their abusive partners is understandable, but nevertheless limits the extent to which the results can be applied to abused women in general. We can gauge some of the perceptions from the few women still involved with partners, but they might have vastly different perceptions of the justice response than other women who remain with partners.

Immediately after the last incident in which the police had been involved, 41 (of 62 or 66.1%) left the relationship. Twelve women (19.4%) had been separated from their partners when the assaultive incident occurred; another six women (9.7%) continued or resumed the relationship and three (4.8%) reconciled and broke up with their partners several times.

The racial background of the majority of the male partners was Caucasian (45 of 67 men or 67.2%) or Aboriginal (15 men or 22.4%) with seven men (10.4%) of visible minority status: three of Central/South American ancestry, two African-Canadians, one of Asian descent and one from Southeast Asia. One partner was a visitor to Canada, who no longer lived here, having returned to his homeland.

The employment rates of the male partners are similar to that of the women: full-time employment was 39.7% (23 of 58), part-time or seasonal employment was 12.1% (7 men), and 29.3% were unemployed (17 of 58). Six men (10.3%) were retired or semi-retired, two (3.4%) were not employed because of a disability and three were currently incarcerated (5.2%). The men's educational levels were as follows: not completed high school (22 of 62 or 35.5%); completed high school (33.9% or 21 of 62); some technical training or university courses (11 of 62 or 17.7%); completed technical school or university (8 or 12.9%).

To the extent that the women knew details of their partner's background, 44 of 57 (77.2%) of the men had a criminal record. The criminal records were commonly for assaults (17 of 42 men or 40.5%), theft/fraud (7 or 16.7%) or drugs (5 of 42 or 11.9%), and three men with assault plus theft (7.1%). Sixteen women were aware that their partner had assaulted an intimate partner in a previous relationship.

Nature of the Abuse

Table 2.6 provides information with respect to the nature of the abuse as described by the women respondents. Including the most current incident, the physical abuse was chronic in over half the relationships. This was more often the case in Regina than in Calgary, which is likely a reflection of the nature of the service being provided: Calgary is a first-appearance court while the program provided by Family Service Regina serves a wider range of clients. Focusing more on physical abuse rather than on psychological abuse is not intended to imply that the latter is not as difficult or as dangerous. However, the police are more likely to respond by laying charges when assaults are physical.

Table 2.6: Nature of the Abuse

Nature of the Abuse	Regina N = 30		Calgary N = 42		Total N = 72	
No physical	1	3.3%	1	2.4%	2	2.8%
Physical 1 or 2 times	6	20.0%	19	45.2%	25	34.7%
Physical 3 to 10 times	3	10.0%	7	16.7%	10	13.9%
Chronic physical	20	66.7%	15	35.7%	35	48.6%

The following quotes illustrate that threats and harassment create debilitating environments within relationships:

> Just before we came here, he started to get more aggressive: stabbing the walls, threatening to kill himself, mind games. The place we rented, he was on the lease. He knew I couldn't kick him out, and he played on that. I called the police a few times. [They] said there's nothing they could do. They told me, "The best thing you can do is look for shelter."

> There were days where he was calling me fifteen, sixteen times a day at work. Threatening, being really abusive and mean and ugly and I was a mess. He'd call me day, night and told me if I didn't answer the phone that he'd get fucking ugly. It was really, really derogatory, really mean, just filthy, beastly talk. That went on for a couple of months. It was out of control.

> I was held hostage in psychosis [partner's mental health issue]. I couldn't move off an 8 1/2 by 11 piece of paper that he put on the floor, in extreme control mode. I would think, I've got to get out of here but I was too frightened to call the police and pretty soon I started crying and he made me sit down, started ordering me around.

To provide a more in-depth sense of the abuse experienced by the women respondents, we present the following quotes that describe the nature of the violence. In all cases, the police laid charges.

> A nice man turned into a monster. Most of the men work on rigs and they do a lot of drinking and drugs and there's only a couple of women in the town, so they've all slept with those, so, there you go. [The abuse was] verbal first, and then physical. And jealousy ... The most serious [incident] he broke my hip, three pins in my hips and that's why we're not together. The police were involved before. He's been charged. Guess he just didn't learn his lesson the first time, the second time.

> The most serious incident was one night we were out. He had his semi-truck with him and there's a bunk on it. He wanted to stay in the bar and I didn't want to stay, so I was like "I'm going to lay down in the truck." And when I woke up he was hitting me and he had blackened my ears, there was blood coming out of my ears and, and he was choking me (pause). That, for me, was the most serious time.

> He confined me to a basement. Basically kept me away from my children for a month. Locked me in the house, unplugged the phone cord, the store was across the street. He would make sure that I stayed in the bedroom and everything was locked up. So he went to the store so I wouldn't leave.

> The most serious incident was probably the last one where he got mad at me over not wanting to make a job interview for him. He tried to strangle me and I broke away and he pulled my hair and he hit me and he split my lip open. He cut my arm open with his fingers, and when he split my lip open and blood started to come all over the place, he was shocked at what he had done. He quit and I ran and by the time I came back and he threatened me again if I ever did anything or if I ever left that he would kill me. I believed him.

Police Involvement

With respect to police involvement, of 61 women asked this question, the majority (96.7%) had previously called the police from one or two times (22 or 36.1%), to three to ten times (25 or 41.0%), to over ten times (11 or 18%). In several cases, neighbours had also phoned or the woman had asked friends to phone for her. But in each of these cases, the women had phoned more frequently than the neighbours.

The few women who had not previously involved the police cited several reasons for not doing so: they did not yet see the abuse as serious enough, had alternative strategies, feared repercussions from their partner if they called the police, or their partners prevented them from calling by using force.

With respect to the most current police involvement, the police laid charges in more than half the cases; a smaller proportion were dual charges. The majority of the accused were men but woman were solely charged in two cases and men and women were dually charged in eight cases, for a total of 14% of the total. Regina's respondents all had Family Service Regina's Domestic Violence Program to assist them with the court process. Therefore, none of these cases involved women being solely charged. All had circumstances in which the police either laid charges or assisted them in acquiring an emergency protection order.

Table 2.7: Police/Justice Response to Most Current Incident

Police Response	Regina N = 30		Calgary N = 42		Total N = 72	
Male charged	15	50.0%	37	88.1%	52	72.2%
Female charged	0	0%	2	4.8%	2	2.8%
Both charged	5	16.7%	3	7.1%	8	11.1%
Protection order	10	33.3%	0	0%	10	13.9%

While not all women were pleased with how the police responded during the most current police involvement (see Table 2.7), the majority believed that the police took their safety into consideration and another third did not agree that this was so. Nevertheless, of the women who were asked whether they would phone the police if the violence were to recur, three-quarters replied that they would.

Women's Contact with the HomeFront Domestic Court Caseworkers

In Calgary, after the police have laid assault charges, victims are contacted by the HomeFront domestic court caseworkers (DCCW) and offered assistance and information either in person in the first appearance courtroom or by telephone shortly after the police charges are laid. When these interviews were conducted from 2003 to 2004, this internal justice system response was specific to the accused appearing in the HomeFront first-appearance court. The victim's interaction with the court caseworkers, while often brief, enabled workers to determine their wishes with respect to the accused, make referrals to other community agencies and provide feedback to victims about how the plea court case was proceeding.

It is commonly acknowledged that after police involvement, not all women want their partners to go through the criminal justice system. Furthermore, the impact of their partner's "honeymoon" tactics and/or their intimidation often result in many victims not following through with justice system processes. Traditionally, however, victims have had little say in the system, except to refuse to co-operate or recant their testimony if the case proceeds to trial court.

In the HomeFront first-appearance court, however, the court team, with input from the HomeFront domestic court caseworkers, takes into account the victims' wishes about what happens with the charges. Of the 12 women who answered a question about whether they wanted the charges to proceed to court, two-thirds (9 women) did, while the remainder (3 women or 33%) wanted the charges dropped.

Of the 42 interviewees, 30 (71.4%) remembered having been involved with the HomeFront court caseworkers, while 4 women (9.5%) had no such contact (8 women did not specify contact or were unsure because of the number of calls from agencies such as Victim's Services and mandated perpetrator treatment agency partner checks). Of those who were not involved, one respondent clarified that she had no contact because she had no phone and would not open nor respond to the letters that were mailed to her.

Of 27 women who responded to the question about whether they found the HomeFront court caseworker helpful, over half (55.6% or 15 women) stated that they did, another 5 (18.5%) had mixed opinions and one-quarter (25.9% or 7 women) did not find the worker helpful.

The respondents were asked what aspects of their contact they found helpful or not helpful. Among the positive responses, most cited the information and/or the emotional support provided by the HomeFront staff. Fifteen women reported that the information provided by the caseworkers was invaluable:

> It was always the same lady that went with me. She would tell me ahead of time what was going to happen ... and more or less what I could ask for to the judge. What my rights were. Without her I wouldn't have known what was going on. I probably wouldn't have shown up.

> [*Did you find the domestic court caseworkers helpful?*] Yeah, they were. They took me to that little room and chatted with me and gave me pamphlets. I still have them in my purse. She [the worker] called me. She told me everything that was going on.

> She explained her role: she talks with the Crown prosecutor and lets them know my side. She would be phoning to let me know the outcome of the situation and she would be my representation personally. It felt very good actually (laughs). When she phoned me the day of the trial to let me know the outcome, she explained the peace bond and she explained it clearly to my mom.

> She called me. She explained everything that is gonna happen, that could happen. After, she phoned me to say, "He said he's 'not guilty.'" I said to her "I am very nervous, I don't know ..." She said, "Be calm. I am not a lawyer but we're gonna ..." I don't remember what else she said but everything is really comfortable. I feel secure. She was telling me every step.

> [*Did you find that involvement helpful?*] Oh absolutely. Just preparation of what to expect, that made me feel better, the not knowing is scary but when you know how it's gonna work, where do you sit,

> what do you do... So it was a great help, a great comfort. They gave me the tips, yeah, not look at him, keep your eyes you know, on us, no matter what they ask of you, if you need to say something look at the judge, 'cause the judge would ask me questions as well.

Of 19 women who were asked whether they found the domestic violence court caseworkers supportive, the majority (17 of 19 or 89.5%) stated that they did. Ten women who reported positive experiences with caseworkers described them as being emotionally supportive:

> [*In which way was she helpful to you?*] Emotionally ... [She was] very good at explaining everything to me and being there for me, she sat right beside me, she held my hand, she went for breaks with me.

> [*What did you think their role would be?*] Support, a supportive role. [*Did they fulfill this role?*] Yeah, even just beyond, I mean they took the time afterwards, "Do you want something to drink, to sit down?" asked me how I felt about the whole situation. It was great, it wasn't just like, "It's done, goodbye." They actually cared. It was a very good experience.

> They believed me ... They didn't doubt or question my integrity.

> [*Were you involved in the case?*] No, not really. If I'd wanted more, I could've had more, they offered me more. I didn't want it, I was quite happy with what I had. [*If you received information about the case, what kind?*] I received it from — victims advocate (DCCW) called me, Val from Court Prep called me when they found out, and the Victims Assistance unit called me.

However, one respondent who was pleased with the support also felt the need for more than was offered:

> I don't think there was enough contact. She would phone me and that was about it. It was helpful because he was lying to me about what went on and she phoned me and told me the truth. He was

getting mad because I knew the truth and he was hiding a lot of things. [*So, more involvement would've been helpful to you?*] Yeah.

Two women did not accept the services of the court caseworkers as they believed that they could deal with their situation alone:

[*Did you find their involvement helpful?*] Not really (laughs). They might be useful to other people, but I have to handle things myself, that's the only way I feel comfortable.

[*Was their involvement helpful?*] Not really. As I said to her, I already knew the steps. I felt that if I needed help, I would get help. I'm sorry to say it that way. Don't get me wrong, I think that she was trying to help. But, I've had counselling for this and I didn't want to make things worse than what they already were. [*So, if you wanted help then you would seek out the counsellor?*] Exactly.

Another woman commented that it was confusing because several agency representatives were contacting her:

Some other ladies were constantly phoning me up and asking if they could meet with me, so I went down. I had several of them calling me and getting me all mixed up and confused with who was involved with me and what was happening. [*Was that the Court Preparation Program, or was she through the HomeFront court?*] I'm not sure, they didn't really give me details as to where and how. [*Kind of confusing?*] Yeah.

One woman claimed that the caseworkers did not respond to her needs as a member of a minority group, but she did not elaborate on what these were. Another respondent stated that she was not really asked about her disability.

Fifteen women were asked whether the HomeFront court caseworker took their wishes into consideration. More than half (9 women or 60.0%) replied yes, 2 women (13.3%) were mixed and 4 (26.7%) said no. Unfortunately, most did not elaborate on their reasons for this perception. One who did not believe that this was the case, and had previously complained about not receiving up-to-date information on her partner, commented:

> I felt I had a right to know what was going on and, they made me feel totally useless. I'm really mad that they didn't tell me that there was court the day he got out, because I wanted my input on some of the things that I knew were going to happen and did, and I never got that chance.

Two women appreciated that the court caseworkers did take their wishes into consideration and stated:

> Yes, absolutely, absolutely. She even said to the judge, "Mrs. ____'s recommendations are..." So they took my recommendations and they did it.

> When I was informed that they were going to elevate the charges, I believe that they passed that information on to the Crown prosecutor.

Finally, of 18 women who were asked whether they believed that their safety was a priority for the HomeFront court caseworkers, the majority (16 of 18 women or 88.9%) stated that this was so. None provided further explanation. However, several who were not pleased with the caseworker's responses to them described the following:

> [*Was anybody giving you information about your case?*] Well, this one girl from the domestic court, I called her up, crying. I said, "Listen, I need to talk." She said, "Well, call a counsellor." [*The same woman was upset because she believed that the domestic violence court worker had contacted child welfare about her.*]

> I did go to a couple of hearings with [partner], and I had a couple of questions. They didn't have the time of day, didn't answer the questions, the answers that I was expecting anyway.

Several respondents complained that they were not kept up to date on the case as promised:

> They were supposed to inform me of what was going on. I had gone to [another province] for a funeral and they said, "He's been charged with___ and he'll be in the Remand Center for two weeks." So I thought, "Oh good." Because they have a system where if they've served time for something else they get off way sooner, he was off in three days. He had been out for three days before this woman called me, so that wasn't protecting me. I told her, "I need to know the minute he gets out. Please call me. If I'm not home, please leave a message on my answering machine." Well, he had been out harassing me and three days later I get this call from [the worker] saying he was out.

> She would never call me to let me know what was happening, so I just took it in my own hands to go to court myself to say, "Okay at least that way I'll know what's happening."

In summary, several respondents raised serious concerns such as not being provided up-to-date information about their partners as they had expected or having negative interactions with the HomeFront court case-workers that resulted in them not perceiving these staff as resources to help address their needs.

In general, however, the research respondents who were positive about the HomeFront caseworkers found the information and emotional support that they provided valuable. Without this input and contact, some would not have attended or testified throughout the court process.

Family Service Regina's Domestic Violence Program

In Regina, all domestic-related police reports (whether charges are laid or not) are forwarded to Family Service Regina for follow-up by their Domestic Violence Program. In some situations, domestic violence workers meet with victims immediately, either at the scene or at the police station. In general, contact is made as soon as possible after receiving the referrals in recognition that there is a period of time when victims are more likely to reap the benefits of supportive intervention.

Domestic violence workers complete risk assessments and develop comprehensive, practical safety plans with victims. Action is then taken to make the plans work. This might involve physically helping with moving households, providing transportation to shelters or safe places, arranging police escorts to retrieve personal belongings, assisting in obtaining emergency intervention orders or peace bonds, providing accompaniment to report incidents, advocating for funds needed to relocate, changing locks or obtaining a telephone, or making appropriate referrals that engage other needed community services that will maximize safety.

It is essential that basic needs — food, shelter, clothing, medical services and, for victims in fear of losing their children, legal advice — are met in a timely manner. Victims' current levels of resources and knowledge of workable strategies are assessed and assistance is given to connect victims with the community services able to provide for their basic needs. With safety and basic needs taken care of, victims are able to focus on meeting emotional needs. Domestic violence workers help victims identify their existing support network and, according to their expressed needs and comfort levels, decide upon referrals such as therapy or support groups.

The Domestic Violence Program includes a specialized victims services component that assists victims through the criminal justice process. This necessitates working closely with others in the criminal justice system in order to be effective as both a liaison and advocate for victims. On the practical side, domestic violence workers provide transportation and accompaniment for victims in their dealings with the Regina Police Service. These include delivering completed witness statements, attending follow-up interviews, having injuries photographed and reporting subsequent incidents of violence and breaches of protection orders.

The workers provide updates regarding the status of investigations and facilitate meetings with investigating officers. In high-risk situations, victims are updated with each court appearance. Court Services provides same-day information regarding the outcomes of show cause and bail hearings, which is necessary in order to adequately plan for the safety of victims and their children. In such cases, victims are encouraged to provide information at hearings, either on their own or through the domestic violence workers, concerning fears they have for their safety or the safety of their children and other loved ones. Upon release from police cells or by the court, copies of protection orders are obtained and passed on to victims. The details of the orders and the victims' roles and responsibilities in enhancing their effectiveness are explained. Along with other community agencies that work with victims of crime the Domestic Violence Program facilitates an adult victim/witness court orientation session that is offered monthly.

Family Service Regina's involvement with victims does not end with the sentencing of abusers. As a result of a policy concerning provincial corrections staff notifying victims who want information regarding specific applications and crucial dates related to incarcerated offenders, the Domestic Violence Program has become an important link between the Regina Correctional Centre and victims of domestic violence. This enables the agency to keep victims informed, to allow them input into vital decisions and to better plan for their safety. A similar, albeit less formal, working relationship has been established with Probation Services. Referrals to Correctional Service Canada allow victims to receive important information related to offenders serving time in federal institutions.

Women's Comments about Family Service Regina's Programs

All of the 30 interviewees had been involved with the Family Service Regina Domestic Violence Program, one in response to a previous incident, the rest regarding more recent events. The women commented most often about the supportive nature of the FSR domestic violence worker, the importance of having the processes of the justice system explained to them, court accompaniment, receiving information about the accused's court or prison status and the support groups offered by the agency.

Fourteen women mentioned the supportive nature of their contact with the FSR domestic violence worker, primarily describing their availability, willingness to provide information and referrals, and the extent to which they reached out to the women.

> [FSR worker] was the best thing that happened to me. She helped me tremendously. I don't know if people understand the brain-

washing process that goes on along with abuse, but they have a way of wheedling back into your life mentally and emotionally [and] you're not able to fight for yourself. All I had to do was tell [FSR worker], "This happened, what should I do?" and she was wonderful. Really good emotional support. I can't say enough great things about Family Services. Basically the only information I got was from Family Services. If I wouldn't have been involved with Family Services, I wouldn't have known what was going on.

The counsellor from FSR was always there for me, phoning, "Are you doing okay? How are things going?" She was just a godsend to me. I, I don't know where I would be without her.

They're just really good to have. At first I thought they were a pain in the ass. Like the first phone call, I thought, "Like what's it to you? What are you gonna do about it?" Then, later on when I spoke to [FSR worker] and she had called a couple of times, I thought, "Wow, this woman's really good." I didn't really understand her role but once I did, yeah, it was, she's great.

Absolutely. They never tired of a dumb question. They didn't give their opinions but they gave good information about how different services could match my different needs. I knew that if I ever called them up and I needed a shoulder to cry on, they would be there for me and if they could, they would come and see me or I would go and see them. I found that they were very firm in their boundaries in terms of safety and that was really helpful to me at that point.

In all honesty, I think she saved my life. Whatever I needed, she was there for, just really put a voice of rationality. She wasn't sympathetic but she was very empathetic, just kind of made me believe that, yeah, I have some flaws but they're nothing where my head should be put through a wall. I might be as bossy and you know a classic A-type personality (laughs) but that doesn't mean that I deserve to be half-strangled. She put a lot of things into perspective.

Fourteen women spoke about how helpful it was to have taken the court preparation course offered by FSR and to have the FSR worker accompany them to court or to the police to get an emergency intervention order.

> If it wasn't for her, I don't know where I'd be. She was very supportive and she went with me to the police station. If she hadn't gone down with me, I wouldn't have gone, I was so afraid. That was a big step for me and the fact that she went with me made all the difference. I still get the odd phone call from her. "How are things going?" So she's been really good.

> She was right there with me the whole time. When I testified she was there, she would walk me into court. His family are very aggressive, in-your-face people. His mother, his dad, they're all like that. They'd be sitting there, staring at me walking into the courtroom and she escorted me in and she escorted me out and she was just right there.

> Oh, excellent, excellent. [FSR worker] came to every court date with me. She would inform me, like there had been so many cancellations throughout the period, I mean you never know. [FSR worker] would call and let me know, "It's been cancelled ..." The second time, last year, I phoned Family Services. [FSR worker] is the one that I spoke to. Picked me up and we went to the police station together and took my statement. They set me up for photographs because, of course, I needed them.

> When that trial went through, I was upset and my ex and his girlfriend at the time, mocked me when they walked out of the courtroom. Really mocked me, like "Ha, ha, you lost, we won," and my worker just came out and said, "You know, the situation's already bad enough. Why don't you leave it alone?" She said that to all of them. She stepped up for my rights. She did everything that I needed and she was there for a shoulder to cry on whenever I needed to talk. I just had to pick up a phone or go down to the office or you know. I'm still in contact with her today.

> [FSR worker] let me know exactly when the court dates were if they
> got changed or when he was in jail, she let me know he was getting
> released early so warning [me to] keep an eye out.

Eight women commented on the importance of receiving information
about what had transpired in court or of letting them know that the perpetrator was being released from prison:

> She's been a godsend because they don't keep you informed of
> anything. You have no idea. [FSR worker] really helped me with
> that. Oh, wonderful. She has always kept me informed of court
> dates, cancellations, she's flagged warrants so we know when he
> was picked up. She has a lot of respect from the police, I believe,
> and the justice system and so they respond to her if she wants to
> know something. She's been there with me the whole way.

> [FSR worker] would call and let me know what happened each
> time [ex-boyfriend] went to court, each time that he postponed it
> or fired his lawyer. There was so many reasons that he kept putting
> it off. [FSR worker] was good. I was angry because "How can he get
> away with this? How can he keep putting it off?" I didn't think that
> was fair but [FSR worker] told me exactly what was going on when.

While five women respondents mentioned having been offered but
choosing not to attend the support groups for women victims of intimate
partner violence offered through the agency, another five women described
having been members of the groups and what they gained:

> They've been put me through an abuse group, where I learned how
> it was, you know, that I was better and what abuse was. Basically it's
> helped me out a great deal and I'm starting to get my confidence
> level and my self esteem back up. So they were very, very helpful.

> She encouraged me to come to the support group on Wednesday
> nights. I didn't find it super helpful because I found it pretty victim-
> orientated. I didn't feel ready at that time to share with a lot of people

I didn't know. The drop-in support groups through the day were more valuable because it was a learning system where the information came out and we processed it together. That group of people was a bit more constant. I felt I could share more with them and I found that approach of being able to respond to information, give it back to the leaders, test it out on them so that you could check out your thinking was really helpful.

The support group I attended for quite a while. I might even now go again.

Finally, nine women made comments about their experiences with the FSR Domestic Violence Program more generally.

Out of everybody I've had to deal with in all of the system here, they were the most helpful. They reached out. They let me know that they were there for a variety of things. I could always pick up the phone and talk to [FSR worker]. She always checked in with me. They're the ones who got the DVERS [Domestic Violence Emergency Response System] unit installed in my home, which finally let me sleep. They stuck with me through that.

I find Family Service Regina to be an excellent organization in meeting the needs. They've got many counsellors working with them, different programs in place. It is actually the exact same kind of centre that we ran up north and I know that it works. It's grass-roots. It's flexible enough because it's not government to respond to needs as they arise and to respond in creative ways. The domestic violence section of Family Services is really helpful, which is to me, number one: contacting people and supporting women who are at the bottom of the curve.

Excellent. They're the only ones that ever helped me. If it wasn't for [FSR worker], I wouldn't have known where to go. I still phone her. They were good to me. They found me a safe place to live and they phone me quite a bit. I still keep in contact with [FSR worker].

She does a lot. [*That's been three years now?*] Yeah, 'cause my ex-husband is still bothering me.

Summary

The two justice programs highlighted in this chapter have several major differences. HomeFront is an internal justice system response to assist victims through the accused person's first appearance in the HomeFront specialized domestic violence court. The domestic court caseworkers assess the victims' safety, present their wishes to the court team that debates the options for the accused in first-appearance court and provides victims with information about the process and outcome of the court proceedings. The contact is thus often relatively brief but concentrated on a critical period for many victims — after the police have laid charges through to the disposition in first-appearance court. In Calgary, this can lead to the charges of low-risk and first-time offenders being stayed with a peace bond with the condition of attending batterer treatment. Court preparation when the case proceeds to trial, longer-term counselling and support, and help acquiring restraining and emergency protection orders are typically referred to other agencies in the city.

In contrast, Family Service Regina's Domestic Violence Program is offered by an agency external to the justice system, but starting at the same point as the HomeFront workers. The reach of the program extends past the point at which cases are concluded in trial. The program is holistic, offering court support and preparation, assistance in acquiring emergency intervention orders, long-term counselling and support groups. The differences largely stem from the diverse court responses to domestic violence in the two cities.

Although the programs are distinct, we can make a number of preliminary conclusions based on the interviews with women involved with both the HomeFront domestic court caseworkers and Family Service Regina's Domestic Violence Program. Although not all the women were satisfied with the way the police had dealt with them, almost all valued the safety the police presence gave in the immediate crisis. In Calgary, the women received phone calls from many workers who offer assistance (HomeFront domestic court caseworkers, victims assistance workers and the three agencies that offer perpetrator treatment, which each conduct partner checks). Many of the women found this confusing. The fact that Regina's programs are largely offered under the umbrella of Family Service Regina is an advantage since many individuals do not follow through with external referrals.

Any specialized domestic violence programs that take women's perspectives into consideration and provide her with realistic expectations about what the justice system can accomplish are helpful. Women whose partners' cases proceed to trial are often subjected to unfair and questionable cross-examination from defence lawyers. Some of the judges' rulings indicated the need for specialized knowledge of the dynamics of intimate partner violence. In particular, custody and access issues are often intertwined with the criminal justice system and either exacerbate the violence or are ignored. In short, while specialized approaches make a difference for many women whose partners are charged, some women still fall through the cracks and are left vulnerable to abuse by their partners.

Most victims go through many phases while in an abusive or violent relationship. The common response to early abusive incidents is to deny the problem or minimize its significance. These coping mechanisms are typically reinforced by the abusers. For victims who grew up with abuse and violence, it is natural for them to deny and minimize the violence, as what is happening may seem normal. Once victims recognize the abuse to the point that denial is impossible, they often go through a phase of internalizing the blame. This, too, is reinforced by abusers who typically blame others for their abusive and violent behaviour. For many victims, even those who start out with healthy self-esteem, being abused instills doubts about their worthiness and abilities and slowly diminishes their hope that anything should or could be different. Low self-esteem, shame, fear and isolation make seeking help a difficult and courageous step.

While timely intervention does not guarantee that victims will not go back to abusive or violent relationships, those reconciling with partners will return with a safety plan in place, with the barriers of secrecy and isolation broken down, with the knowledge that there is someplace they can call for assistance and support, and with valuable information to help them look at their relationships more objectively and with less tolerance for abuse and violence. Although it is recognized that justice system interventions do not address all the needs of victims of domestic violence or the complicated dynamics present in violent relationships, justice system interventions do provide immediate, and sometimes longer-term, protection. More importantly, the justice system temporarily breaks the cycle of violence, creating a window of opportunity for victims to take advantage of the community supports that are available, such as those offered by Family Service Regina and HomeFront.

As a major institution, the justice system does more than control and punish; it reflects, shapes and reinforces society's attitudes. As such, justice system involvement has the potential to provide clear messages to both victims and abusers. Regardless of how well abuse has worked for them in the past, whether charges are laid or not, an appropriate justice system response makes it clear that society does not deny, minimize or normalize their abusive behaviour. For those abusers who believe it is their right to have power over, abuse and then blame their partners and other family members, the justice system has the potential of shifting the balance of power somewhat and making it clear to both victims and abusers that victims are not "less than" in the eyes of the law and the abuse and violence is not their fault; abusers are responsible for their behaviour and it is neither appropriate nor justified.

For victims whose fear has immobilized them, whose self-esteem has plummeted, whose decision-making ability has been eroded and who see few options and little hope, justice system involvement will offer validation and the opportunity for external supports to come into play. Victims will see that they do have options, there is hope and, most importantly, that they do not have to make difficult decisions or deal with their situation alone. So while a justice system response is essential on its own merits, its importance is greatly enhanced when criminal justice officials take advantage of the many opportunities for community support.

Notes

1   This Community University Research Alliance (CURA) project was funded by the Social Sciences and Humanities Research Council of Canada to compare the efficacy of the community and justice responses to woman abuse in the major cities in the three Prairie provinces.

CHAPTER THREE

From Shelter Worker to Crown Attorney: *One Woman's Journey*

Rekha Malaviya

Working in the field of domestic violence is very challenging. The hours are long and the stakes are very high — it involves the well-being of vulnerable women and children. Some cases are incredibly heartwarming and other cases are absolutely heartbreaking. Despite the challenges and frustrations, I have worked in this field for 18 years. I started in 1989 when I began my first job in a shelter. I worked at Osborne House, the second largest women's shelter in Canada, for ten and a half years. While working at Osborne House, I set out to learn as much as a layperson could about the justice system and how it worked. I have always been fascinated with the law. On my days off work, I used to spend mornings at the Law Courts Building just to watch court proceedings. I did this out of personal interest, but also because I thought I could help shelter clients better if I knew more about the justice system.

My impressions of the legal process, as a layperson, were not positive. I was amazed to see Crown attorneys with briefcases full of files for a morning in court, when it seemed to me that all that energy and focus should go into just one case at a time. I was coming from a job in which each client was given my full attention for as long as she needed it. I knew that as a shelter worker my role was very different from the Crown attorney's, but to see the prosecutor handling 80 files in one morning seemed untenable and unorganized to me. Little did I know, at the time, I was getting a glimpse of my future.

My journey from the shelter to the courtroom has been challenging, but the goal of empowering women has always been very meaningful and important to me. In some sense I never really left the shelter: in 2004 I became the chair of the board of Osborne House. I feel my life has come full circle, and I have the privilege of combining my two passions, law and service to my community. I'll begin the story of my journey at Osborne House, where I learned critical lessons about domestic violence from the women who sought refuge there.

The Osborne House Years

I began my job at Osborne House as a crisis intervention counsellor. Working on the crisis line was as rewarding as it was challenging. There was satisfaction in knowing that a woman who was reaching out for help could find support on the other end of the line. I could validate and normalize what she was feeling, increase her awareness of what her experience was about and try to play some small role in empowering her to make choices that would keep her safer. I could truly understand why she didn't feel she could leave the situation she was in or, if she had, why she felt she had to go back. Although it was never realistic to assume that we were all she needed, it was gratifying that when she did need us, we were there. She expected us to be able to do something for her and knew we were on her side.

The successes made the overwhelming nature of hearing the clients' stories worthwhile. I remember "Lindsay" who came to Osborne House repeatedly over the years. She was among the most seriously beaten down women I ever met — physically and emotionally. I remember an occasion when Lindsay called the crisis line and I could barely understand what she was saying. I asked her if she was injured and she said "no." Knowing her history, I asked her, more specifically, if any bones were broken. She said "yes," her jaw. Injury had become so normalized for Lindsay, so common, it didn't even seem to her worth mentioning.

She, understandably, had no self-esteem and no strength to leave once and for all, but she had amazing strength in what it took to survive. It was devastating to see her come in so regularly and always return to her husband. I often felt we were doing nothing to help, but she kept coming back. Then, one day, when she came into the shelter, she had a packed suitcase. I remember the counsellor who greeted her crying because she was so happy. Although Lindsay did once again return to her partner, she remained in the shelter a little longer. The suitcase was symbolic of a *huge* step she had taken towards emotionally letting go, just a little. The next time she came in, she came *before* he assaulted her. She always knew when it was about to happen and, for the first time, picked up the phone to let us know she was coming before she was hurt. Again, she went back, but what a massive leap forward! Lindsay's situation truly helped us understand how important it is that we be open to alternative ways of defining success: a lesson that became very important to me in my future as a Crown attorney.

Other experiences at Osborne House shaped how I viewed the dynamics of domestic violence and the consequences of it. I suspect that no other event during my time at Osborne House hit me as hard as Judith's murder. When I met Judith I understood that there are many types of abuse: psychological, physical, sexual, emotional, financial, and I thought I truly grasped all the potential consequences. However, I was to discover that I still had much to learn.

Judith came to Osborne House very early during my time as a counsellor. In 20-plus years of marriage, her husband, a respected businessman in his circles, had *never* laid a hand on her. The abuse and control she suffered was extreme but exclusively emotional and psychological. He repeatedly warned her that leaving was not an option and, that if she did, she would have to watch over her shoulder for the rest of her life, because he would disfigure her so that no other man would look at her. In talking to Judith, it was clear that she had very good reason to fear this was true. Still, she returned. I understand now as I did then that she needed to do so because there was safety in following his instructions and in being near him in order to gauge his attitudes and behaviours towards her.

Then one day he got physical, putting a headlock on their 16-year-old daughter. This was the one thing that Judith would not tolerate. Due to his threats, exceptionally extensive plans were put in place to obtain a new identity for Judith and relocate her to another province. She and her daughter did so and we all felt relieved, until July of 1991 when we heard he had murdered her. He had hired a private detective, and when Judith had been located, her husband waited outside of her apartment building, shot her and then killed himself.

Experiences like these have influenced me in indescribable ways, and shaped the way I worked with women in the shelter. They continue to influence the way I now work as a Crown attorney.

Making the Transition to Law

In 1997 I made the decision to go to law school. I continued to work at Osborne House on evening shifts and weekends and during the summer to finance my education. When I graduated I applied to article with the Manitoba Department of Justice. I learned, before my articling year ended, that I would be going directly into the Domestic Violence Unit (DVU) of prosecutions when I was admitted to the bar. I was ready ... I thought! I had learned so much about domestic violence during my years at Osborne House, but I soon discovered I still had *so* much to learn about the law. I was completely unprepared for the challenge of integrating my past life with my new role as Crown attorney.

One of the first things I had to learn was to change my language. When a criminal charge is laid, the person alleging the offence is a "complainant," not a "victim." It is up to the judge, not me, to determine whether someone is a victim. In law, a woman only becomes a victim when the alleged offender is convicted. I also learned that women no longer perceive my role as being one of a "helper." This has been a hard lesson and one I didn't want to learn. I'm not surprised by this anymore, but it still makes me sad. Often I am perceived as the enemy. I am frequently on the receiving end of a lot of anger from the friends and family of a complainant when I am not able to "put the guy away" and, at the same time, the target of the complainant's anger if I keep trying to pursue the prosecution. Although my priority is the same as it was at Osborne House (helping victims of violence), I am now the bad guy who never seems to do anything right.

Certainly there are complainants who appreciate our efforts and don't try to push us away. But often we have to work on behalf of women who do create barriers and are angry if we pursue a case. Having overcome my emotional reaction to being cast in the role of bad guy, I am now able to approach situations to minimize animosity. Thankfully, women like Lindsay and Judith taught me so much and I have learned to be patient and diligent and appreciate that success needs to be measured in terms of each woman's needs and capacities at a particular moment in time. Through Lindsay I learned that very small steps can be very far-reaching. Judith's life and death reinforced in such a tragic way the fact that we can never minimize abuse just because there are no physical injuries. Their lives remind me of the complex circumstances complainants face, of the importance of respecting their knowledge about their partner and finding respectful ways of handling cases to help women and their children to be safe.

I am forever grateful that I understand as much about domestic abuse as I do. I can keep telling women that assaults against them aren't their fault, aren't deserved, aren't provoked, aren't caused by alcohol. I can offer them support and direct them to resources. I can't, however, be their counsellor anymore and this was an extremely difficult thing to let go of. One of the biggest challenges I faced when I started in the DVU, was learning not to spend half an hour on the phone with each complainant. It's simply not possible — between the files that each of us has to review and the time we're out of the office and in court, our days are full to overflowing and the overtime never stops. This is one more reason why I'm grateful I know about the services available to women in my community. If I can't be a counsellor anymore, then at least I know how to connect the women to the necessary services in their community.

My Life as a Crown Attorney

Each of us in DVU usually has about 300 files assigned to us at any given time. This does not include circuit courts or in-custody matters that potentially could add another 300 files for review. Files are equal to incidents that lead to an arrest, not individuals. Often in nasty cases, an accused individual will generate four or five files (incidents) that can be disposed of in one court hearing. We are not exactly understaffed — there are 18 of us — but we all do feel overworked. When I started to experience this first-hand, I thought back to my criticisms of Crown attorneys when I was observing court as a layperson. Not surprisingly my outlook has entirely changed! Instead of disparaging my colleagues for having to manage briefcases full of files, I'm amazed at how well they do it. This is not to say that they do a haphazard job. On the contrary, Crown attorneys work *hard*. We can only keep up the high volume of files by being very organized. We take pride in our work and recognize the significance of it. While I've never been a nine-to-five sort of person, the hours we log in a day shock me. But we all do it, because it's important!

We also face challenges from our own colleagues who work in other areas of law. Some fellow prosecutors maintain that what we do in DVU is not "real law." In my humble opinion, our work is not only "real law" but additionally requires something far more. Not only are we Crown attorneys in DVU required to have an intimate understanding of the Criminal Code, the rules of evidence and the roles of the players within the system, but we must also recognize the humanness of the circumstances with which we are dealing and the longer-term repercussions of the choices we make. We must deal with emotions that rarely exist in any other prosecution and attend to them while still fulfilling our legal and ethical responsibilities. I've never come across a victim of a car theft who is torn about whether or not to proceed because the accused is the sole provider for a family. For the victims, car thieves are criminals; domestic abusers are parents and partners. In order to facilitate a positive outcome, we must remain sensitive to this emotional connection between the victim and the accused, and operate effectively within legal precedent and the rules of law.

Finally, the work itself is hard. When I moved from shelter work to becoming a Crown attorney, I wasn't prepared for the fact that in criminal proceedings we hear the "worst of the worst." I hadn't realized how overwhelming it would be to hear day after day about the awful things people do to one another. I certainly did have some sense of that working on the crisis line, but in the shelter there was less consistency and intensity to the awfulness, and so much more hope in between.

Different courtrooms deal with different stages of the legal process. Some courtrooms hear guilty pleas and conduct sentencings. Other courtrooms are set aside for trials, others do bail hearings. The worst weeks in our rotation through various court hearings are those in custody (bail) courts. For the most part, only those who have committed the most serious offences or have the most extreme criminal histories are detained (held in custody). In these cases they have to appear in bail court to apply for a release (bail) and a judge has to rule on the matter. For five straight days we have to read bail files — countless numbers of them — the worst of the worst. It is like being on the front line. This is why specialization is so important. We work with a team of 17 colleagues who have all done their rotation in bail court. They understand. We are a cohesive group and give each other a great deal of support, and we have an incredibly astute supervisor who understands the emotional toll and ensures we don't get that rotation too often.

A Prosecutor's Perspective on Mandatory Charging

When I moved from shelter work to prosecution, some of my attitudes towards social policy began to shift. As a shelter worker, my ideas of the benefits and pitfalls of mandatory charging were based on my conversations with women on the crisis line. Although I've always felt that there are advantages and disadvantages, I began to rethink the merits of this policy from my new perspective.

There has been much intense debate about whether the concept of "zero tolerance" exists in Manitoba, and, if so, whether or not it is a good thing. Some of this controversy seems to be a result of thinking that police don't need evidence to make an arrest. However, mandatory charging in Manitoba requires that there are reasonable and probable grounds to arrest. To some extent, the evidence required in addition to a complaint may be quite nebulous (this is the nature of domestic violence work). The evidence could be something as imprecise as the complainant's demeanour or as concrete as injuries or, in exceptional cases, the presence of witnesses.

A mandatory charging policy avoids putting victims of domestic violence in a position where they are forced to make a choice about pressing charges. It has historically been demonstrated that leaving the decision to the victim can create increased risk to his/her safety and can cause intense internal conflict because of the confusing and ambivalent feelings victims often have towards their violent partners. It can be critical in many circumstances that the victim is able to convey to the accused that a decision about charging or proceeding with prosecution is beyond their control. Complainants are frequently relieved to hear that they can honestly tell their partners that the choice is not theirs to make. Threats designed to make victims "drop the charges" have less weight when complainants are able to tell their partners they do not have that kind of control over the process. Particularly in cases where the victim prefers that the prosecution proceed, this knowledge can be extremely comforting.

It is often the case that the most vulnerable victims of domestic violence are the ones at the greatest risk of significant bodily harm or worse. That vulnerability is created and fostered in part by fear, isolation, lack of support and the beating down of a victim's self-esteem or trust in their ability to make decisions that will increase safety for them and their children. Some critics claim that mandatory charging policies are patronizing and disempowering. However, it is my experience that this policy may afford far greater protection for those who do not have the awareness or strength to remove themselves from very dangerous situations, but are willing to call 911 when incidents escalate. In such cases, law enforcement and, subsequently, prosecutions and the courts have critical roles to play not only to protect these individual victims and their children, but also to ensure that on a societal level the message is clear that domestic violence will not be tolerated.

If law enforcement policy encourages police to intervene, specialization of Crown attorneys, courts and corrections becomes crucial. When justice agencies become involved in the dynamics of domestic violence, the system must recognize the complexity and volatility of these cases. Anyone familiar with the havoc that domestic violence wreaks is aware that there are an enormous number of factors at play. All of the components of the justice system — the police, prosecutions, courts and corrections — must co-operate in order to provide effective interventions.

Notwithstanding my position that mandatory charging is a good thing, it has become apparent to me that, although such situations are rare, individuals will try to "use" the policy for malicious purposes. This includes abusers trying to use it as another weapon in their arsenal of abuse, which is another reason why specialization is beneficial. It is far easier to recognize a "fake" complaint when one is surrounded by the "authentic" ones.

It is very upsetting to know that the resources of police, Crowns and courts are being used for reasons other than those for which they were intended. It is frustrating because dealing with these situations requires us to take time and energy away from legitimate matters. Although these situations are relatively infrequent, they certainly do exist and we become a "tool" used by a vengeful partner to carry out a personal vendetta. We have a responsibility to do our best to weed out such files. It is, however, not always easy to recognize them and it is important that we not automatically set them aside at the risk of including genuine abuse in our filtering out.

Difficult Decisions: An Everyday Reality

Crown attorneys in DVU make difficult decisions everyday — often, many times each day. It is critical that we do so, however, only after being fully informed of all of the nuances of any given file. Decisions can include whether to proceed with a charge, what position to take on sentencing, whether to have a charge laid, whether to have a child witness interviewed, and so on. When I started out as a Crown attorney, I had no idea of the number and nature of the decisions I would need to make and of the complexities inherent in each case.

One of my colleagues was recently troubled by a file he had involving an adult victim who had experienced childhood sexual abuse by a family member. This victim had suffered emotionally immeasurably over the years and was feeling that she was finally at a place where she could put the abuse behind her and move forward with her life. Then she received a subpoena (summons to court) to testify against her abuser.

These cases are extremely challenging because of the intense human trauma, the timing of disclosures, the lack of corroborative evidence and all of the other factors we must consider. My colleague was noticeably upset and concerned about what action to take. The allegation was very serious; however, for evidentiary reasons, he believed that a conviction was possible but not highly likely. He was also concerned about the potential impact that testifying could have on the complainant. Should he have her testify and relive her experience only to find, in the end, that the accused was not found guilty? Or should he decide, before the trial date, not to proceed?

In consultation with the victim and her family, he chose the latter approach — a decision they all supported — but he was still very concerned about how she would cope with the lack of closure. In discussing resolution of the matter with all involved, he learned that what the victim wanted

— more than anything else — was an apology. She got it. Although the accused can hardly be said to have been held accountable in a court of law, he did read, in an interview room with only the lawyers and the parties present, an apology to this victim and to her family members. This veteran Crown shared that he had to choke back tears when a relative of the victim, leaving the room, thanked him and told him, "You've given her her life back." Whether this is a failure or a success depends entirely on how you measure it. If conviction is the measure of success, he failed. If the victim's best interest is the measure of success, I think he succeeded. There is a difference between a formal and an informal resolution. Sometimes an informal resolution is the best we can get ... and sometimes it is also the best resolution.

One of my earliest complex and serious cases involved a six-year-old victim named "Jamie." Certainly, I had learned by then how limited my role was, how little control I had over the outcome, and that it was not my place to "save" victims. Still, I was committed to seeing that justice was done and to ensuring that this little girl's experience with the system did not add to what she had already been through.

An extended family member had been charged with sexually abusing her over a period of time when she was four years old. Jamie had to testify at the trail and the accused was convicted. The Court of Appeal overturned the conviction based *strictly* on a legal technicality. It explicitly said that it wasn't that the Court didn't believe what she said, but that the judge had made an error in law that couldn't be overlooked. Recognizing that people, children in particular, are affected by the court process in any number of ways, Jamie seemed to have coped surprisingly well. It was not until after she'd testified that we learned that she had been throwing up after finishing in court.

All that stress, and the accused's conviction was not upheld! I had to determine whether to try the case again. Given how difficult this had been for Jamie, we — her parents and I — made a decision not to put her through it again. Hopefully, this little girl will *always* know she was believed, if not "in law," then by a number of people: by the Child Victim Support Services worker, by me, by the trial judge, maybe even by the Court of Appeal judges. One can only hope that will mean something to her some day.

Victim's Expectations and the Law

There are consequences to all of our decisions. We work hard to ensure that complainants are aware of the reasons for these decisions, particularly when the victim doesn't agree with the approach being taken. It would be exceptionally easy for us simply to insist that every case proceed to prosecution. We have, however, rules that we must follow, guidelines that we must heed and ramifications that we must consider.

In every case a Crown attorney is required to meet the standard of "a reasonable likelihood of conviction" in deciding to proceed with a prosecution. If it is our assessment that a case cannot meet that standard, we have an obligation to put an end to the matter. This standard is higher than that which guides the police (reasonable and probable grounds) and explains, to some degree, why we will stay proceedings (i.e., drop charges) in some cases where police choose to lay them. We measure "reasonable likelihood of conviction" based on the law and on our perceived ability to meet the ultimate test, which is whether we feel there is sufficient evidence to prove our case "beyond a reasonable doubt."

Domestic violence usually occurs behind closed doors and is often not witnessed by others. The case becomes one person's word against the other's. In these instances, the law in our country requires that if a judge feels it even possible that the accused's version of events *could* be true, the judge must acquit. That is an *incredibly* high standard. An abuser's denial of responsibility, self-righteousness and need to be "right" can be dangerously reinforced when he hears a judge say "not guilty." A victim who returns to such a relationship will incessantly be reminded that the complaint was found to be "untrue," that the abuser was "innocent," that the victim was "not believed." Is this a risk worth taking — is the trauma to the victim worthwhile — when the likelihood of conviction is reasonable or possible but slim?

What of situations in which children have witnessed the violence? Often police officers prefer not to obtain statements from children, not wanting them to feel they have to "take sides" or fearing that having to retell the tale will be traumatic. Sometimes, however, the children are the only "independent" witnesses to an assault. Providing their observations to the court has the potential to solidify our case. It becomes a matter of weighing the risk. How much consideration should be given to the potential message that children receive when other adults take them and the situation seriously? How do we weigh this against the trauma of testifying? Does this make involving them worthwhile?

The goal should be to stop the violence. At least as important should be ensuring that the victim is aware that help will be available if needed. Among my long list of fears is that a victim will choose on a future occasion not to call police because she has had such a terrible experience with the criminal justice system. If we push and pressure a woman into testifying, for example, despite her protestations, particularly if the end result is an acquittal, who are we helping? In such a case, even if the accused is convicted, what if she returns to him? The next time she may choose not to call 911 because of her alienation from the justice system, and she may be badly hurt or worse. How could we call that success? These are the difficult decisions we weigh everyday.

Who Defines Success?

One of my greatest pet peeves is hearing people complain that our system isn't working because we are not putting abusers in jail. It amazes me that this is the criteria so often used to determine whether we have been successful. The reality is, many different outcomes can be a success.

The traditional definition of success for a prosecutor is conviction. However, obtaining a conviction is highly dependent on the complainant's co-operation. All too often complainants are not prepared to testify. In some of these cases, typically with first-time offenders and a less serious charge, we can delay the case and bargain with the defence that if the accused will attend, participate in and complete an abusers' treatment group, we will drop the charges. We will pursue this option only if the victim agrees to it and if the accused attends one of the approved programs. We call this a delayed remand; in reality, it is a form of diversion. However, when the alternative is little likelihood of conviction, it seems like a very good solution. The victim gets what she wants: her partner receives treatment to stop the abusive behaviour. The accused has an opportunity to learn different choices to stop the abusive behaviour and has the added incentive to complete the program because dropped charges means no criminal record. The prosecutor gets what she/he wants if the treatment program is effective and we never see the couple again. This would not be a traditional concept of success for a prosecutor, but it is one of our measures of success in DVU. Sometimes our difficult decisions involve proceeding with a case against a victim's wishes. We don't do this easily or take the decision lightly, but sometimes the circumstances are so dangerous it would be socially and legally irresponsible not to prosecute. A recent case of mine comes to mind.

I was in the midst of a prosecution a short while ago in which 10 minutes prior to the start of the court hearing, the complainant quite willingly outlined the circumstances that gave rise to the charges. I have become very familiar with "Kim" and "Ron" over the years as Ron has a very lengthy history of violent behaviour (primarily towards Kim) and drug use. While Kim is normally very ambivalent in the weeks leading up to Ron's court appearance, in the end she is always co-operative and willing to reaffirm what has occurred.

On this particular occasion, the allegations were by far the most serious. Ron had assaulted Kim a week earlier and flashed a gun around in front of some acquaintances. A day or two later, he pointed the gun at her, shot a bullet into the doorframe not six inches from where she was standing and verbally threatened her. The police arrested him near her home with the loaded gun in his possession. The case went to trial.

Before the trial, I attempted to arrange meetings with Kim to review her testimony and the court process in greater detail, but she didn't respond to my calls. I finally saw her the morning the trial began, and her openness in sharing the details of the incident left me with every confidence that all would be well once in the courtroom. I was absolutely overcome with shock when, between the time of our meeting and her attendance in court 10 minutes later, she suddenly "forgot" everything that had occurred and said it was all a blur.

I can understand why: fear, love, concern that her children would be taken away if the truth came out and so on. My understanding, however, left me no less frustrated. The allegations were among the most serious I encountered. This was a very dangerous man. Thankfully, I had some recourse. The police officers investigating this matter were extremely diligent and thorough. It is very significant that when they obtained a statement from Kim, they videotaped it and ensured that, prior to providing it, she had sworn an oath on video to tell the truth. Due to changes in the law (notwithstanding Kim's complete unwillingness to co-operate on the stand), I was able to put the facts before the court through the videotaped statement. As a result, the accused faces the prospect of many years of incarceration.

My former "shelter self" thinks how disempowering and patronizing of me to have decided that I would protect Kim from the accused and interfere with the choice she was making. What a contradiction between what I learned working in a women's shelter and the nature of my job today. My priority was Kim, and I believe I did the right thing ... though, if I'm being honest, I have to admit I also had a disturbing thought in the back of my mind: *What will I say at the inquest?*

We Can't Do It Alone

We have two sizable shelters for abused women and their children within the city and eight others throughout the province. There are numerous programs and services available with mandates specific to domestic violence. While I would never suggest that we have all that we need, especially in rural and First Nations communities, Manitoba has come a long way in establishing a wide variety of resources for victims of domestic violence and for their partners.

We have a *joint* responsibility — those in the criminal justice system *and* those in social services — to work together to ensure that justice is done and that victims are safe. This is particularly true in high-risk situations. When women have a history of abuse they often have numerous agencies involved in their lives. These agencies really need to learn to work together.

While working at Osborne House, I met "Bev," who was being stalked by her partner. Not only was our shelter involved with Bev, so was Child and Family Services, which was monitoring the needs and safety of the children; a probation officer who had been assigned to supervise the offending partner; and the police, who had been called on numerous occasions, were aware of the situation, as were various Crown attorneys who'd prosecuted the numerous charges against her partner. Yet at no time had all of these involved parties come together. It appeared that not one of the agencies was truly aware of the threat this individual posed to Bev.

He was charming, as so many abusers can be. I mean no offence whatsoever when I say that the probation officer had been completely taken in by him and had absolutely *no* idea of the history of this relationship. This was to be expected, as the only information the probation officer would have received was that relating specifically to incidents for which the offender had been convicted and whatever version of the story the offender provided to him. Any other history, including threats which couldn't be proven in a court of law and behaviours which were abusive but not "criminal," would not have been known to him. Numerous police officers were aware of bits and pieces but police resources were such that a dedicated group of officers could simply not be assigned to the file.

It took hours to coordinate a meeting with all of the people involved. Bev was quite willing to provide her consent to have the information shared between agencies. It was only through that meeting that we were able to ensure that *everyone* had all of the relevant information. I will never forget the look on the probation officer's face when he recognized how he had been manipulated. Through this sharing of information and a commitment to continue, we were able to formulate a protection plan with Bev, which ultimately ensured her safety. It shouldn't have been that difficult.

I'd like to think this is changing. I have recently had the opportunity to attend COHROU meetings. COHROU is the Criminal Organization/ High Risk Offenders Unit of Probation Services. The number of offenders supervised by COHROU is necessarily small because surveillance is so incredibly intense. Assessment criteria are extensive and offenders accepted for supervision by COHROU are the extreme cases — whether because of their level of violence or, most importantly, the risk they pose to the victim. A sub-unit of COHROU supervises those convicted of offences involving domestic violence. Supervision can mean that an offender is required to connect with a probation officer daily. COHROU staff often go to offenders' residences to ensure that they are consistent with court orders and that the offenders are complying with the restrictions placed on them by the courts, including curfews and requirements that they abstain from alcohol.

COHROU staff also try to maintain regular contact with the victims of the offenders to ensure their safety or determine the status of the relationship.

My meetings with the domestic violence subunit of COHROU are great! At the table once a month are representatives from the provincial correctional facility, Victim Services, the Winnipeg Police Service, Employment and Income Assistance, Probation Services, and the Crown. We discuss various cases and decide how best to deal with them. For example, one of our cases dealt with an offender who was being supervised by COHROU but who had contact with the Employment and Income Assistance worker and whose partner had had regular contact with Victim Services, particularly while the offender was being prosecuted by our department. This individual was very familiar to the police and had undergone programming while incarcerated. It was a wonderful and fascinating discussion, and the plan we devised was a cohesive and informed one. This type of communication and coordination is essential to successful interventions. We need to find forums for including staff of non-governmental agencies like shelters or counselling programs. One of my current priorities as chair of Osborne House is to try and establish this sort of networking among agencies in the city.

The first step in all of this is communication. This is as basic as having a conversation with all service providers to better understand the complainant's perspective or situation. As a Crown attorney, I have frequently stated that I wish service providers would more actively seek the permission of their clients to speak with the Crown to ensure that all relevant information is available to them. While this is done to some extent, it needs to become a regular practice.

Law: Its Limitations and Potential

Our legal system is based on precedent. The decisions made in each case are based on similar cases that have gone before it. Judges really don't have the ability to veer far from past practices or judgements. Our Courts of Appeal exist to put a stop to judges who try to impose extreme sentences where such a sentence has not been imposed before in similar circumstances. We are bound not only by the courts that have set the tone for years and years before us, but by Parliament where laws are made.

Despite this weight of tradition, we can maintain our efforts towards progress and continuing improvement. For example, quite possibly as a result of the specialization of DVU Crowns, conditional discharges in cases involving domestic violence — essentially, outcomes which do not result in a criminal record — are now rare. They used to be exceptionally commonplace. Judges in our courts are more aware of the seriousness of domestic violence and Crowns are trained to reinforce that message. Furthermore, Parliament has recognized the special circumstances of domestic violence. Legislation now specifies that violence in an intimate partner relationship be treated as an aggravating factor (i.e., more serious than a similar level of violence among strangers). We will continue to push — incrementally — and attitudes will change, as will community sentiment. As society's awareness increases and justice personnel learn and share their knowledge, slowly but surely the justice system will improve its response to domestic violence.

I had occasion to speak to service providers and academics at a conference, and in preparing for this, it occurred to me that what we do at these conferences is talk about the problems. We focus on what's *not* working, which is extremely important. It is only by identifying the gaps and weaknesses that improvements can be made; but, at the same time, it is *so* important to celebrate the victories! We have come *so* far in this country, most specifically in Manitoba, in addressing the scourge of domestic violence. Criminal harassment is a crime! Raping one's wife is a criminal offence! A person will be arrested for abusing his/her spouse! Within our lifetime, this has not always been the case. A victim's stalker will no longer be able to further terrorize her by cross-examining her in court.

In Manitoba, we have 18 Crown attorneys in the Domestic Violence Unit and a Victim Services Program. Our aim is to ensure better results for victims of domestic violence. We no longer charge women who recant their original complaints. We have greater protection through more accessible protection orders. There is a far greater diversity of background and experience on the bench ensuring judges more closely reflect the gender and ethnic makeup of our community. So we are making progress.

One of the most helpful innovations — successes — of late is a change in the administration of our specialized court identified as "the Front End

Project." This project involved extensive planning and co-operation with all the key justice personnel, the police, the prosecutors and the judges. Recognition of its impact has been received nationally when they were awarded the gold medal in public administration. On the heels of this award has come a gold medal from the United Nations — that is an international award!

The administrative details are too lengthy and complicated to explain in this chapter; however, I will mention two of the consequences of the Front End Project that have incredible potential for better processing domestic violence cases.

1. There has been a significant reduction in delays from the start of a case to its disposition. Where it might have taken years, in the past, for a domestic violence matter to wend its way through the system, the streamlining of the system has reduced timelines to months. A quicker resolution of a case has tremendous advantages for prosecutors and for the families involved.

2. The project has led to effective Crown attorney ownership of a file. Although the original intention of the specialized court was to facilitate Crown ownership, lengthy delays in cases made it more and more difficult for a prosecutor to always have control of a particular offender's file. Speedier resolution of cases now makes this an achievable goal. Ownership means following the case from its start, even if it goes from the Provincial Court to the Court of Queen's Bench to the appeal court. Ownership means that if a particular offender reoffends, the same Crown attorney will handle the case again. This provides continuity and familiarity with the case, which benefits the victim and the prosecutor. The victim doesn't have to tell and retell the story over and over again, has an opportunity to develop a sense of trust, and can establish a good working relationship with the prosecutor. It is also valuable to the prosecutor because she/he gets to know the accused's patterns of behaviour. This knowledge makes for more powerful arguments from the Crown at the court hearings. This can have *substantial* benefits when an abusive relationship has a long history. Two specific cases illustrating these advantages come to mind.

Case 1

"Joe" and "Lexie" had been in a relationship for a number of years. Since 2003, 41 charges were laid against Joe arising from allegations relating to domestic abuse. Until last year, Lexie had been adamantly opposed to prosecuting Joe. It had been her position that she was strong enough to deal with the abuse and did not need the criminal justice system to intervene on her behalf. She had maintained this position angrily and consistently despite the diligent and supportive efforts of Terry, a DVU Crown attorney. Lexie attended bail court in support of Joe's applications to be released and regularly wrote letters advocating for him. According to Terry, she "called often and even swore at me ... but eventually she got sick of it all and stopped making excuses [for him]."

As a result of Terry's faith and unwillingness to give up, and with the ongoing support of a victim services worker, Lexie ultimately acknowledged the abuse. For the first time, she was ready to testify. Joe was sentenced to a period of incarceration as a result of guilty pleas entered when he recognized that Lexie was going to testify. Joe is now being supervised by COHROU.

As Terry says, "When we think of complainants we often think of victims, but Lexie reminded me of just how tough these women are." Were it not for the understanding of a Crown attorney like Terry, her knowledge of the couple's history and her relationship with the victim (regardless of how adversarial), Joe would probably be free today to continue his abuse.

Case 2.

"Lenny" has faced 78 charges since 2002. Most of them have been crimes directed at his former wife. Most of his behaviour consists of stalking, although he has been convicted of assaulting her and of uttering threats to her and their grown son. He had no criminal record of any significance prior to 2002. The file was not assigned until a criminal harassment charge was laid in 2003. Since then, the same Crown attorney has had almost exclusive involvement in conducting each and every hearing related to Lenny.

Lenny's wife, "Sue," had tried for most of their 30-plus years of marriage to support and encourage him and to tolerate his abuse until finally she could endure no more. Still, she bore him no ill will, and she and their adult children were prepared to continue to provide him with as much emotional support as possible. But then the chronic and ongoing harassment began, and ultimately they could not take anymore. Much of Lenny's difficulty was that, for over half his life, his world has been his family. In his mind, he had done everything for them, including provide for them. Now he was retired, he had lost his immediate family, and he had alienated his extended family on both sides as well as his friends because of his behaviours. He had nothing else.

Prior to the assignment of the file, no consistent pattern was identified from the regular arrests. Every file was handled by a different Crown attorney and, because Lenny was a charmer and *always* admitted his offences and showed "remorse," it was easy to accept his claims that he was just a sorry old man (though he wasn't yet 60) and would never do it again.

Once the file was assigned and only one Crown attorney took conduct of each prosecution, it was obvious that he made these promises each and every time. The situation was compounded by Lenny's drinking, but the difficulty had been that this was viewed as a separate issue. On one occasion, a Crown attorney unfamiliar with the file consented to Lenny's release on bail when the only allegation was that he had failed to abstain from the consumption of alcohol. The difficulty was that the drinking fuelled Lenny's obsession and severely compromised his judgement. The assigned Crown attorney's position was and always had been that the drinking simply formed a different aspect of the ongoing harassment.

On the last few occasions when Lenny appeared before the court, the assigned Crown attorney had ensured that *all* of the history was before the court. This included transcripts of previous sentencing hearings so that it was clear that he had, each and every time, promised to stop. As a result of the Crown attorney's understanding of all of the history and the willingness to take many extra steps to ensure that each judge clearly saw the "big picture," what would otherwise be perceived as "minor" breaches were now being taken seriously. Very recently, Lenny was sentenced to the maximum jail term available on a summary conviction for a breach. Lenny is also being supervised by COHROU.

It is very important to note that, in both these cases, success was not achieved in a vacuum. Without the assistance of Probation Services and Victim Services, far less positive results would have been possible.

Conclusion

Some days I wonder why I have chosen to work in such a stressful field and why I have stayed for so long. I think it is my belief that things can change. People change. I have seen it at Osborne House and in court. Laws change and systems change, and all of this can add up to more resources and more support for people seeking safe, respectful homes for themselves and their children. There is no greater joy than to see an abused woman discover her strength and change her life. Those of us who work in the field are the "supporting actors" who assist these women in their starring role as heroes in their own lives.

PART II

Criminal Justice: Different Models of Specialization

CHAPTER FOUR

Specialized Domestic Violence Courts: *A Comparison of Models*

Leslie M. Tutty, Jane Ursel and Fiona Douglas

In the past, assaults between partners were seen as private matters and treated differently from similar assaults committed by strangers (Fusco, 1989). Today, however, the criminal justice system intervenes in a substantial proportion of domestic violence cases in Canada and the United States (Tsai, 2000; Ursel, 2002). This has been the result of broad policy changes over the past two decades. These policy changes have occurred at all levels of the justice system, including the police, prosecutions, courts and corrections.

Entry into the criminal justice system is usually victim initiated, typically, through a telephone call to the police during a crisis. Yet, according to the 2004 General Social Survey, relatively high proportions of victims choose not to involve the police: only 37% of women victims and 17% of male victims made such contact (Ogrodnik, 2006). One of the frequently cited reasons for these low rates of contacting the police is the view that the police and the criminal justice system are not helpful to victims. Over time, critiques of the justice system response to domestic violence have resulted in a number of policy and practice changes that put greater emphasis on the safety of victims and on holding offenders accountable for their assaults. One of the consequences of these changes has been the introduction of specialized criminal courts.

This chapter, the first in the second section of this book, introduces our discussion on the criminal justice system response to domestic violence. We begin with a brief overview of how the criminal justice system works, how to understand the terminology used by our authors and what to look for in assessing different models of court specialization. We review the various rationales for developing specialized domestic violence courts and the different models of specialization that exist in Canada. We conclude with the research results of a comparison of courts in four Canadian cities, three of which had implemented different models of specialization and one which was not specialized. This comparison of different models of courts is rare in the published literature and presents numerous challenges. Nevertheless, comparisons are the best way to determine the benefits of each model, and we will call the reader's attention to cases in which the comparisons are limited by non-identical procedures.

Understanding the Criminal Justice System

As stated above, entry into the criminal justice system (CJS) is typically through a call to the police, usually by the victim, but sometimes by a family member, friend or neighbour. The police respond and determine whether there is sufficient evidence to conclude that a crime has occurred. In determining what constitutes sufficient evidence, police guidelines stipulate there must be "reasonable and probable grounds that a crime has occurred." If such evidence exists, the police charge the offender if he/she is present or issue a warrant for her/his arrest if the accused is not present.

There is a hierarchy of evidence required in the CJS, which serves to screen out cases at different levels of intervention. While the police can arrest on "probable grounds," the prosecutor is mandated to proceed with the case only if they have a "reasonable likelihood of conviction." If the case goes to trial, the judge must determine if the accused is proven guilty "beyond a reasonable doubt." This hierarchy of required evidence/proof is the basis of our justice system, which assumes that "a person is innocent until proven guilty." This helps explain why there are many more calls to the police than people arrested, many more arrests than prosecutions and many more prosecutions than convictions. Individuals are often very frustrated by the drop-off of cases from arrest to conviction; however, this is the price we pay for a justice system based on the underlying belief system of safe-guarding an individual's innocence unless there is compelling evidence to the contrary.

Once an accused person is charged, the police have two options for proceeding. If the offender does not appear to be a current threat to the victim or the community, they can release the accused "on his/her own recognizance." This means the accused undertakes to keep the peace, have no contact or communication with the victim and promises to appear on their assigned court date. Police can also stipulate other conditions if deemed necessary, for example, a weapon prohibition. If the accused is thought to pose a risk to the victim or if he has a long prior record, the police will arrest him and hold him in custody (jail) until his bail hearing.

At a bail hearing, the prosecutor, referred to as a Crown attorney in Canada, will typically present the case for keeping the accused in jail, and the defence lawyer will typically present the case for release of his/her client on bail. Whether the individual is detained in custody or released on bail, the next step is for the prosecutor to determine whether or not to proceed with the case. If, for whatever reasons, the accused agrees to plead guilty, the matter proceeds to a sentencing hearing and the jobs of the prosecutor and the defence lawyer are quite straightforward. The prosecutor presents the facts of the case, the defence lawyer responds and both "speak to sentence," meaning that they suggest a sentence that they consider appropriate in the particular case. Often the prosecutor will highlight the seriousness by suggesting a more serious sentence and the defence lawyer will point out "mitigating" circumstances that would suggest a less severe sentence. This is the nature of the adversarial legal system within which the defence lawyer and the prosecutor work.

However, practice is usually more complex than the simple process outlined above. Often guilty pleas are a result of a plea bargain, which may occur for a variety of reasons. Frequently, the prosecutor offers a deal to the defence lawyer to drop some of the more serious charges if the accused is willing to plead guilty. Those who wonder why prosecutors would do this should keep two considerations in mind. First, prosecutors have their eyes on the high burden of proof they must meet (beyond a reasonable doubt) in order to get a conviction. Second, in all cases, but particularly in domestic assault cases, prosecutors must assess how strong their witness is. If the prosecutors are concerned that the victim/witness will not testify or may change their story on the stand, they may see a guilty plea as the best way to achieve some consequences for the crime. In jurisdictions such as the Winnipeg Family Violence Court, the Crown attorneys often meet with a reluctant victim/witness to tell her/him that they would be willing to proceed on lesser charges and recommend counselling for the accused if the victim/witness will testify. If the victim agrees, the prosecutor will call the defence lawyer, indicating that they have a willing witness; often this results in a guilty plea. This process has been referred to as "testimony bargaining" (Ursel, 2000, 2002).

Finally, in a number of specialized domestic violence courts, prosecutors implement a form of diversion. This typically occurs in cases in which (1) the victim won't testify; (2) the accused will not plead guilty; (3) the crime is a first offence; (4) it is not a serious charge; or (5) the victim is consulted and concurs. Such "diversion" results in the Crown proposing to the defence that if the accused is willing to attend, participate and complete a treatment program for batterers, the prosecutor will remand the case (delay the court hearing). If the accused successfully completes the program, the charges may be dropped. This is a very attractive offer to defence counsel because the accused will not have a criminal record, his/her charges will be stayed and hopefully, the treatment will be effective and there will be no further abuse. However, not all specialized courts provide a diversion option. For example, in the Yukon court (see chapter 8 in this volume) accused persons are offered treatment only after they have pled guilty, and their sentences are withheld until completion of the treatment program.

In cases in which the accused and defence have no interest in entering a guilty plea, the Crown must seriously assess the reasonable likelihood of conviction if they proceed to trial. The critical determinant of "likelihood of conviction" in domestic assault cases is the co-operation of the victim/witness (Dawson & Dinovitzer, 2001). As Crown attorney Rekha Malaviya explained in chapter 3, many factors go into the difficult decision of whether to proceed to trial. A large proportion of cases in which the accused pleads "not guilty" ultimately end in a stay of proceedings, otherwise known as "dismissed for want of prosecution." Formally, a stay of proceedings means that the Crown will not prosecute the case unless new evidence justifies doing so. A 12-month time limit exists for deciding to proceed in cases that have been stayed. In reality, stayed cases are seldom proceeded with in the year-long period because the underlying problem, the reasonable likelihood of conviction, has not been overcome in this time.

Each time a sensational criminal case is covered in the media, considerable criticism emerges with respect to "settling for a guilty plea" or "failing to prosecute" or "failing to convict." However, these cries of indignation seldom take into consideration the complexities of a case and the reality that justice personnel must conduct themselves within the requirements of the law. If we are not willing to abandon our dearly held belief that a person "is innocent until proven guilty," we must assess the justice system within the restrictions that this belief system imposes, particularly the escalating burden of evidence/proof required as a case proceeds through the system.

Given the complexities of the law and the special issues encountered in domestic violence cases, such as reluctant witnesses, we can appreciate why the traditional criminal justice system response to domestic violence cases would be less than satisfactory. Beginning in 1990, provinces across Canada began to consider specialization as a better way of handling domestic violence cases. As stated in the introduction to this book, the administration of our federal criminal code occurs at the provincial level. Thus, each province, and indeed, municipalities within provinces, have selected different strategies for specialization. However, to date, all of the specialized courts established in Canada have operated within our standard court structure.

Court Structure

Two primary levels of criminal courts exist in Canada: the Provincial Court and the Court of Queen's Bench (the higher court).[1] The Provincial Court hears the overwhelming number of criminal cases, probably over 75% of all criminal matters. However, the Criminal Code of Canada does provide that when a charge is a serious charge (indictable offence), the accused pleading not guilty has a right to have his/her case heard either in the Provincial Court or the Court of Queen's Bench. An indictable offence indicates that, if convicted, a sentence of incarceration could be imposed for two years or more. If a person is sentenced to two years or more, they are held in a federal prison. Few accused persons opt for a hearing in the Court of Queen's Bench; however, as a general rule, the more serious the charge and the consequences the more likely the accused will be tried in the Court of Queen's Bench. In most provinces, more senior, experienced Crown attorneys prosecute cases in this higher court.

Because most criminal matters are heard at the Provincial Court level, domestic violence specialization occurs there. However, strategies have been introduced in some jurisdictions to deal with domestic assault cases that may end up with a trial in the Court of Queen's Bench. Some of our authors use the term "vertical prosecution." This means that the Crown attorneys who specialize in "domestic violence" will prosecute the case if it proceeds to the Court of Queen's Bench. In some jurisdictions, the special-ized prosecutor will also stay with the case if it goes to the Court of Appeal.

Appeal courts handle appeals from a dissatisfied defence lawyer or a dissatisfied prosecutor. Just because a lawyer is unhappy with the judge's verdict or sentence does not automatically lead to an appeal hearing. The lawyer must apply to have her/his appeal heard and stipulate the grounds on which an appeal is justified. The appeal court judges will determine whether the applicant has grounds to appeal. Many applications are turned down, but if they proceed to be heard, vertical prosecutions would provide for the Crown attorney who started the case in the specialized court to follow the case to an appeal court.

Some authors prefer to use the term "Crown ownership" of a file (case). This includes the concept of vertical prosecution but also means that the same prosecutor will handle the accused person's case if he/she comes back on a second or third reoffence over the years. Since our specialized courts are revealing that a small percentage of offenders are chronic reoffenders, this type of "ownership" of a file is very effective as Crown attorney Malaviya has indicated in chapter 3.

Another term that the reader will encounter is "judicial review." In most courts, both traditional and specialized, once the case has been ruled on as not guilty or guilty and the accused has been sentenced, the judge's involve-ment in the case is over. However, the process of judicial review, as described in the Yukon specialized court in chapter 8, provides ongoing monitoring of the offender's progress by the judge. It typically takes the form of an offender appearing back in court periodically to report on his/her progress, usually until their court-mandated course of treatment is complete. The practice is very time-consuming for judges; thus, it is more likely to occur in jurisdictions with smaller populations or a smaller volume of cases.

The Rationale for Specialized Domestic Violence Courts

In the past two decades, specialized domestic violence courts have become widespread across North America as one mechanism to more effectively address intimate partner violence. The reasons for developing specialized domestic violence courts are many. First, domestic violence cases often involve overlapping concurrent charges relating to separate incidents with the same partner. In the absence of specialized courts, a number of prosecutors could be proceeding on different components of the case without knowing of the other related incidents (Buzawa & Buzawa, 2003). Specialized courts enhance the possibility of consolidating all matters and proceeding on the full range of offences rather than fragmenting cases throughout the system.

Second, specialization was designed to respond to the common criticism of the traditional legal process that it did not protect victims and that offenders were seldom arrested and prosecuted. Prior to specialization, sentences for assaulting intimate partners were typically lenient, not befitting the "serial" nature of the crime (Bennett, Goodman & Dutton, 1999; Jordan, 2003). A very serious concern was that within the traditional system, victims were often revictimized during the justice process (Buzawa & Buzawa, 2003). One example is that victims who recanted their testimony could be held in contempt of court and confined to prison, despite the fact that their reason for not testifying was because they were being threatened by the offender (The Honourable Judge Mary Ellen Turpell-Lafond, RESOLVE Research Day, Keynote Address, 2003).

The term "specialized court" has become a short-hand term for a broad range of related services that support or interact with the court. Most specialized courts operate in tandem with victim support programs, government or community treatment agencies and often specialized police units, Crown prosecutors, and probation officers (Babcock & Steiner, 1999; Shepard, 1999). In fact, there are many different models of specialization. Some specialized courts involve judicial review processes, other courts emphasize rigorous prosecution, and still other models of specialization emphasize programs to support and advocate for victims in order to assist them through the court process (Hoffart & Clarke, 2004). Studies have found that victims who use advocacy programs and protection orders are much more likely to testify or have their cases completed in court (Dawson & Dinovitzer, 2001; Weisz, Tolman & Bennett, 1998; Barasch & Lutz, 2002).

Three basic principles underlie specialized domestic violence courts, some of which are incorporated into separate courts (the early Ontario model) and some which are combined in one court (Clarke, 2003). These principles are (1) early intervention for low-risk offenders; (2) vigorous prosecution for serious and/or repeat offenders; and (3) a commitment to rehabilitation and treatment. The early intervention strategy fits with what have become known as "problem-solving" courts, in which those who commit crimes because they need treatment for drugs or mental health issues are offered the opportunity to receive such assistance in the hope that they will not reoffend (Van de Veen, 2003).

The first principle, early intervention, is exemplified in the Yukon court specialization, the Calgary HomeFront model and the Ontario specialized courts. A variety of procedures are used by Canadian specialized courts that focus on early intervention. Some require the accused to plead guilty before attending batterer intervention programs; others stay the proceedings with a peace bond. Some use judicial or court review in which the accused periodically return to court to review their compliance with treatment (Gondolf, 2002; Healey, Smith & O'Sullivan, 1998).

The speed with which the court facilitates the accused starting treatment also varies based on the court processes. In Gondolf's four-site evaluation of batterer interventions in the United States, the length of the program was less important than the time it took to begin the program. The men in the programs with pretrial mechanisms were much more likely to stay in treatment (Gondolf, 2002, p. 214).

The second principle, vigorous prosecution, emphasizes Crown attorneys working with police and victims to ensure the strongest prosecution effort possible. This emphasis encourages police to record the victim's statements and injuries at the time of the incident through photographs, videotapes, audiotapes and tapes of 911 phone calls. This thorough ongoing process of evidence collection results in prosecutors being less dependent on the victim's willingness to testify (Dawson & Dinovitzer, 2001). This strategy is also likely to utilize vertical prosecution and/or Crown ownership of a file so the specialized prosecutors "keep" the case from first appearance, through to trial and possibly appeal court. File ownership will also ensure that the same offender will return to the same prosecutor for subsequent offences over the years. A recent U.S. study of a court with specialized prosecutors found that convictions for domestic violence offences were significantly related to lower rates of recidivism (Ventura & Davis, 2005).

The third principle, rehabilitation and treatment, is evident in the sentencing patterns of judges in specialized courts. Court-mandated treatment has become the most frequent disposition in a number of jurisdictions with specialized courts. The emphasis on treatment is not limited to convicted offenders, as many specialized prosecutors offer peace bonds or delays in proceeding to enable the accused to attend treatment in the hope of having charges dropped.

Given the centrality of treatment programs to most domestic violence court initiatives in Canada, the next section briefly reviews the literature on the effectiveness of these programs. Understanding the limits as well as the potential of treatment is especially important since many women victims stay in or return to potentially dangerous partners in the hope that they will change as a result of group treatment (Gondolf & Russell, 1986).

Research on Court-Mandated Treatment Programs

Numerous evaluations of treatment for men who abuse their intimate partners have been conducted.[2] However, in this chapter, we focus on evaluations of court-mandated programs. One key question about batterer treatment programs is whether court-mandated offenders benefit in comparison to those who self-refer or receive no treatment at all. Edleson and Syers (1991) compared six treatment conditions and found that, at the 18-month follow-up, the men involved with the courts had lower levels of violence than "voluntary" group members. Similarly, Rosenbaum, Gearan and Ondovic (2001) found that court-referred men who completed treatment had significantly lower recidivism rates than self-referred men.

Some randomized clinical trial studies of batterer intervention programs have been conducted. Palmer, Brown and Barrera's 1992 study in Ontario randomly assigned a small sample to a 10-week treatment group and compared it with a "probation only" control group. Those assigned to treatment reoffended at a significantly lower rate than those in the probation only group. A recent meta-analysis of 22 mostly quasi-experimental evaluations of domestic violence treatment (Babcock, Green & Robie, 2004) found no differences between treatment models (the Duluth feminist-informed model compared with cognitive behavioural approaches, for example) but that treatment had a significant but small effect on recidivism in addition to the effect of being arrested.

Two more recent randomized clinical trials, one in Broward County, Florida, and the other in Brooklyn, NY (Jackson, et al., 2003), raised serious questions about batterer intervention programs when neither found statistically significant differences between violations of probation or rearrests in men randomly assigned to either treatment or a control condition. These conclusions, using the "gold-standard" of experimental research designs, created significant concerns about the effectiveness of treatment. Gondolf (2002) has responded with critiques of the implementation of the last two studies. In at least some instances, random assignment did not occur, the groups were characterized by high dropout rates and it was difficult to access victims for follow-up reports, casting doubt on the interpretation of the findings.

It is interesting to note that three studies, one in Canada (Ursel & Gorkoff, 1996), one in the United States (Gondolf, 1999) and one in the United Kingdom (Dobash, et al., 2000), found similar evidence that court-mandated treatment programs did reduce recidivism and/or reduce the level of abuse and control in the couple's relationship. Ursel and Gorkoff's Canadian study examined a sample of convicted offenders from the Winnipeg Family Violence Court, comparing recidivism rates of individuals who received and completed court-mandated treatment to those who did not receive court-mandated treatment. This study was limited to recidivism rates as measured by rearrest and did not undertake partner interviews. The authors concluded that treatment did have an effect on reducing recidivism; however, the degree to which the recidivism was reduced was influenced by two factors (1) the criminal history of the accused and their related sentence, and (2) the history and experience of the treatment program.

The Winnipeg recidivism study compared 551 convicted offenders who were ordered to attend and completed a court-mandated treatment program to 1,479 offenders who received other sentences not involving treatment. Two years after completion of their sentences, individuals who were sentenced to probation and received treatment from an established program had a higher reduction in recidivism than individuals on probation who received treatment from a very new and less experienced treatment program. Offenders sentenced to a maximum security jail did not have as large a reduction in recidivism if they had completed treatment as did offenders in the minimum security jail with an established treatment program (see chapter 5 in this volume). While this study was limited to examining only one measure of reoffending — recidivism that led to CJS re-involvement — it is notable that the results are similar to the studies conducted by Gondolf and Dobash et al., who had the added benefit of follow-up interviews with partners.

Gondolf's multi-site evaluation assessed four batterer treatment programs, with variation on whether referrals were made before or after trial, length of program (from three months to nine months) and whether additional services were offered. Rather than the cessation of violence, Gondolf (2002) refers to "de-escalation of assault," finding that, while nearly half of the men in the four treatment sites reassaulted their partners at some time in the nine months following program intake, two and a half years later, more than 80% had not assaulted their partner in the past year (based on partner reports) and, among those who did, the severity of the assaults were reduced. This fits with the points raised by Jennings (1990), who has questioned whether the absolute cessation of violence during treatment was a fair standard, whereas in treatment programs for other problems such as alcoholism, clients are expected to relapse and to learn from these experiences to help them resist in the future.

A subgroup of about 20% of the referrals was identified as dangerous men who continued to assault their partners despite intervention. Gondolf concluded that such offenders need a different approach as they did not seem to experience any change in behaviour regardless of the intervention. Further, he recommends screening for severe substance abuse and psychological problems that are associated with dropping out (Gondolf, 2002). Gondolf recommends providing programs as early as possible and shifting the focus from program length to program intensity (p. 214). For example, as soon as possible after charges and during the crisis when motivation tends to be the highest, offenders could attend counselling three or four times per week for the first four to six weeks.

The United Kingdom study conducted by Dobash and colleagues (2000) examined reabuse patterns in a 12-month follow-up study of two groups of offenders, men who had completed a treatment program (51 men and 47 women partners) and a control group of men with some other form of CJS intervention (71 men and 97 women partners). Dobash et al. found little difference in the rearrest rate of the two groups in a 12-month follow-up. Seven percent of the men in treatment and 10% of men in the control group were rearrested within one year, very similar to the Winnipeg data that indicated that on average about 10% of offenders reoffend within one year (see chapter 5). The most important findings from the U.K. study were the reports from the women partners of the two groups of men. According to the women, 33% of the men who had treatment committed a subsequent act of violence compared with 70% of the men in the control group, a statistically significant difference. Furthermore, individuals who had ceased or reduced their violent behaviour had also reduced their controlling behaviour.

In summary, while there has been considerable skepticism expressed by victim's advocates about the effects of batterer intervention programs for court-mandated clients, the research supports its utility for a relatively large proportion of those charged with assaulting intimate partners. The proviso that some repeat offenders and others with co-occurring problems such as substance misuse and psychological problems are not amenable to the models currently in use suggests the need to conduct further research on identifying these subgroups and developing appropriate interventions.

Research on Specialized Domestic Violence Courts

The specialized domestic violence courts in Canada present an interesting variety of models designed to provide more effective interventions. While a select few have been evaluated, most reports are not published and are difficult to access. We rely heavily on Clarke's best practices review (2003) for the evaluation findings reported in this section.

Winnipeg established the first dedicated family violence court in 1990 and appointed dedicated Crown attorneys, supported by a women's advocacy program for women whose partners were charged (Ursel, 1998a, 2000, 2002). According to Ursel's evaluations, before specialization the most common sentences for convicted offenders were conditional discharge, probation and fines. After specialization, sentencing patterns changed dramatically: supervised probation (most often with a condition to receive treatment) and incarceration became the most frequent outcome of a conviction.

Ontario developed a system of 22 specialized domestic violence courts with plans to have one in all 54 jurisdictions in the province by 2004 (Clarke, 2003). An evaluation by Moyer, Rettinger and Hotton (2000, cited in Clarke, 2003) focused on the initial model where some sites used early interventions and other used vigorous prosecution In Ontario's early intervention model, the accused pleads guilty as a condition to being mandated to treatment. Moyer et al. reported that case processing times were significantly reduced, a higher proportion of accused entering the program pled guilty as compared to the year before the project was implemented and treatment started soon after referral. Victims in the early intervention sites were significantly more likely to be satisfied with the case outcomes than other victims.

In 2000, while not creating a fully specialized court system, Calgary established HomeFront, a specialized initial or docket court that is a critical point of entry into the regular court system. Accused who are considered at low risk of reoffending can have their charges stayed by a peace bond at the docket court. The Crown prosecutor reads the particulars of the offence into the record and has the accused acknowledge its accuracy, so that this information is on file in the event of a reassault (Hoffart & Clarke, 2004).

While some community stakeholders expressed concerns about the decriminalization of domestic assault charges, Hoffart and Clarke (2004) clarified that "those with Peace Bonds tend to make quicker linkages with treatment and are less likely to drop out than those without Peace Bonds" (p. xiii). They also noted that offenders who received peace bonds were mandated to treatment in a timely fashion in the hope that they would be less resistant to such intervention in the immediate aftermath of police contact. Early case resolution is a key principle of the model and refers to the ability to set court dates quickly so as to facilitate rapid referral of eligible offenders to treatment. As Hoffart and Clarke (2004) summarized:

> About 46% of the cases were concluded within two weeks from the first appearance in the Domestic Violence Docket Court (a mean of 37 and a median of 17 days). About 86% of the HomeFront cases were resolved within two adjournments or less. (p. xiii)

Evaluations of two American specialized courts in San Diego (Peterson & Thunberg, cited in Clarke, 2003) and in Brooklyn (Newmark, Rempel, Diffily & Kane, cited in Clarke, 2003) provided positive findings with respect to baseline data that compared variables such as time to disposition, proportion of offenders being placed on probation or mandated to treatment and recidivism rates.

Research on a specialized court in the Yukon using an early intervention model and judicial review (Hornick, Boyes, Tutty & White, chapter 8 in this volume) concluded that cases were seen significantly more quickly, fewer victims were unwilling to testify, offenders were fast-tracked into counselling and recidivism rates were reduced.

In summary, few evaluations of specialized courts have been conducted and most have focused on only one model. Comparative research is complex, however. The context of the communities in which the courts are established is critical and must be documented and captured in any evaluation. Despite the challenges, further research is essential in understanding which components of specialization make the most difference in holding offenders accountable and in safeguarding victims. Further research could have direct application by identifying best practices so that the justice and community services can revise and enhance their responses to those affected by intimate partner violence.

The Current Comparative Court Study

A four-city study recording criminal justice processing of domestic violence cases was undertaken in the three Prairie provinces in the period 2001–04.[3] Court data from the year 2002 were collected in Winnipeg, Regina, Calgary and Edmonton using the measures developed and implemented for 12 years by RESOLVE Manitoba in its ongoing assessment of the Winnipeg Family Violence Court.

Three of the four cities had implemented some form of specialization. Winnipeg had the longest running program of specialization, providing a broad range of specialized professionals and dedicated courtrooms. Winnipeg also had the highest volume of cases. Calgary's specialization at the time of data collection was limited to its first-appearance court, HomeFront, developed in 2000, while Edmonton developed a specialized trial court in

2001. Since the Edmonton data was collected in the early stages of the city's specialized justice response, not all cases were sent to the specialized court, an important limitation with respect to the interpretation of the data presented here. Finally, Regina had no specialized court in 2002 and serves as a comparison city.

Table 4.1 presents a summary of the specializations associated with the courts in each of the study sites. It highlights the fact that, even without specialization, Regina had several key aspects of a specialized approach including offender treatment and the availability of Family Service Regina to provide support to victims while their partners, who had been charged, proceeded through the justice system. Indeed, all four cities provide victim support in some manner.

Table 4.1: Program Characteristics by Court Site

	Winnipeg	Regina	Calgary	Edmonton
Specialized court	Full: All Provincial Court Hearings	None	First appearance	Trial Court
Police teams	Yes victim support	None	Yes vigorous investigation	Yes victim support
Specialized Crown prosecutors	Yes	No	Yes	Yes
When mandated to treatment	At sentencing and "stayed" low-risk first offenders	At sentencing	At First Appearance Court for low-risk offenders stayed with peace bond	At sentencing
Support for victims	Women's Advocacy Program	Family Service Regina	DV court caseworkers	DV follow-up teams
Dedicated judges	Only in first two years	No	No	No
Specialized probation	Yes	No	Yes	No
Judicial review	No	No	No	No

A number of important distinctions are also apparent between the four jurisdictions even when they have apparently similar programs. For example, both Winnipeg and Calgary provide for an early counselling referral and resolution; however, they provide this option very differently.

The Calgary HomeFront court mandates treatment at an early stage (often one to two weeks after charges have been laid) for low-risk offenders who have taken responsibility for their behaviour by accepting a peace bond. The hope is that earlier intervention, when the crisis of having been charged is relatively fresh, will lead to positive change during offender treatment. The term "mandated" is typically used when an accused has been sentenced. Using the term in connection with charges being "stayed" without a guilty verdict indicates the unique nature of the process in Calgary. Although the charges are stayed, the actions of the accused are monitored by probation officers and if, for example, the individual does not complete treatment as required, the original charges could be brought back before the court. The Calgary court will also expedite a quick referral to counselling for accused who plead guilty.

In contrast, the Winnipeg early referral to counselling occurs through the process of a delayed remand. In cases of low-risk — typically first-time offenders whose partners will not testify but agree to the early referral option — the Winnipeg prosecutors offer to delay the court hearing and refer the accused to a designated treatment program. The prosecutor offers to stay proceedings if the accused attends and completes the treatment program. In the Calgary court, the case is stayed before counselling, and in the Winnipeg court, the case is stayed after the treatment program is successfully completed.

A distinction also occurs in the approach to police victim-support teams in Edmonton and Winnipeg. Both Winnipeg and Edmonton use specialized follow-up teams in which a police and a social worker follow up on calls originally responded to by a regular responding officer. The specialized team in Edmonton follows up on serious offences against which charges have been laid and which are before the courts. In Winnipeg, the police-social worker teams respond to households in which the police have often been called but there is insufficient evidence to lay a charge. These are cases flagged by the responding officers as having potential to escalate. The specialist team visits the household upon agreement of the complainant and checks to see if there is further evidence that might result in a charge as well as making referrals to services for both the complainant and the alleged accused. This program was designed to intervene before, what was feared to be, an eventual escalation.[4] The Calgary Police Services' Domestic Conflict Unit does not include social workers and is largely an evidentiary team, conducting vigorous in-depth investigations in the most serious assault cases.

Finally, in 2002, only Winnipeg and Calgary had specialized probation and none of the courts studied used judicial review, perhaps a reflection of the enormous caseloads in cities that would make such reviews both onerous and expensive.

Research Results

In total, this study examined data for 5,205 accused individuals: 3,163 in Winnipeg, 798 in Regina, 920 in Calgary and 324 in Edmonton. The much larger volume of cases in Winnipeg reflects their longer history of specialization; cities with specialized courts may experience a similar increase in volume over time. Throughout this analysis, various tables may indicate a lower total number of individuals than the totals noted above because of missing information. For example, our total for ethnic origin of accused in the four cities is 4,727 (90.8%) because details on the ethnic origin of the accused are not always provided in the files.

The first analysis of interest describes the characteristics of accused persons charged with assaults against intimate partners and how these compare across the four cities. As can be seen in Table 4.2, the ethnic origin of the accused varies across the cities.

Table 4.2: Ethnic Origin of Accused by Court Site

	Winnipeg N = 3,033		Regina N = 507		Calgary N = 850		Edmonton N = 298	
European origin	1,425	47.0%	192	37.9%	575	67.6%	196	65.8%
Aboriginal origin	1,341	44.2%	307	60.6%	97	11.4%	59	19.8%
Other*	267	8.8%	8	1.6%	178	20.9%	43	14.4%

* Immigrant and visible minorities.

The analysis of the data in Table 4.2 indicates that the ethnic characteristics of the accused are significantly different across the four locations (chi-square = 509; p < .000, phi coefficient = 0.33, indicating a moderate effect).[5] These differences suggest that the cities have some unique demographic characteristics. Winnipeg and Regina have a much higher concentration of persons of Aboriginal origin while Calgary and Edmonton have a higher proportion of immigrants according to census Canada statistics. With respect to the age of the accused, across the four jurisdictions the average age was 34.05 years (N = 5,189, s.d. = 9.8 years). Notably, while the age range was large (from 15 to 81 years), most of the accused were in their early thirties, perhaps indicating the possibility for changing their abusive behaviour.

When we consider the gender of the accused (see Table 4.3), statistically significant differences occur across the four sites, with Winnipeg reporting the highest number of women accused and Edmonton reporting the lowest (chi-square = 363; phi coefficient is .26, indicating a moderate effect). Edmonton is not the best comparison, however, because it only handles trial cases, which are the smallest percentage of all cases involving arrests. Nevertheless, the percentage of women accused is still considerably higher in Winnipeg at 16.5% than in Calgary at 13.0% and Regina at 9.6% of all persons arrested. It is important to note that approximately 7% of the accused women in Winnipeg and 9% in Calgary are a result of dual arrest situations.

Table 4.3: Sex of Accused by Court Site

	Winnipeg N = 3,163		Regina N = 798		Calgary N = 880		Edmonton N = 324	
Male	2,631	83.2%	721	90.4%	766	87.0%	268	82.7%
Female	522	16.5%	77	9.6%	114	13.0%	26	8.0%
Other*	10	<1%	0	0	0	0	30	9.3%

* The other category includes a small proportion of cases with multiple offenders, some all male, some all female, some mixed male and female offenders.

In assessing the characteristics of the accused, prior criminal record is important, especially with respect to previous crimes against persons (CAP). A prior record is an important risk factor in assessing the potential threat of the accused to the victim. Any history of prior violence, particularly prior domestic violence, typically indicates a relatively high likelihood of reoffending. The data in Table 4.4 indicate statistically significant differences in the rate of accused with a prior record appearing before the four courts (chi-square = 707; p < .000; phi coefficient is .37, indicating a moderate to strong effect). Individuals in Calgary were much less likely to have a prior record of crimes against persons, while those in Winnipeg had a much higher rate. This may reflect the fact that the data on recidivism on the accused persons in Calgary were from the first-appearance court (the total sample of those accused), while a number of cases from the other locations may have been dismissed or dealt with in other ways. Further, as of 2002, the Winnipeg specialized court had been in place for over a decade.

Table 4.4: Prior Record of Accused by Court Site*

	Winnipeg N = 3,137	Regina N = 728	Calgary N = 898	Edmonton N = 324
Prior record	82.8%	77.9%	60.8%	70.1%
Domestic assault	48.1%	14.3%	4.9%	15.1%
Sexual assault	3.2%	3.0%	8.8%	3.1%
Other CAP**	17.4%	36.5%	16.9%	21.9%
All CAP	68.7%	53.8%	30.6%	40.1%
Other	14.1%	24.0%	29.7%	29.9%
No prior record	17.2%	22.1%	39.2%	29.9%

* The N for prior record is lower than total cases due to missing information.
** CAP - crimes against persons

Since the Calgary HomeFront model is unique, because the bulk of its effort occurs in first-appearance court, let's first examine the outcomes in this specialized court. As is evident in Table 4.5, in the year 2002, while more than one-third of the accused pled not guilty at first-appearance court and proceeded to trial, over half (56%) took responsibility for their acts, either by agreeing to have their cases stayed with a peace bond (34%) or by pleading guilty (22%). Both of the latter groups were court mandated to conditions that include batterer intervention programs, substance abuse treatment and probation, either as a condition of the peace bond or of their sentence after pleading guilty. As noted previously, attending treatment as a condition applied to a peace bond would not typically be considered being "court-mandated to treatment," but in the HomeFront court, probation services monitors the conditions applied to the peace bonds and takes action if an accused does not complete his/her requirements. Importantly, these conditions were applied in a relatively short period after the police laid charges, and changes to the system of intervention meant that they could start batterer intervention treatment within days of having attended the HomeFront court. Further, since trial court is expensive, these procedures likely resulted in substantial financial savings, although a cost-benefit analysis was not conducted for this research.

Table 4.5: Calgary HomeFront First-Appearance Court Outcomes

Outcome	Frequency	
Guilty plea	194	22.0%
Stay of proceedings	7	0.1%
Stayed with peace bond	296	33.6%
Dismissed for want of prosecution	1	<0.1%
Accused deceased	1	<0.1%
Withdrawn*	35	4.0%
Pled not guilty	346	39.3%
Total	880	100%

* The charges are not deemed to have enough merit to present at first-appearance court and have been withdrawn by the Crown.

A common concern with respect to the criminal justice system is conviction rates. While most specialized court personnel maintain that conviction should not be the primary or only measure of success, it is an outcome of interest. An overview of the outcomes of the four courts in Table 4.6 provides comparative data on conviction rates. As explained above, Calgary's conviction rate is substantially lower because it puts a great deal of emphasis on early referral to counselling with a stay and peace bond.

One common assumption made by the general public is that domestic violence cases are unique in the percentage of cases that do not result in a conviction as compared to other crimes against persons. This expectation has arisen from understanding that victims of a domestic assault are often reluctant to testify against their assailants. However, as difficult as domestic violence cases may be, they do not have dramatically different conviction rates than general assaults against a non-family member.

Table 4.6: Comparative Conviction Rates by Court Site

	Winnipeg N = 3,163		Regina N = 798		Calgary N = 880		Edmonton N = 324	
Guilty plea	1,654	52.3%	425	53.3%	258	29.3%	140	43.2%
Guilty verdict	52	1.6%	12	1.5%	29	3.3%	30	9.3%
Total conviction	1,706	53.9%	437	54.8%	287	32.6%	170	52.5%

* Because Calgary's major specialization is at first-appearance court, these data are not directly comparable. The Calgary guilty plea rates are different in Table 4.5 and 4.6 because a proportion of accused changed their plea after the first-appearance court.

In order to make such a comparison, we took the findings from our 2002 study of domestic violence cases in the four courts and compared the court outcomes with a national data set on all crimes against persons, which was reported in 2003. Although there is a year difference between the current data set and the national data set, the comparison sheds some light on the fact that conviction rates for crimes against persons whether they are assaults against strangers or family members, tend to have about a 50% conviction rate (see Table 4.7).

Table 4.7: Conviction Rates of Crime Against the Person at the National Level Compared with DV Courts by Site

	Canada* CAP 2003	Winnipeg	Regina	Calgary	Edmonton**
Total number of cases	118,692	3,163	798	880	324
Convictions	48.5%	53.9%	54.8%	32.6%	52.5%
Acquittals	6.2%	1.1%	<1%	15.4%	44.8%
Stays	40.9%	44.3%	42.4%	34.9%	2.5%

*Source: Statistics Canada, CANSIM, 252-0015 and Product # 85-002-x (www40.statcan.ca/l01/cst01/index.htm).
Note: Adult Criminal Court Survey data are not reported by Manitoba, Northwest Territories and Nunavut.
**This number refers to cases that proceeded to trial.

The conviction rates of Winnipeg, Edmonton and Regina are all somewhat higher than the national rates. Again, the Calgary HomeFront court stands out with a much lower rate of conviction overall, since at the time of data collection, its model focused more on early intervention for low-risk offenders rather than vigorous prosecution. Without the option of their charges being stayed with a peace bond early in the process, many would have pled guilty and their case would have been characterized as "convicted."

If convictions are not the only way to hold accused accountable or support a victim's need for safety, an alternative "successful" outcome is a stay with consequences in low-risk cases. One model of a stay with consequences as practised in the Calgary court is a stay with a peace bond and/or counselling. In Winnipeg, the practice is to stay proceedings upon successful completion of counselling. The data in Table 4.8 compares the stay rates and patterns in the four courts. Calgary and Winnipeg have the highest rate of stay with consequences, including stays of proceedings with counselling and stays with peace bonds with various conditions attached.

Table 4.8: Stay of Proceedings Rate and Consequences by Court Site

	Winnipeg N = 3,163		Regina N = 798		Calgary N = 880		Edmonton N = 324	
Stay of proceeding	861	27.2%	337	42.3%	32	3.6%	8	2.5%
Stay with peace bond	216	6.8%	1	<1%	357	40.6%	Not specified	
Stay with counselling	324	10.2%	0	0%	n/a	0%	Not specified	
Subtotal stays with consequences		17%		<1%		40.6%	Not specified	
Total stays	1,401	44.3%	338	42.4%	389	44.2%	8	2.5%

Although Regina and Winnipeg have similar overall stay rates, the absence of specialization in Regina results in little use of "stays with consequences." The Edmonton court data is the least comparable because it only records cases set for trial, thus the bulk of cases stayed would not show up in this data set. Further, we have no information from Edmonton on the total number of cases stayed or whether they ever used "stays with consequences."

Table 4.9 summarizes the consequences for the relatively small number of cases involving a not guilty plea that proceeded to trial. Clearly, all jurisdictions are characterized as having a relatively small number of cases resolved through trial. However, the profiles of the trial outcomes differ substantially across the various courts.

Table 4.9: Rate of Trial Hearings and Outcomes by Court Site

	Winnipeg N = 3,163		Regina N = 798		Calgary N = 880		Edmonton N = 324	
Set for trial	94	3.0%	33	4.1%	170	19.3%	175	54.0%
Trial Outcomes*								
Guilty verdict	52	55.3%	12	36.4%	29	17.1%	30	17.1%
Not guilty	33	35.1%	15	45.5%	17	10.0%	46	26.3%
Dismissed	8	8.5%	6	18.2%	124	72.9%	98	56.0%
Discharged	1	1.1%	0		0		1	0.5%

* Percentage of outcomes calculated by number of trials.

Once again, Edmonton is unique in this data set because it only deals with cases set for trial, thus it is not surprising that it has the highest percentage of trial cases. Interestingly, Calgary has a high rate of cases set for trial relative to Regina and Winnipeg. The reason for this is unclear given that their specialization is limited to first appearances.

Finally, Table 4.10 presents data with respect to the sentences handed down to accused persons who were either found guilty by the court or pled guilty.

Table 4.10: Sentences for Convicted Offenders by Court Site

	Winnipeg N = 1,706		Regina N = 437		Calgary N = 287		Edmonton N = 170	
Probation	1,356	79.5%	317	72.5%	225	78.4%	92	54.1%
Incarceration	492	28.8%	79	18.1%	59	20.6%	30	17.6%
Fine/Restitution	258	15.1%	33	7.6%	48	16.7%	40	23.5%
Conditional discharge	192	11.3%	78	17.8%	8	2.8%	8	4.7%
Absolute discharge	27	1.6%	2	0.1%	1	0.3%	2	1.2%

One of the anticipated outcomes of court specialization was a change in sentencing patterns (Ursel, 2002). However, the differences in Table 4.10

are ambiguous. There are as many differences between the three specialized courts as there are differences between the specialized and non-specialized courts. This may be a reflection of the fact that specialization in Alberta is partial — Calgary only has a first-appearance court and Edmonton, only a trial court.

Our descriptive analysis of the differences in court outcomes and sentencing indicates some clear differences between the four courts. However, at the descriptive level, it is difficult to specify the cause of these differences. For example, Winnipeg stands out as having the highest proportion of offenders sentenced to jail. This could be an indication of a more severe sentencing practice, but it could also be a reflection of the much higher prior record rates for crimes against persons among accused in Winnipeg (three times higher than Calgary). Similarly, Winnipeg has the highest guilty verdict rate at trials: 55.3% relative to 17.1% in Calgary and Edmonton and 36.4% in Regina (Table 4.9). While this could be an indication of very successful prosecutors, it is more likely a reflection of the very small percentage of cases set for trial — that is, more rigorous screening rather than more rigorous prosecution.

These caveats indicate that comparative analyses of different court models must be careful to control for the characteristics of the accused and the crime as well as the screening practices of prosecutors before reaching conclusions about the most effective models or practices. One limitation of the current study is an inability to control for all relevant variables because partially specialized courts resulted in partial information. For example, in Edmonton, specialized only at the trial court level, it was not feasible to track information for accused persons whose cases did not proceed to trial. Typically, only about 15% of all accused have their cases set for trial. Thus, this comparative study provides a cautionary tale about the importance of having sufficiently comparable court processes to provide comparable data sets and facilitate meaningful comparisons. As the first comparative court study of its kind in Canada, this study calls attention to the critical factors to be considered when assessing the more detailed court evaluations in the following chapters.

Conclusions

The momentum for specialized domestic violence courts in the criminal justice system is increasing. Since the data for the above comparative study were collected in 2002, specialized courts have been opened in North Battleford and Saskatoon, Saskatchewan, and in Moncton, New Brunswick. Further, specialization in Calgary was extended to include a trial court in 2005. Finally, a committee of service providers and justice personnel in Regina are developing a proposal for a fully specialized court in their city and the concept of specialization is under review in British Columbia. Thus, it is timely and important to consider existing studies of specialized courts in Canada.

This chapter has laid the groundwork for understanding how the criminal justice system works and the goals and objectives of specialization. It has also provided a brief overview of studies that look at the impact of court-mandated treatment on an offender's likelihood of reoffending. Research in this area is of growing importance given the tendency for specialized courts to put greater emphasis on treatment interventions as a form of diversion and a condition of sentence. The chapter concluded with some preliminary findings from the first comparative court study involving specialized domestic violence courts in Canada. The reader is invited to assess the merits of each court model presented in the subsequent chapters in light of the "lessons learned" from the comparative court study.

Notes

1   This is true only for some provinces. It is more accurate to say "there are two primary levels of criminal courts in Canada: provincial courts and superior courts." In Ontario the superior court is called the Supreme Court of Ontario. It would be accurate to say it is the Court of Queen's Bench in the provinces included in this study.

2   Canadian studies include Augusta-Scott and Dankwort (2002) in Nova Scotia; Montminy, et al. (2003) in Quebec; Palmer, Brown and Barrera (1992); Barrera et al. (1994), Scott and Wolfe (2000), Tutty, et al. (2001) in Ontario; and McGregor et al. (2002) in Alberta.

3   This Community University Research Alliance (CURA) project was funded by Canada's Social Sciences and Humanities Research Council from 2000 to 2004 to compare the efficacy of the community and justice responses to abuse of women in the major cities in the three Prairie provinces (Tutty et al., forthcoming).

4   The Winnipeg police and social worker program operated for three years as a pilot project. Modified in 2005, police now work in conjunction with victim service staff addressing similar situations.

5   While inferential statistics are normally used on samples from populations, the four research sites constitute a mix. Winnipeg, Calgary and Regina represent the entire population of cases, but Edmonton is a subset of all DV cases.

CHAPTER FIVE

The Winnipeg Family Violence Court

Jane Ursel and Christine Hagyard

The Winnipeg Family Violence Court (FVC) came into operation on September 15, 1990; it was the first specialized domestic violence court in Canada. This chapter provides some history of how and why it began. It outlines the major components of this specialization and follows with an analysis of the influence the specialized court has had over time.

As the first author of this chapter, I should reveal that my relationship to this court is complex. I studied the court response to domestic violence cases from 1983 to 1990, prior to specialization, first as an academic and later as a government employee. I worked in government for five years from 1985 to 1990 before returning to academic life in the summer of 1990. During my time in government I held several positions. I was the first provincial coordinator of Wife Abuse Services, in which capacity I played an active role in the development of these services. I set up the Women's Advocacy Program in 1986, which became an integral part of the specialized court when it was introduced. I was also part of the implementation committee that met regularly and planned for the introduction of the specialized court. Thus, I have not been a disinterested observer, and it is best for the reader to know this. Having a foot in each world, academe and government, has given me some unique perspectives on the specialized court and some unique opportunities, not the least of which has been my ability to collect the Family Violence Court data for the full 17 years of its operation.

The History of the Winnipeg Family Violence Court

The change that led to the implementation of the Winnipeg Family Violence Court (FVC) began in the early 1980s, when Attorneys General across Canada began to issue directives to the police forces under their jurisdiction. They were responding to the complaints of women's groups that there was a "double standard" in the justice system — "If you hit a stranger, it's a crime; if you hit your partner, that's too bad and you needed counselling." In short, the police did not usually arrest in response to a domestic violence call. In 1983, the Manitoba Attorney General issued a directive to the police to lay a charge if there were reasonable and probable grounds that a crime had occurred, regardless of the relationship of the accused to the victim. This was the legal standard for all crimes — it had just not been applied in cases of intimate partner violence. While this may not have seemed particularly radical (it did seem fair and just), it began a process in Canada that has now resulted in six jurisdictions having specialized courts. Further, similar courts have been set up in England and Australia, often based on the Canadian model.

Why did such a simple directive shake up the system? In Manitoba, for the first time in our history, we could count the occurrence of assaults against women by their partners through police arrests! It is true that emergency women's shelters, just beginning to grow in number across Canada in the early 1980s, were telling us about the large number of women seeking safety; however, there is nothing like police statistics to get public attention. In Winnipeg, this meant that the number of spousal abuse cases coming to court increased and newspaper court reporters began to take notice. A similar circumstance arose in Ontario in 1997 (see Dawson and Dinovitzer, chapter 6 in this volume).

Before specialization, spousal abuse cases were heard alongside shoplifting, break and enter and the wide variety of criminal offences that appear in Provincial Court. We began to see disturbing headlines in our press — for example, "Days of Terror Net Suspended Term" in the *Winnipeg Sun* of December 18, 1987. The lack of serious consequences for individuals found guilty or who pled guilty to beating their wives was coming to the public's attention, and it did not conform to the public's idea of justice.

In Winnipeg, government officials in the Departments of Justice and Family Services and in the Women's Directorate began to meet to discuss a possible specialized court. At this time, we were fortunate to have a very open-minded group of decision-makers: our Chief Judge of the Provincial Court, our Director of Public Prosecutions and our Minister of Justice, who had been a court reporter and had "seen it all." These key actors were willing to dare to change an old and revered system, a system that clearly was not able to respond effectively to the growing number of domestic assaults that were coming through the courts. The press, always up for a good headline, published dire statements by esteemed judges and outraged defence lawyers that domestic violence cases did not belong in the court. But interestingly, they appeared to be the voice of the past. Public opinion surveys were conducted by the Winnipeg Area Study in 1985, two years after the first directive to lay charges in cases of intimate partner violence; in 1991 after the introduction of the court; and again in 1995, two years after a more rigorous directive to charge was introduced, all of which indicated overwhelming support for these policies (Ursel, 2006). The community at large believed that assaulting a family member was a crime and it was time to hold offenders accountable.

What began as a directive to charge put a process in motion that substantially changed how domestic violence cases were treated in the criminal justice system (CJS) in Manitoba. One of the themes we explore in this chapter is the extent of integration in the CJS. A change in one component of the system affects the entire system over time, causing each component, from the police to corrections, to change their policies and practices in order to adapt to the new circumstances. Figure 5.1 documents the sequence of policy changes, and the following section describes their implementation in specialist programs and services.

Components of Specialization

To assess the comprehensiveness of the justice response, it is helpful to know the size of the population it serves. Manitoba has a population of one million people, two-thirds of whom live in the City of Winnipeg, approximately

670,000 residents. Several of the specialized components exist in towns outside of Winnipeg, which will be highlighted in the following description.

Figure 5.1: Critical Criminal Justice Policy Changes

---

* **1983** — Directive to police to charge, regardless of relation of accused to victim
* **1986** — Woman's Advocacy Program, for women whose partners are charged
* **1990** — Winnipeg Specialized Domestic Violence Court
* **1992** — Corrections-Domestic Violence Initiative
* **1993** — Mandatory arrest policy, Winnipeg police
* **1996** — Criminal Code amendment to oblige courts to consider abuse of spouse or child as an aggravating factor in sentencing
* **1999** — *Domestic Violence and Stalking Protection Act*
* **2001** — Special Domestic Violence Unit in provincial prison

---

The cases that are seen in the specialist court include "all cases in which the accused is in a relationship of trust, dependency and/or kinship." This includes intimate partner abuse, child abuse and elder abuse. In partner abuse cases, the Crown guideline states: "Domestic assault for the purposes of this policy, is defined as physical or sexual assault or the threat of physical or sexual assault of a victim by a person with whom they have or have had an intimate relationship, whether or not they are legally married or living together at the time of the assault or threat" (Prosecutors Guideline, April 2000). The components of specialization are listed below roughly in the order that an individual encounters them in the justice system.

1. **Police**: At the entry level, the police label all cases which are domestic, and all police officers on duty are the first responders and usually the arresting officers. The Winnipeg Police Service has 10 specialized staff: a domestic violence coordinator, eight officers who specialize in follow-up investigations in two of the busier police districts, and an officer/instructor in charge of domestic violence training at the police academy.

2. **Victim Services**: The Provincial Victim Services Program employs 52 staff who are employees of the Manitoba Department of Justice. In Winnipeg this includes three relevant programs with 16 staff. The Domestic Violence Unit (formerly the Woman's Advocacy Program)

has eight counsellors who provide specialist services to spousal abuse victims whose partners have been charged. An early intervention program is made up of five staff members who work with domestic violence victims who have called police but whose partners haven't been charged. Finally, two staff members support victims of all homicide cases, including surviving family members in domestic homicides. During court hours at least one staff member is available for court attendance and at least one other assists individuals applying for protection orders (see Busby, Koshan & Wiegers, chapter 9, and Laurie, chapter 10 in this volume). The Victim Services staff meet with women to respond to their questions, explain the court process, do risk assessments and protection planning as well as provide court accompaniment and referrals.

3.   **Crown Prosecutors**: The Domestic Violence Unit consist of 17 Crown attorneys who specialize in the prosecution of all Winnipeg domestic violence cases. This unit utilizes a practice called "file ownership," a process to ensure that the same prosecutor will handle the same case even if it goes to a higher court or to an appeal court, and especially if the accused reoffends. The intent is to have a single prosecutor handle the case so that he/she becomes very familiar with the accused's pattern of behaviour. The other benefit is that the victim will only have to deal with one prosecutor, minimizing the number of times she has to tell her story. The prosecutors in this unit sometimes also do circuit court, that is, they prosecute cases in communities outside of Winnipeg that have a visiting rather than a resident court, judge, prosecutors, and so on. As a result, because a high percentage of cases in circuit court involve domestic assaults, the smaller communities get the benefit of a specialized prosecutor when they otherwise wouldn't.

4.   **Judges**: In the first two years, 14 selected judges sat in the domestic violence court. However, since 1992, all of the Provincial Court judges have rotated in the domestic violence courtrooms.

5.   **Court**: Within the Winnipeg Provincial Court, the entire process for hearing domestic violence cases is specialized. The specialized process includes a domestic violence bail court, several courtrooms that daily hear guilty pleas and sentence the offender, and two trial courts for

adjudicating cases in which the accused enters a not guilty plea. In total each day, five or more courtrooms hear family violence matters (depending on the number of trials), adding up to a minimum of 60 hours of court time per week.

6. **Corrections**: There has been a dramatic expansion of domestic violence treatment programs in Manitoba as a result of specialization. Since 1992, all correction facilities, including jails and probation offices, throughout the province have trained staff who offer treatment programs for offenders. The purpose of this expansion was to ensure that all convicted offenders receive a treatment program from corrections that is free of charge and available throughout the province. In addition, the local provincial prison that services most Winnipeg offenders has a specialized unit within the prison that provides intensive treatment and interventions for individuals who are in prison for domestic offences. Corrections only deals with convicted offenders. In cases involving individuals who receive a stay of proceedings with an order for counselling, the treatment is provided by non-governmental agencies.

Domestic Violence Court Cases

The information presented in this chapter represents a decade of data collection in the Family Violence Court. We collected information on all cases directly from the docket and coded all of the details of each case from the Crown attorney's file. Thus, the data presented are not a sample but the total population of individuals who have been charged. For the decade 1992–2002, we have data on 30,554 separate cases involving a total of 22,732 individuals. The difference between cases and individuals is accounted for by repeat offenders.

Our unit of analysis is the individual accused, not the charges with which he/she enters the system. It is not uncommon for individuals to have five or more charges when they have their first court appearance, some of which may be dropped. However, if they plead guilty or are found guilty of any of the charges, their case is counted as a conviction. We calculate the stay rate and the conviction rate from the point of arrest. This is important because some authors count the outcome from the point at which the prosecutors decide to proceed with the case. The latter starting point produces a much higher conviction rate.

In the first two years after the court opened in 1990, the volume was relatively low and there were dedicated judges hearing the cases. After 1992, the volume rose dramatically and every judge in the Provincial Court had a rotation through the specialized courtrooms. For the purposes of this chapter, we are reporting on the period between 1992 and 2002, a decade in which the volume and the personnel in the court remained relatively constant. Finally, the Winnipeg Family Violence Court, like the Calgary HomeFront Court (Tutty, McNichol & Christensen, chapter 7 in this volume), hears all family matters, spousal abuse, child abuse and elder abuse. However, for this discussion, we only report on the spousal abuse cases, which constitute about 83% of the total. Given the high percentage of women victims and male accused, we have used the pronoun she for victims and he for accused for simplicity, although, we clearly recognize the fact that a small percentage of victims are men and a small percentage of accused are women.

Our findings are presented in three sections. In the first section, we look at the effect specialization has had on the volume of cases coming to the attention of police and the courts. In the second section, we outline what we know about the victims and the accused, and in the third section we examine the outcomes of being arrested, including how many cases proceed to court, how many are stayed and the impact of different case outcomes on the incident of recidivism. Finally, we conclude with a brief discussion of some of the challenges to the specialized court.

Specialization and the Increase in Cases

The event that triggers the involvement of the CJS is usually a call to police by the victim because she fears for herself and/or her children. In Winnipeg, most calls are 911 emergency calls, although in some cases the incident is reported after the fact on a non-emergency line. Over the decade approximately 82% of the calls to the police were made by the victim, 8% of the calls were made by a friend or neighbour, 5% by children or family member and 5% were institutional, that is, by a social worker or hospital staff. Figure 5.2 shows the change in arrest rates from 1983–2002. This figure provides a clear indication that arrest rates have increased with time; however, the greatest increases have occurred since court specialization (1990–91).

Figure 5.2: Spousal Assault Arrest Rates in Winnipeg 1983–2002 before and after Specialization

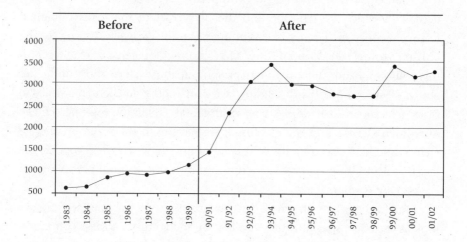

One of the most interesting findings from our data is the evidence of the extent to which the various components of the justice system were integrated and how changes within these components affected the public and the police. Keeping in mind that almost 90% of the calls to police were initiated by the victim and/or her family, these calls appear to have increased as new components to the specialized justice system were added. This is documented in Winnipeg police records that report that calls for service labelled as "domestic" rose from 9,685 in 1990 to 14,662 in 2000.

The other factor that explains the rising arrest rates is police behaviour at the incident. Winnipeg police records indicate that the ratio of arrest to calls for service rose from 7% in 1990 to a peak of 36% in 1993 and 1994 and has fluctuated between 25–30% since. Changes in the behaviours of both victims and police can separately affect the arrest rate. The combination of high calls and a higher ratio of arrest produces a rapid increase in arrests.

Two factors appear to have provoked changes in the likelihood of victims calling police and in the likelihood of police making an arrest: (1) the accumulation of policies encouraging intervention within the CJS, and (2) dramatic incidents that attract high-profile media coverage. When an incident or an innovative program such as the Family Violence Court receives high media coverage, potential victims become more sensitive to risk, are more aware of available resources and are therefore more likely to call police for help. Shelters and crisis lines also experience an increase in calls under those circumstances, as potential victims seek help and advice from many sources. At the same time, police are aware that it is a "sensitive" issue and tend to follow policy more strictly.

Figure 5.2 illustrates the impact of both policy initiatives and high-profile incidents on arrest rates. The peak in 1993–94 reflects the introduction of a strict mandatory arrest policy by police that attracted a great deal of debate and media coverage, and the peak in 1999–2000 reflects sustained and intense media coverage of a tragic dual domestic homicide.[1] Thus, fluctuations in rates can be explained by situational events; however, the more or less consistent rise in arrests over the 20 years of policy change can be largely attributed to these policies and their impact on the public and on police.

Further evidence of the interaction effect between public perception of the justice system and the likelihood of calling the police is found in the 1999–2000 National Transition Home survey conducted by Statistics Canada (Locke and Code, 2000). Women who were resident in a shelter at the time of the survey were asked about their previous violent assault and whether they called the police. The study revealed that the jurisdiction in which police were most likely to arrest, Manitoba, was also the jurisdiction in which women were most likely to call the police.

Dual Arrest

This rising arrest rate has caused some critics of the CJS to warn that mandatory arrest rates can lead to dual arrests (countercharging). This occurs when police respond to an incident and both the man and the woman claim that they are the victim and police charge both of them. Dual arrests are a problem for two reasons. The most obvious is the terrible effect it has on a victim who calls for help and ends up being charged. The police in Winnipeg have implemented training to assist officers in identifying the dominant aggressor and reduce the number of dual arrests. These arrests are also a problem for the prosecutor because, if both the husband and wife have been arrested, they both have a vested interest in denying the incident, resulting in very high stay rates in cases of dual arrest.

We examined the incidence of dual arrest in the year prior to the mandatory arrest policy and compared it to a number of years after the policy was introduced. We found that in the year prior to the policy (1992–93), the police arrested a single accused person in 94.5% of the incidents, with dual arrests occurring in 5.5% of the incidents. In the year the mandatory arrest policy was implemented (1993–94), the police arrested a single accused in 93% of the incidents, and dual arrests occurred in 7% of the incidents. The highest rate of dual arrests occurred in 1997–98, when it reached 9%, and then it dropped to 7% in 2000, staying at that level for the next three years, suggesting that the police training to identify the dominant aggressor may have made a difference. Calgary reports a 9.7% dual arrest rate but they do not site "before" data (Tutty et al., chapter 7 in this volume). Thus in Winnipeg, the before and after effect of mandatory arrest has meant an increase of 2–3.5% in dual arrests, depending on the year. It is interesting to note that despite the fact that dual arrests occur in some circumstances, this has not resulted in a decline in calls to the police. Ultimately policy-makers must assess which poses the greatest risk to the security of women and children: our past experience of police reluctance to charge in most circumstances or the present experience of police error in charging too many people in a small percentage of cases. To date, policy-makers in Manitoba continue to support the mandatory arrest policy.

In Winnipeg we have found that community attitudes change when there is a consistent message from the police, the courts and corrections that spousal assault is a serious crime that can pose serious risks for the victim and will result in serious consequences for the offender. As a result, there are more calls to the police and an increase in the volume of cases in the courts and in corrections.

Accused and Victim Characteristics

Because our data are taken from prosecutors' files, it is an offender-based data set. As a result, we tend to have more information on accused persons than on victims; however, we will present the victim characteristics when the data permit. Table 5.1 provides a summary of the major demographic characteristics of the accused and the victim.

Table 5.1: Accused and Victim Demographic Characteristics*

Characteristic	Accused $N = 30,706$	Victim $N = 32,086$
Gender		
Male	83%	16%
Female	17%	80%
Male/Female	< 1%	4%
Ethnicity**		
European origin	49%	46%
Aboriginal origin	39%	36%
Other	12%	17%
Average age	33 years	32 years

* The fact that the number of accused and victims exceed the number of cases (30,554) is a result of the fact that there are a few cases of multiple accused and more frequently multiple victims.
** The ethnicity of the victim was known in only one-third of the cases.

People of Aboriginal origin make up approximately 13% of the population of Winnipeg, but make up 39% of the accused in FVC where ethnic origin was known. Aboriginal accused and victims were overrepresented by a factor of three. However, it is important to recall the numerous national incidence studies conducted by Statistics Canada (1999, 2004), by Amnesty International (2004) and by Aboriginal women's groups, which consistently report that Aboriginal women are three times more likely to be abused by an intimate partner than non-Aboriginal women. Tragically, their presence in the FVC may be an accurate representation of the incidence of violence in their lives.

The average age of victims was 32 and the average age of accused persons was 33. The range in age was 18 to 87 for the accused and 16 to 83 for the victims. While the range in age was broad, the majority of victims and accused were relatively young. If any comfort is to be had from these statistics, it is that research shows that earlier intervention in the cycle of violence is more likely to break that cycle.

Information on the relationship of the victim and the accused indicates that the most frequent cases heard in FVC involved abuse in ongoing relationships: 36% common law, 20% boyfriend-girlfriend and 16% husband and wife. However, 24% of all cases involved ex-partners: 9% ex-common law, 8% ex-boyfriend-girlfriend and 7% ex-spouse. The fact that so many relationships were intact, at least at the time of their court case, gives some insight into why victims were so often reluctant to co-operate with the prosecution. It also highlights the importance of early intervention and treatment programs, because many of these couples would reconcile.

Another factor of interest is the number of accused who assault their ex-partner. This suggests that the actual percentage of victims who were women was probably closer to 84% than the 80% listed for single victim or all female victims. In the 4% of cases listed as male/female victims, the usual scenario involved a man assaulting his former female partner in the presence of her new partner or friend. Thus, the primary or intended victim was the woman, but often her male companion would be assaulted as well.

We have information on the education and employment history of the accused but not the victim. The data indicate that persons listed as unemployed (16%) or on welfare (33%) and persons with a lower than average education were overrepresented in the FVC, as they generally are in most criminal courts. Critics of the justice system point to this overrepresentation of the disadvantaged as further evidence of the negative consequences of criminalizing domestic violence matters. However, it is important to recall that 90% of the calls to the police come from the victim and/or her family. If the victims are as disadvantaged as their accused partner, this typically means that, unlike a middle-class victim, they may have no other source of help but to call the police. While most victims will concede that calling the police would be their last resort, we know that middle-class victims have more resources[2] to protect them from this last resort (Strange, 1995). So, if a victim or her family has no other source of help but to call the police, is it unjust for the police to intervene and, where evidence of a crime exists, to arrest?

The overrepresentation of accused persons with low income and low education is an issue. However, one way to assess whether the arrest was appropriate, whether the person arrested really did pose a threat to the security of the victim, is to examine the accused's history of prior violence. All risk assessment measures indicate that past behaviour is one of the best indicators of future behaviour and on that basis the prior records of the accused imply a serious level of risk.

Table 5.2: Prior Arrests of Accused in the Winnipeg Family Violence Court 1992–2002

Spousal N = 28,843*	# of Cases	% of All Cases	% of Cases with Priors
Has a prior arrest	23,518	82%	
Domestic	11,236	39%	48%
General assault	5,885	20%	25%
Sexual abuse	711	3%	3%
Child abuse	99	< 1%	< 1%
All crimes against persons	17,931	62%	76%
Other prior arrests	5,587	19%	24%

* There was missing information on prior record for 6% of the cases.

Based on the assumption that past behaviour is a good predictor of future behaviour, the finding that 82% of the accused had a prior arrest for some criminal matter suggests a serious potential for risk among the accused. Most importantly, Table 5.2 indicates that 48% of those prior arrests had been for domestic offences and 76% of the prior arrests had been for some crime against a person. This suggests that persons being arrested could reasonably be considered as posing a significant future risk to the victim.

The Court Process and Outcomes

In traditional court studies, the issue of conviction rate and sentencing is of primary concern. However, one of the distinguishing features of the specialized court is its commitment to providing an effective intervention to the cycle of violence, and this may not always be a conviction. In Manitoba, the guidelines for the prosecution's Domestic Violence Unit encourage vigorous prosecutions but not at the expense of revictimizing the victim. In a sense, the Manitoba model lies between the more traditional model in the Toronto K Court, which puts a high premium on convictions (Dawson & Dinovitzer, chapter 6 in this volume), and the Calgary model, which prioritizes treatment over conviction for low-risk cases (Tutty et al., chapter 7 in this volume).

As Dawson and Dinovitzer (2001) point out, the most important determinant of case outcome is the strength of the evidence that is based upon a victim's co-operation with the prosecution. It is well documented in the literature that victims are often extremely ambivalent about testifying against their partner (Ursel, 1998a, 2002; Dawson & Dinovitzer, 2001). Prosecutors have two strategies for dealing with the unpredictability of victim testimony. First, they can encourage the police to take photos and/or audiotape or videotape the victim's statement at the time of the incident, which may allow them to proceed without victim testimony. The second option, not uncommon in Winnipeg, is that the Crown can negotiate with the victim about what outcome she would like to see, with the hope of gaining a guilty plea and a joint sentencing recommendation with the defence. This has been described as "testimony bargaining" (Ursel, 1998a).

A typical bargaining process unfolds in the following way: a victim indicates to the Crown that she will not testify as a witness because she cannot afford having her husband jailed. The prosecutor then asks the victim what outcome, ideally, she would like. More often than not, she simply wants the violence to end; she does not want to leave her partner or see him go to jail. In response, the Crown attorney might offer to drop the most serious charge that could lead to a jail sentence and recommend probation and court-mandated treatment in exchange for her testimony. If she agrees, the Crown notifies the defence that the victim will testify and, most often, the case is resolved through a guilty plea.

In circumstances in which the victim refuses to co-operate because she does not want her partner to have a criminal record, the Crown can recommend a delay in the case and offer the accused a potential stay of proceedings if he attends, participates in and completes a treatment program. A stay will occur when the Crown receives a report from the treatment program verifying the accused's participation. This is similar to the Calgary HomeFront process (Tutty et al., chapter 7 in this volume). A "stay with counselling" typically occurs when the accused is judged to be of lower risk and the victim agrees with the treatment option. Because the prosecutors are reluctant to put an uncooperative witness on the stand,[3] one of the features of the FVC is a relatively high stay rate. However, often these are stays with consequences, either treatment or a peace bond or both.

Type of Charge and Court Outcome

In Winnipeg, as in the other courts reviewed in this book, the accused most frequently enters the CJS with the charge of common assault. However, a large number of accused are charged with multiple offences at the time they are arrested. A frequent combination is common assault and breach of a court order and uttering threats. There are two ways that we can calculate charges: a gross count to determine all the charges by case and their frequency, which adds up to more than 100% because of multiple charges, or a net count, in which we record only the one most serious charge with which an individual enters the system (eliminating multiple charges). Table 5.3 identifies the charge characteristics calculated both ways.

Table 5.3: Types of Charges in the Winnipeg Family Violence Court by Case[1] 1992–2002 (*N* = 30,554)

Types of Charges	Frequency of All Charges by Case		Frequency of Most Serious Charge by Case	
Common assault	18,749	61%	16,934	56%
Breach	13,214	43%	3,773	12%
Uttering threats & criminal harassment	6,185	20%	3,039	10%
Assault with a weapon	3,526	12%	3,133	10%
Aggravated assault & ACBH[2]	3,229	11%	3,220	11%
Sexual assault	418	1%	418	1%
Murder[3]	37	< 1%	37	<1%

1 Counting charges by case means that if an accused has four counts of common assault on a single case, we count it once and not four times.
2 ACBH — assault causing bodily harm.
3 Murder includes charges of first- and second-degree murder, manslaughter and attempted murder.

The second column in Table 5.3 indicates that only half (56%) of the individuals charged had common assault as their most serious charge. If we combine all of the indictable charges (i.e., all subsequent charges excluding breaches), we find that a third of the accused had an additional, indictable offence charge. This, combined with the high prior arrest rate, indicates that the FVC is dealing with a significant number of serious assaults.

Case Outcomes

Over the decade under review, the conviction rate in FVC has increased from a low of 45% in 1995–96 to a high of 55.8% in 2001–02, which is similar to the conviction rate in Toronto's K Court of 55.6% (Dawson & Dinovitzer, chapter 6 in this volume). Interestingly, the increase in conviction rates seems to have occurred in conjunction with the appointment of a committed prosecutor who was the supervisor of the Domestic Violence Unit. She formalized the process by which a charge may be stayed with counselling and increased the conviction rate at the same time. This is yet another indicator that all the best policies won't necessarily make a difference unless there are committed personnel to carry them out. To capture the change in conviction rates over time, Table 5.4 presents the court outcomes for the full decade in the second column, for the first two years (1992–94) in the third column and for the last two years (2000–02) in the fourth column.

Two factors account for the increase in conviction rates in the last two years under review. The most obvious is the 10% increase in guilty pleas; however, the other factor is the dramatic reduction in cases set for trial. In 1992–94, 960 cases were set for trial with 332 or 35% resulting in guilty verdicts. Trials are risky for prosecutors because of the high rate of victims who do not show up to testify (as measured by cases dismissed or discharged). In the last two years under review, only 216 cases were set for trial, less than a quarter of the number set in 1992–94. Furthermore, of those that did proceed to trial in 2000–02, 47% resulted in a guilty verdict.

The other change in court outcomes is the introduction of the treatment option with a stay of proceedings. In 1992–94, there were no documented cases of stay with counselling; however, in 2000–02, 706 or 9% of cases

Table 5.4: Court Outcomes 1992–2002 and Selected Years

Court Outcome	1992–2002 N = 30,546		1992–1994* N = 7,469	2000–2002** N = 7,586
Guilty plea	14,089	46%	44%	54%
Guilty verdict	695	2%	4%	1%
All Convictions	14,784	48%	48%	55%
Stay of proceedings	10,736	35%	34%	26%
Stay with peace bond	2,410	8%	9%	8%
Stay with counselling	1,135	4%	0%	9%
All Stays	14,281	47%	43%	43%
Trial Not Guilty	479	2%	3%	1%
Dismissed/Discharged	943	3%	6%	<1%
Accused deceased (Number not percentage)	59		5	22

*1992–94 total set for trial (332 guilty + 186 not guilty + 442 dismissed) = 960.
**2000–02 total set for trial (101 guilty + 79 not guilty + 36 dismissed) = 216.

were disposed of in this way. This is particularly important because when we look at recidivism rates for those who had a stay of proceedings; the individuals who had a stay with counselling had half the recidivism rate of those who had a stay with a peace bond. This has very important policy and practice implications for prosecutors.

Sentencing

One of the first and most dramatic changes to have occurred with the introduction of the specialized court has been the shift in sentencing. In the seven years prior to specialization, the most frequent sentence for a convicted offender was "conditional discharge." This can be interpreted as "Yes, the accused did the crime, but there is no treatment ordered, no punishment and they are not left with a criminal record after the discharge period ..." — in short, no consequences. When specialization was introduced, the most frequent sentence became probation, and the second most frequent sentence, incarceration: there are now serious consequences for domestic violence offences.

Table 5.5: Sentences for Convicted Offenders in the Winnipeg Family Violence Court

Number of cases[1] resulting in sentence N = 14,784 or 48% of all accused		
Probation	10,180	69%
Incarceration	3,707	25%
Fine	2,222	15%
Conditional discharge	2,144	15%
Absolute discharge	278	·2%

1   Number of cases are less than the total number of sentences and percentages are greater than 100, because offenders frequently have two or more sentence outcomes per case for example, three months in jail and two years probation.

The overwhelming majority of the convicted offenders receive a sentence of one to two years probation and court-mandated treatment. In all cases in which we have full information (90%) on the conditions of probation, 81% included court-mandated treatment. It is further important to note that 98% of the sentences to jail were to the local provincial jail, which has the special Domestic Violence Unit. This ensured that most offenders would have the opportunity to attend and complete the treatment in jail.

A serious consequence does not imply a single-minded focus on punishment. All of the offenders who are incarcerated and 81% of the offenders who were on probation would receive treatment. Further, with the stay-with-counselling option introduced in the latter two years, we find that approximately 10% of those individuals whose cases were stayed also had a treatment imperative. Thus, while the Winnipeg FVC is not a treatment court like the Yukon model (Hornick et al., chapter 8 in this volume), it does place a high priority on treatment for offenders and accused.

When we consider sentences by the most serious charges, we find that the highest rate of incarceration (38%) was for those who were convicted of sexual assault; the second highest rate (34%) was for persons who had been convicted of major assaults (aggravated, ACBH, etc.), and the third highest rate (32%) was for those convicted of breaches. While incarcerating individuals convicted of breaches may seem extreme, because it is generally assumed that breaches are "minor offences," our data indicate that persons sentenced with breaches had one of the highest rates of recidivism. Thus, their sentences may have been quite appropriate when considering the risk they pose to the victims.

Recidivism

One of the greatest concerns for victims, service providers and CJS personnel is whether the offender will commit a violent act again. For the victim, this is a measure of her risk; for the criminal justice system, it is a measure of its efficacy. Therefore, recidivism is a central issue to any assessment of differing court models of intervention. Within the CJS, recidivism is typically measured in terms of the accused's reappearance in the system due to a subsequent arrest. These are the data we have available to us in the FVC.

However, this is a crude measure at best because an abuser may reoffend in a new town or city and that offence would not show up in the Winnipeg data. The other limitation is that the abuser may continue to abuse but his partner (either the original victim or a new partner) may not call the police. The most thorough measure would be follow-up interviews with the partners of abusive men; unfortunately, these are expensive and time-consuming studies that are only occasionally undertaken. However, several partner follow-up studies have been conducted (Gondolf, 2002; Dobash et al., 2000), typically to assess the outcome of treatment programs, whether court ordered or voluntary.

The FVC study has several measures of recidivism and factors that are correlated with recidivism. Overall, our decade of data indicates that approximately 10% of accused did reoffend within one year, and within the decade about 40% reoffended at least once. Table 5.6 presents an analysis of individual accused, their number of offences over the decade and the relationship between number of times they have reoffended and their conviction rates.

The first row of Table 5.6 indicates that 60% of all of the individuals in the 10-year data set offended only once, and their conviction rate was the lowest at 37%.[4] In these cases, if the charge was common assault, there were no aggravating factors and the victim concurred, these individuals would be the most likely candidates for a stay with counselling or stay with peace bond. In the second row, we see individuals who had reoffended once accounting for 21% of the individuals; on their second offence their conviction rate increased to 48%.

Table 5.6: Spousal Abuse Reoffence Pattern and Conviction Rate Winnipeg Family Violence Court 1992–2002

Single/Repeat Accused	Number of Individuals	% of All Individuals	Conviction Rate
Single offence	13,469	60%	37%
1 Reoffence	4,819	21%	48%
2–3 Reoffences	2,923	13%	54%
4–5 Reoffences	855	4%	57%
6–9 Reoffences	396	2%	62%
10–23 Reoffences	122	<1%	67%
Total	22,584	100%	46%

Table 5.6 indicates that, with every increase in number of reoffences, the conviction rate rises. It is significant to note that 34% of all individuals reoffended three times or less and 60% had a single offence. Thus, 94% would not be considered chronic reoffenders. The 34% of individuals who reoffended three times or less would be likely candidates for sentences of probation and treatment or short incarceration and treatment. In contrast, the 122 individuals who reoffended 10 to 23 times were clearly chronic reoffenders. While these individuals constituted less than 1% of the accused in a decade, they posed a major threat to their victim(s) and a major challenge to the system. A preliminary analysis of one-third of these chronic reoffenders indicates that they always targeted the same woman (the original victim), condemning her to a life of terror unless an effective solution could be found.

To achieve a more accurate measure of recidivism, we selected all accused from one year, 2000, and checked to see how many of the individuals who were arrested in 2000 had reoffended by the end of 2003. This standardized the time during which they had to reoffend (three years). We looked at this group and assessed their reoffence rate by the court outcome and by two categories of reoffence. The first category is all criminal code offences other than breach and the second category is all breach offences. Table 5.7 presents our findings of reoffence by court outcome.

Table 5.7 reveals that, overall, 40% of accused persons who appeared before the FVC in 2000 reoffended. The highest category of reoffenders were those individuals who had been convicted either by a guilty plea or a guilty

Table 5.7: Recidivism Rate by Court Outcome
and Type of Reoffence

N = 2,443				
Court Outcome	**# Individuals**	**New Offence***	**Breach Only**	**Total****
Guilty plea	1,150	391 (34%)	195 (17%)	51%
Guilty verdict	27	11 (41%)	4 (15%)	56%
All Convictions	1,177	402 (34%)	199 (17%)	51%
Stay of proceedings	800	216 (27%)	40 (5%)	32%
Stay with peace bond	211	44 (21%)	21 (10%)	31%
Stay with counselling	199	30 (15%)	4 (2%)	17%
All Stays	1,210	290 (24%)	65 (5%)	29%
Trail Not Guilty	28	5 (18%)	3 (11%)	29%
Dismissed/ Discharged	28	7 (25%)	4 (14%)	39%
Total	2,443	704 (29%)	271 (11%)	40%

*Any new offence other than breach.
**All percentages are row percentages.

verdict, and the highest recidivism was for those who were convicted through trial (56%). In the category of individuals who had a stay of proceedings, the lowest recidivism rate was for stay with counselling (17%), the lowest rate of recidivism in all categories. If we separate out breach offences from other offences, we have a reoffence rate of 15% for stay of proceedings with counselling, with breaches accounting for the other 2% of arrests.

Interestingly, stay with peace bond appears to have no more effect in reducing the overall recidivism rate than a stay with no conditions or consequences. However, a significant percent of their reoffences involved breaches, so perhaps the peace bond provides a measure of protection for the victim. If the accused becomes threatening or engages in behaviour associated with abuse (such as drinking), the woman at risk can call the police who can arrest for a breach, hopefully before an assault has occurred.

Assessing recidivism sometimes feels a bit circular because the judgements that go into determining whether to prosecute a case or decisions about bail or sentencing are similar to the factors that predict recidivism.

Thus, when we read recidivism statistics, we need to read them with the understanding that much screening occurs at the prosecutorial and judicial level that predicts reoffence patterns. For example, those accused deemed most eligible for a stay with counselling will be selected by the Crown for this outcome because they are the least likely to reoffend, given past behaviour. Our data indicate that, indeed, these individuals have the lowest recidivism rate.

This is important when we come to policy implications. The selection into stay with counselling may be the factor that produces the effect, that is reduced recidivism, rather than the counselling. If we find that a stay with counselling is associated with the lowest recidivism rate, we should not conclude that all offenders would cease or reduce reoffending if they received a stay with counselling. Some of these offenders are very dangerous, and if they were given a stay with counselling, they would most likely reoffend and a victim's safety would clearly be at risk. However, what may be a very sound policy implication is that, for those who receive a stay of proceedings, including counselling as a condition could provide the most effective outcome.

Court-mandated treatment for offenders is a frequent outcome in specialized courts. Thus, a final measure of recidivism to consider is the effect of treatment on an offender's likelihood to reoffend. The Ursel and Gorkoff study (1996) cited earlier did a detailed comparison of recidivism among offenders who had completed treatment and among those who had no court-mandated treatment. At an early stage in their study, they discovered the necessity of separating offenders sentenced to probation from those who had been sentenced to jail because these two populations had very different abuse histories and very different patterns of reoffending. In the Winnipeg data set, offenders who were incarcerated had an average recidivism rate of 49%, while offenders who were on probation had an average recidivism rate of 28%. Thus, when attempting to assess the impact of treatment, it is critical to treat these as two populations.

The Winnipeg recidivism study followed 551 convicted offenders who received and completed a court-mandated treatment program: 419 who were sentenced to probation and 132 who were sentenced to jail. This group of treatment program graduates were compared to a control group of 1,151 offenders who received a probation sentence and no treatment and 328 offenders sentenced to jail without treatment. We then compared the recidivism rates of these two groups two years after they had completed their sentence.

An additional factor was found to be important in the impact of treatment, and that was the degree of experience of the treatment program providers. This was still in the early days of the Winnipeg Family Violence Court and many programs were rapidly starting to deal with the increasing volume of cases. Thus, we matched up offenders with and without treatment by category of sentence and by experience of treatment program providers. All of these factors were observed to have an effect, as indicated in Table 5.8.

Table 5.8: Recidivism Rates of STIP* Graduates vs. Control Group Offenders by Site of Program and Sentence

Program Site	Program History	Control Group	STIP Graduates	Difference in Recidivism
Medium/Maximum security jail	New program	48.6%	39.5%	10.1%
Minimum security jail	Established program	48.6%	25.0%	23.6%
Probation general program	New program	28.2%	21.7%	6.5%
Probation specialized DV	Established program	28.2%	14.0%	14.2%

* STIP — Short Term Intervention Program.

While this study was severely limited to one measure of reoffending, recidivism, it is interesting to note that their results were very similar to the studies conducted by Gondolf (2002) and Dobash et al. (2000), who had the benefit of follow-up interviews with partners.

Conclusion

Court specialization is a phenomenon that is expanding across the country. Six provinces have pursued this strategy because the former, non-specialized courts seemed a poor fit for responding to the unique challenges that domestic crimes present to the justice system. In Winnipeg, we have found that specialization has encouraged greater support for the victim and has placed more emphasis on treatment for the abuser. Specialization is associated with many challenges, not the least of which is coping with the increased volume of cases. Recently, the provincial judges and prosecutors co-operated with police and corrections to introduce a new administrative system, the "Front End" project, whose purpose is to streamline the processing of cases and reduce delays. This system appears to have already reduced delays.

While solving administrative problems is important, the most essential measure of the effectiveness of a CJS focus on domestic violence is the safety and well-being of actual or potential victims. The results of our study suggest that the specialized response is more effective and "just" than the past non-specialized response. Reducing domestic violence is a long-term process, and we shouldn't expect radical reductions in a short time.

There are, however, some early indicators that specialization is correlated with improvements in safety. In the past, Manitoba, like the other Western provinces, tended to have one of the highest female domestic homicide rates in Canada. However, in the decade 1993–2003, Manitoba had the lowest female domestic homicide rate in Western Canada and the third lowest rate in the country. It is hoped that this pattern will continue and that, over time, we may see a reduction in the abuse of intimate partners as well.

Notes

1   In February of 2000 a man with a long prior record of domestic assault killed his common-law wife and her sister. There was massive media coverage of this case because the sister called 911 four times before the dispatcher sent a car out. On her last 911 contact, the sister was being stabbed to death in the midst of the call. When the police arrived, both women were dead. The media attention increased calls to the police for a year and a half. The police services review of the incident led to officers interpreting the arrest policy strictly, responding to all calls labelled domestic and arresting the accused (in cases with evidence of a crime).

2   Middle-class women appear less likely to use any public service and use shelters less than lower-income women. Wherever possible, they choose a

solution that does not bring them and their circumstances into the public sphere.

3   The prosecutor's reluctance to put a reluctant victim on the stand stems from the fact that often cases will come back to the court two or three times before the victim realizes that the arrest alone is not a sufficient deterrent to her partner and she becomes ready to testify. If she had been put on the stand in an earlier case when she was reluctant and denied the incident at trial, this denial could be used by the defence to challenge her credibility in the later case when she is ready to testify. Thus, we see that in the later years of the decade under review, the number of cases set for trial drops dramatically. If the victim is reluctant and unlikely to testify, the case typically does not get set for trial.

4   Eventually some of these single-offence individuals may reoffend, and this would be particularly true of those whose case fell in the last two years of our data collection. Some may simply not have had time to reoffend.

CHAPTER SIX

Specialized Justice: *From Prosecution to Sentencing in a Toronto Domestic Violence Court*

Myrna Dawson and Ronit Dinovitzer

On March 8, 1996 — International Women's Day — Arlene May, a 39-year-old mother of five, was shot to death in her Collingwood, Ontario, home by her ex-boyfriend Randy Isles, who then killed himself. The next day, on March 9, 1996, the *Toronto Star* launched its award-winning, eight-part series that examined society's response to spousal abuse. What the *Star* reporters concluded upon completing their investigation was that the criminal justice system was not responding to spousal abuse, at least not in any meaningful way, nor had it ever seemed to do so. While Arlene May's case was not one of those focused upon in the series that examined cases processed in Toronto, her experiences with the criminal justice system as she tried to remove herself from a violent relationship did parallel some of the experiences of the victims highlighted in the series.

Focusing on the criminal justice process, reporters Rita Daly, Jane Armstrong and Caroline Mallan followed 133 domestic violence cases that occurred during a one-week period in Toronto, resulting in 230 charges. For eight months, as these cases were tracked through the criminal justice system, the reporters found that few of the accused were jailed, most received little more than a slap on the wrist and many cases often fell apart because a victim was coerced or frightened and changed her story. If the victim did not co-operate, charges were usually withdrawn by the Crown or dismissed by the judge. What these reporters uncovered was not a surprise for many already working with the primarily female victims of spousal abuse, but it did shine a spotlight on a system that was ineffective.

The coroner's inquest into the killing of Arlene May by her ex-boyfriend further galvanized the issue. The inquest lead to more than 200 recommendations that spoke to the need for building a response system that brought together all sectors involved in cases of domestic violence. Again, the inquest highlighted what many working in the field already knew: that fragmented services — working in isolation but often serving the same victims — were a key concern when responding to cases of domestic violence that involve complex and related concerns by a number of individuals and agencies.

These events — Arlene May's murder and subsequent inquest, and the *Toronto Star* series — are often credited for bringing about changes in the way the criminal justice system in Ontario now responds to domestic violence. By directing attention toward an inefficient process, they in effect forced the political will that was required to commit resources to improve a woefully inadequate response to a serious social problem. That same year, the first two domestic violence courts were established in Toronto at Old City Hall and North York with the aim of providing a more effective response to domestic violence than traditional criminal courts and related processes. In 1997, when these two courts were up and running, additional domestic violence courts were implemented in Brampton, Hamilton, London, North Bay, Oshawa and Ottawa. In 2001, the Ontario government made a commitment to introduce domestic violence court programs to all of its 55 jurisdictions. As a result, Ontario's Domestic Violence Court (DVC) program may currently be the most extensive in Canada.

The DVC program is a mechanism for bringing together teams of specialized personnel, including police, Crown attorneys, staff in the Victim/ Witness Assistance Program (VWAP), as well as those working in probation services, the Partner Assault Response (PAR) Program and community agencies involved in providing services to victims and offenders in cases of domestic violence (Ministry of Attorney General, 2001). When a DVC program is fully operational, it should include the following components: (1) a domestic violence court advisory committee; (2) trained specialized domestic violence Crown attorneys; (3) investigation procedures and specialized evidence collection by police; (4) a case management system;

(5) a partner assault response intervention program; and (6) expanded training for all criminal justice actors involved in the criminal justice processing of domestic violence cases (ibid.).

The first two courts implemented in Toronto each had a specific focus — North York was based on an early intervention model and Old City Hall was modelled after what is referred to as a "coordinated" or "enhanced" prosecution response. As additional courts were implemented in various jurisdictions across the province, a hybrid model gradually evolved in which both models were incorporated in each of the courts. In other words, within the same jurisdiction, specialized teams would deal with first-time offenders using the early intervention model and with more serious or repeat offenders using the coordinated prosecution model. Because the first two courts influenced the other DVC programs that followed, this chapter will describe these two courts in detail, including their structure, processes and primary objectives. Focusing on a snapshot of time, we then describe the types of cases heard in the Old City Hall court, the characteristics of victims and their abusers as well as the criminal justice outcomes. We also present the results from three separate analyses that focus on distinct but related research questions. We conclude by highlighting some issues underscored by these findings, suggesting priorities for researchers who are concerned with understanding the operation and efficacy of these courts, both for those who work within them and for those who are meant to benefit by them — the victims of domestic violence.

The Structure and Process of the Courts

In Ontario, domestic violence is defined as "any use of physical or sexual force, actual or threatened, in an intimate relationship" (MAG, 2001, p. 1). Intimate relationships include heterosexual and same-sex partners; they can vary in length and can include both current and estranged dating, common-law and married couples. Although both women and men can be victims of domestic violence, it is recognized by the Ministry of the Attorney General that in the overwhelming majority of cases, this type of violence involves men abusing women. The Crown Policy Manual (CPM), maintained by the ministry, provides some guidance to Crown attorneys on how to conduct their prosecutions. Beyond providing a general framework for dealing with victims of domestic violence, the CPM specifically addresses when a Crown attorney should withdraw charges and thereby not proceed with a domestic violence prosecution.

In Ontario, where it is generally the police that lay the charge, the police directive is to lay charges in these cases as long as reasonable and probable grounds exist to do so — police discretion beyond that point has been eliminated, leaving it to the Crown to determine whether to proceed with the charge. According to the CPM, withdrawing charges of spouse or partner assault, though within the Crown's discretion, "is not appropriate unless exceptional circumstances exist" and, prior to making such a decision, a Crown attorney must consult with a more senior Crown or with a domestic violence coordinator (CPM, 1993: SP-1, p. 4).

Stressing the importance of sound prosecutorial discretion in these cases (CPM, 1993, p. 3), the CPM provides Crown attorneys with a partial checklist of relevant factors to consider when determining whether to withdraw charges in domestic violence cases. This includes the strength of the case, the history of violence by the defendant, evidence of harassment of the victim by the defendant after charges have been laid, the extent of injuries suffered by the victim and the reasons the victim gives for not wanting the prosecution to proceed. Also to be considered are the results of an interview between the Crown and the victim in which "Crown counsel discusses the public wrong aspect of domestic violence and tries to respond to any concerns the victim may have" (CPM, 1993: SP-1, pp. 4–5). Building on these guidelines, we describe below the first two specialized domestic violence courts implemented in Ontario.

Coordinated Prosecution Model — K Court, Old City Hall
Early in 1997, a specialized Domestic Violence Court was established at Toronto's Old City Hall, located at Dundas Street and University Avenue in the downtown core. Modelled after a specialized court in San Diego, California, this coordinated prosecution court brought together Crown attorneys, members of the Victim/Witness Assistance Program (VWAP), the police, the judiciary, court administration, probation services and community groups that offer intervention or treatment programs for offenders. Referred to as the K Court, after the "K" used by the police to identify domestic violence files, the initial goals of this court were to provide better

support to victims and to ensure that offenders who abused their partners were held accountable for their actions. A key part of this integrated team approach involved collecting additional evidence beyond victim statements to aid in the prosecution of the offender. In the beginning, K Court handled only domestic violence cases from police Divisions 11, 14 and 52, later adding 54 Division, all located in downtown Toronto. The court was staffed by a team of Crown attorneys who prosecuted only domestic violence cases and who were to receive mandatory training in the social, psychological and legal issues often associated with domestic and sexual violence.

Today, in accordance with the 1982 directive from the Attorney General of Ontario, as noted above, K Court Crown attorneys are required to assume an active role in promoting police-laid domestic violence charges. Under this zero-tolerance policy, the police also play a critical role in responding to domestic violence and are no longer expected to ask the victim if she wants the abuser charged. Instead, police must lay charges regardless of what the victim wishes. After police lay a charge, a special reporting form is to be used and an attempt is made to have the victim participate in a video-taped interview that can later be used in the prosecution. Other types of evidence to be collected to lessen reliance on the victim during the prosecution process include photographs of the victim's injuries, 911 emergency telephone tapes and audiotaped statements from the victim or other witnesses to the crime. Prior to the start of a trial in K Court, the victim is to be contacted by VWAP workers and encouraged to participate in an interview. VWAP is meant to familiarize the victim with the court process and provide her with support throughout the trial as well as with referrals to community agencies and services.

The coordinated prosecution model adopted by K Court also provides counselling services to abusers. As soon as a judge stipulates that counselling is a condition of a defendant's sentence, the abuser is referred to an intervention program. These programs usually operate on a group model with one or more leaders directing each abuser to discuss and confront the roots of this behaviour. The program is meant to identify the philosophies and biases that may be used to rationalize and/or justify an abuser's use of violence. There are several treatment objectives, including (1) to help an abuser understand the harm done to his partner, to other members of the family and to the community; (2) to ensure that the abuser accepts responsibility for his abusive and controlling behaviour and does not minimize or deny it; and (3) to help the abuser recognize his abusive actions within the context of power and control rather than anger (MAG, 2001).

Though the CPM is designed to provide guidelines to Crown attorneys across Ontario, the K Court initiative was designed to allow for the more vigorous prosecution of domestic violence cases and to increase co-operation between prosecutors and the police. The initiative is premised on the belief that a commitment to these goals can improve the quality of investigations and increase the number of successful outcomes.[1] Case screening decisions are made by a small group of prosecutors assigned to K Court full-time.[2] This full-time assignment is to ensure that cases are handled from start to finish by the same prosecutor, offering victims more continuity in the process. K Court prosecutors are also expected to meet with all willing victims before trial to discuss the facts of the case, to determine whether victims are ready to testify, to answer questions the victims may have and to show themselves as supportive and understanding of victims regardless of whether they are co-operating with the prosecution. In short, the overarching goals are to provide a sense of continuity to the process for victims, to increase the quality of prosecutions, to increase the likelihood that a victim will co-operate with the prosecution, and finally, to improve service to victims.

As noted briefly above, another central component of the K Court initiative is the systematic collection of evidence by police so that the prosecution need not rely only on victim testimony. Beginning in 1996, the year prior to the implementation of K Court, and continuing into 1998, its first year of operation, Crown attorneys worked with police at the three initial participating police divisions to develop practices for collecting additional evidence. This evidence includes detailed descriptions of the crime scene, the seizure of items that may have been used as weapons, photographs (primarily of victim injuries), transcripts of emergency 911 tapes, medical reports and background information on the relationship between the victim and the offender.[3]

A significant practice in K Court emphasizes the procurement of videotaped statements from victims as soon after the incident as possible, providing that the victims agreed to be videotaped (audio-taping is considered an alternative). The primary goal is to have a videotaped statement recorded immediately after the incident or at least within a 24-hour period. The police are responsible for taping the victim's testimony and, generally, these informal interviews occur at the police station. In extreme circumstances, the police may videotape the testimony in other locations outside the police station.[4] The videotaped evidence may be used by prosecutors in lieu of victim testimony in cases where victims decide not to co-operate with the prosecution. In turn, prosecutors are committed to more actively pursuing the admission of this evidence at trial with the expectation that, because of the strength of available evidence, they will obtain more convictions at trial and a higher number of guilty pleas, all without necessarily requiring the victim to testify at trial.

A final component of the specialized domestic court is the Victim/ Witness Assistance Program (VWAP).[5] While this program is not dedicated exclusively to K Court, this court does generate a large proportion of the clients for VWAP. Victim/witness workers contact victims in all K Court cases by telephone or by letter soon after the bail hearing or detention order.[6] As will be discussed below, this contact can play an important role in preventing future violence because victims are most receptive to information about how to reduce their vulnerability immediately or soon after the crime (Davis, Coker & Sanderson, 2002; Friedman and Tucker, 1997). Practically speaking, victim/witness workers notify their clients about court appearances, solicit their input prior to a guilty plea by their abuser and offer a tour of the court to make victims more comfortable with the process. When victims agree to meet with VWAP workers, it is expected that they will be provided with enough support to prepare them for testifying at trial. The main objective of the program, however, is to support the victim throughout the process regardless of whether or not she chooses to testify.

The success of the above model (and most specialized courts) depends on increased interagency coordination and communication — a key component that the coroner's inquest and the *Toronto Star* series identified as lacking. At Old City Hall, the Woman Abuse Council of Toronto (WACT) is mandated to facilitate this coordination and communication. In the early stages, WACT took the lead role in developing the guidelines and accountability standards used by treatment or intervention agencies, and in coordinating the agreements among the agencies involved. On an ongoing basis, WACT is responsible for coordinating the project-related activities of the intervention agencies, including the collection, analysis and reporting of the program forms that the agencies complete for each offender. WACT also holds regular meetings of senior representatives of the participating agencies to discuss broader policy issues and occasionally calls meetings of senior decision-makers when decisions about policy or funding are required. In short, WACT has been largely responsible for maintaining the specialized court's underlying foundation by promoting continued coordination and communication.

Early Intervention Model — North York

In the same year that K Court was implemented, North York established its first domestic violence court. Similar to K Court, North York's court was created with the primary goal of providing better support to victims but, in contrast to the coordinated prosecution model, North York was concerned with rehabilitating offenders rather than seeking a conviction. Referred to as the early intervention model, this court was to provide treatment for first-time offenders while holding them accountable for their offences. Modelled after a specialized court in Dade County, Florida, this court specifically seeks (1) to encourage offenders to take responsibility for their abusive actions; (2) to provide education programs for domestic violence offenders that place emphasis on the consequences of their actions; and (3) to ensure that there are basic support systems in place for victims and, as part of this, that victims are provided with referrals at their point of entry into the criminal justice system.

At the time this court was implemented, there was a special arrangement to provide counselling and treatment to domestic violence offenders whose cases met key criteria: (1) they were first-time offenders; (2) there were no significant injuries to the victim; (3) the offenders admitted and pled guilty to the assault and were willing to enter a treatment program; (4) the victims were willing to participate in the project; and (5) the offenders had not used a weapon during the incident. In contrast to K Court, this model places emphasis on the offenders' needs as well, focusing specifically on their rehabilitation before the cycle of abuse has been solidified in a relationship to prevent future recidivism.

In this model, the Crown examines each case to identify who is eligible for the program. Before the trial, the victim is separated from the defendant and each are placed in a different room where they are given the opportunity to talk about what they would like out of the court process. At the same time, the accused also meets with the intake person who is responsible for making assignments to specific intervention programs. If the defendant pleads guilty, the presiding judge will impose a conditional bail release with the victim's consent. This order requires that the defendant participate in an approved 16-week batterers' intervention program. While the defendant is in treatment, the victim is to be contacted at least four times by the community agency to assess his/her safety and to offer support services. The defendant is on extended bail while completing the treatment and, therefore, any threats to victim safety or breaches of bail conditions are to be reported to police by intervention program staff. At the conclusion of the intervention program, if there has been no risk or threat to the victim, the defendant comes into court again to be sentenced. If reports from the intervention program as well as the victim are positive, the disposition is usually a conditional discharge accompanied by one year of probation. We describe the North York model because later courts, as noted, evolved into hybrid models that incorporated elements of both K Court and Old City Hall.

A Year in the Life of an Ontario Specialized Court

The data presented here were gathered from files at K Court in Toronto. These files include police investigation reports as well as other documentation collected during the processing of a domestic violence case. This information was supplemented by files kept by the VWAP office. The data collection process involved tracking all cases from the initial charge laid to the final disposition. Cases in which all charges were withdrawn by the Crown attorney were also tracked and reasons for case attrition were documented based on notations in the court files. Case tracking took place from April 1, 1997 to March 31, 1998.[7] Data collection involved regular visits to the court office by the two authors. Information was gathered on over 70 different variables that document the victim, offender and offence characteristics as well as criminal justice variables and outcomes. A total of 474 cases were tracked during this period. Based on the data collected at K Court, we provide an overview of the court, including the characteristics of the cases that were dealt with during a one-year period and their subsequent outcomes (see Tables 6.1 through 6.6 for descriptive statistics).

As part of this study, interviews were also conducted with some victims. Unfortunately, it proved extremely difficult to locate participants and to arrange and conduct the interviews. In total, 60 interviews were conducted, representing less than 15% of the total sample. While this low response rate prevents us from drawing conclusions from these qualitative data, this relatively substantial number of interviews allows us to draw on the victims' comments for illustrative purposes in the discussion and conclusion of this chapter.

Table 6.1: Accused and Victim Characteristics, K-Court, Toronto

Characteristics	Accused N = 474		Victim N = 474	
Gender				
Male	440	93%	44	9%
Female	34	7%	430	91%
Employed	263	55%	—	—
Average Age	35 years		33 years	

What Do the Cases Look Like?

Similar to most research on domestic violence, the majority of victims in our sample were women — 91%. Their average age was 33 years, ranging from 15 to 75 (see Table 6.1). Also consistent with prior research, the majority of the defendants were male — 93% — with an average age of 35 years; the youngest was 18 and the oldest was 75. Overall, the victims and defendants were slightly older in our sample compared with those in other studies (e.g., Schmidt & Steury, 1989). The most common type of victim-defendant relationship was common law (34%) followed by legally married couples (31%) and boyfriend-girlfriend relationships (10%) (see Table 6.2). Close to one-quarter of the victims and defendants were estranged at the time of the incident (8% ex-spouses, 8% ex-common-law partners and 7% ex-boyfriend-girlfriend). The average length of the relationships was almost six years (70 months). In our sample, almost half of the couples had children — one or two children in the majority of cases, but five or more children in several cases.

Table 6.2: Accused-Victim Relationship, K Court, Toronto

Relationship	N = 474	
Common-law partner	159	34%
Legally married	146	31%
Boyfriend-girlfriend	47	10%
Ex-legal spouse	39	8%
Ex-common-law partner	40	8%
Ex-boyfriend-girlfriend	31	7%
Children present	234	49%
Average length of relationship	70 months	—

With respect to the defendant's prior criminal history, more than half the sample (52%) had some type of prior record (see Table 6.3). Of those with prior offenses, 27% had been previously involved with the criminal justice system on charges of violent (non-domestic) offences, 18% for non-violent offences and 36% for prior domestic violence offences. Consistent with prior research examining incident characteristics, 46% of the victims in our sample suffered less serious injuries such as bruises, cuts and black eyes whereas 13% suffered more serious injuries that required medical attention (see Table 6.4). Weapons were used to threaten or assault a victim in 16% of the cases. Finally, when witnesses were present (48%), 14% were child witnesses (usually of the victim and/or defendant), and in the remainder of the cases (34%), witnesses were adults (e.g., relatives, friends or neighbours of the victim and/or defendant). In the next section, we briefly describe how these cases were processed through the court system.

Table 6.3: Prior Record of Accused, K Court, Toronto

Criminal History	N = 430*	
Total with prior offences	225	52%
Prior Record Type**		
Prior domestic offences	81	36%
Prior violent offences,		
non-domestic	60	27%
Other	84	38%

*Information missing in 44 cases.
**Percentage on cases with prior offences.

Table 6.4: Incident Characteristics, K Court, Toronto

Characteristics	$N = 474$	
Minor injuries	217	46%
Serious injuries	60	13%
Weapons used	77	16%
Witnesses present — children	68	14%
Witnesses present — adult	163	34%

What Does the Process Look Like?

Because one of the goals of K Court was to reduce reliance on victim co-operation in the prosecution of domestic violence, we collected information on the types of evidence collected by police and noted in their files what could be used in lieu of the victim's testimony (see Table 6.5). We found that the types of evidence most frequently noted as available in K Court were photographs taken at the scene (32%), primarily of the victim's injuries), followed by emergency 911 tapes (29%) and videotapes documenting the victim's testimony, often taken immediately after the incident or within 24 hours (26%). The victim's statement was also collected in 23% of the cases, other witness statements in 16% of the cases, and medical reports were available in 8% of the cases.[8]

Table 6.5: Case Processing Factors, K Court, Toronto*

Evidence — photographs (injuries/scene)	152	32%
Evidence — emergency 911 tape	139	29%
Evidence — victim's video testimony	122	26%
Evidence — victim statement	110	23%
Evidence — other witness statement	77	16%
Evidence — medical reports	40	8%
Victim met with prosecution	153	32%
Victim met victim/witness assistance workers	247	52%
Victim co-operated	127	27%
Victim co-operated reluctantly	48	10%

*Information based on cases for which the above information was available.

While one goal of the court was to reduce reliance on the victim, a complementary goal was to improve the process to encourage or maintain victim co-operation. To do so, the court focused on increasing interaction between the victims and the prosecutors as well as between the victims and the VWAP staff. Our data on the frequency of meetings among these individuals indicate that the victim met at least once with the prosecutor in about one-third of the cases (32%), and in slightly more than half of the cases (52%), the victim met with a victim/witness assistance worker (see Table 6.5).[9] It is important to note that even if a victim met with prosecutors or victim/witness assistance workers, this did not mean that she co-operated with the prosecution process. Victims may have attended these meetings to request that charges be withdrawn. In total, we found that approximately 37% of all victims co-operated with the prosecution.[10] This figure includes both those victims who co-operated from the beginning and continued to do so throughout the process (27%) as well as those victims who were initially reluctant, but subsequently co-operated with the prosecution (10%). In the remainder of cases, the victims either had no involvement or asked to have the charges dropped and then disengaged from the process. We return to the issue of victim co-operation later in the chapter.

What Do the Outcomes Look Like?

Understanding the effectiveness of any court process entails an investigation of court outcomes. While it is certainly not the only goal of these courts, the prosecution and conviction rate continues to be a key measure of success. Overall, in our sample, prosecution proceeded on charges in 82% of the 474 domestic violence cases (see Table 6.6). In the remaining cases, charges were dropped or stayed. Therefore, the proportion of cases prosecuted in K Court is higher relative to other studies examining the prosecution of domestic violence (Fagan, 1995; Ford & Regoli, 1993; Sherman, 1992), but this is not surprising given that we are examining outcomes in a specialized Domestic Violence Court with a vigorous prosecution policy. In examining the rate of conviction, it should be noted that even if a number of the charges in a particular case were withdrawn, as long as *at least one* of the domestic violence charges was resolved by the accused pleading guilty or being found guilty at trial, the case was considered to have resulted in a conviction. Of those 387 cases prosecuted, then, 81% resulted in a conviction, either through a trial or a guilty plea.

Of those offenders who were convicted, 31% were sentenced to jail with an average sentence length of 111 days (see Table 6.6). The most frequent disposition was a suspended sentence (31%), but conditional discharges were also common (24%). Peace bonds were used to resolve cases in 13% of the cases and conditional sentences in slightly more than 4% of the cases. Probation was always included as part of the sentence with the period of probation averaging 20 months. The average number of days that passed between arrest and trial was 153 days, and the average time between arrest and sentence was 145 days.[11]

Table 6.6: Case Outcomes, K Court, Toronto

Prosecution proceeded*	387	82%
Convictions resulted**	314	81%
Jail sentence imposed***	96	31%
Length of jail sentence	—	111 days

*Percentage based on cases in which charges were laid ($N = 474$).
**Percentage based on cases in which prosecution occurred ($N = 387$).
***Percentage based on cases in which a conviction resulted ($N = 314$).

Examining the Effectiveness of a Specialized Domestic Violence Court

Specialized domestic violence courts, while varying in their emphasis on particular objectives, share some common goals. These include increasing prosecutions, making the process more consistent and less intimidating for the victim to encourage co-operation and creating a process that recognizes and responds to the complexities of domestic violence while, at the same time, making the offender accountable.[12] Though little systematic research has examined the efficacy of specialized domestic violence courts in Canada, we are able to draw on our previous and current research to examine K Court's ability to meet some of the above goals.

Predicting Prosecution

One of the primary goals of this specialized court is to increase the number of cases that are prosecuted while, at the same time, reducing the number of cases that are dropped because the victim does not co-operate.

As we detailed on the previous page, 82% of the domestic violence cases in our sample proceeded to prosecution. This statistic cannot, of course, tell us about the role of victim co-operation in the decision to prosecute these cases. Although it is commonly argued that lack of victim co-operation is the primary reason that prosecutors choose not to proceed in cases of domestic violence, this issue has received little systematic analysis (Davis, Lurigio & Skogan, 1997). In the following section, we discuss how we used the data collected at K Court to undertake a series of statistical analyses in order to determine the relative contribution of a range of factors in the decision to prosecute cases of domestic violence, with a specific focus on the role of victim co-operation.

Using a multivariate statistical technique called logistic regression, we separated out the independent contribution of each of the factors in our model.[13] Specifically, in predicting the likelihood of a case being prosecuted, we were able to assess the influence of victim co-operation, controlling for the influence of a range of variables such as defendant age and gender as well as case characteristics such as weapon used, whether the offender had a prior record for domestic violence or the degree of injury suffered by the victim. We also controlled for the type of relationship between the victim and accused (i.e., whether or not their relationship was intact) and for the type of evidence available (e.g., victim statements, witnesses, photos, video, emergency 911 audiotape or medical evidence). We analyzed the data in two steps: first, we explored the relative contribution of the full range of factors *except* for victim co-operation; second, we introduced the variables for victim co-operation to assess their relative contribution to explaining the likelihood of prosecution. Tables 6.7, 6.8 and 6.9 summarize the direction of significant effects (rather than the actual coefficients), with a positive sign indicating that the variable being examined *increases* the likelihood (or odds) of the outcome whereas a negative sign indicates a *decrease* in the likelihood (or odds) of the outcome. The full tables for all the multivariate results are shown in Appendix 6.A.

In the first step (Table 6.7, Model 1), we found that men were more likely than women to be prosecuted for cases of domestic violence, but that older offenders had lower odds of being prosecuted (see full results, Table 6.A1, Appendix 6.A). The relationship between the victim and defendant was also a significant factor in the likelihood of prosecution: we found that being in an ex-common-law or boyfriend-girlfriend relationship decreased the likelihood that a case would be prosecuted. Our findings also indicated that only one type of evidence — a videotaped statement — significantly increased the likelihood of prosecution. More specifically, cases in which videotaped evidence was available had 2.5 times the odds of being prosecuted compared with cases with no videotaped evidence. Similarly, cases in which the victim met with representatives of the Victim/Witness Assistance Program (VWAP) were twice as likely to be prosecuted compared with cases in which the victim did not meet with the VWAP workers.

Table 6.7: Significant effects of various factors on the likelihood of prosecution

	Model 1 Likelihood of prosecution	Model 2 Likelihood of prosecution
Defendant Characteristics		
Defendant age	-*	-
Male	+	+
Relationship Type		
Ex-common-law	-	-
Boyfriend-girlfriend	-	-
Legal Variables		
Video	+	+
Process Variables		
Victim met with VWAP	+	
Victim Co-operation		
Fully co-operated		+

*A positive sign indicates that the variable being examined increases the likelihood of the outcome whereas a negative sign indicates a decrease in the likelihood of the outcome. The full tables for all the multivariate results are shown in Appendix 6.A

In the second step, we estimated the same model to predict the likelihood of prosecution, but added the variables representing whether or not the victim co-operated with the prosecution. The results of this second model (Table 6.7, Model 2) indicate that in cases where the victim fully co-operated, the odds of prosecution were much higher — more than seven times — than if a victim did not co-operate. In other words, even when we account for the range of factors that predict prosecution, victim

co-operation was independently and positively associated with the likelihood of prosecution. Although our models cannot speak to the influence
of other variables beyond the scope of our data (such as an individual victim's
perception of safety or a victim's hope that offenders would receive counselling), our analysis demonstrates that neither defendant characteristics
nor seriousness of the offence predicted the likelihood of prosecution.

These findings are important because they highlight the key role played
by victim co-operation in the likelihood of a case being prosecuted. More
importantly, the association between victim co-operation and prosecution
shown in our analysis is significant because of the setting from which these
data were collected: a specialized court that is dedicated to prosecuting cases
even in the absence of victim co-operation. Our findings suggest that even
within a setting mandated to proceed without victim co-operation, by
relying on other forms of evidence victim co-operation continued to play
the most significant role in the decision to prosecute.

Predicting Victim Co-operation

Given the importance of victim co-operation demonstrated above, the next
analysis examined what factors might increase the likelihood that a victim
would co-operate with the prosecution. Our goal was to determine what
demographic, situational or process variables were associated with victim
co-operation in the prosecution of domestic violence. Our analysis is restricted
to the 304 cases of domestic violence heard in K Court for which we had
information on victim co-operation.[14]

As indicated in Table 6.8, what we found was, in fact, surprisingly
straightforward: the odds that a victim co-operated with the prosecution were
significantly higher if she met with representatives of the Victim/Witness
Assistance Program (see full results, Table 6.A2, Appendix 6.A). Moreover, if
the victim gave a videotaped statement, the odds of subsequent co-operation
were also significantly higher. No other type of evidence and, indeed, no
other variable was significantly associated with victim co-operation. Victim
co-operation, according to these data, appears to be predicted not by the
nature of the case or by characteristics of the victim or the offender, but by
the victim's interaction with the court system. We will return to these findings
in our discussion.

Table 6.8: Significant effects of evidence and process variables on likelihood of victim co-operation

	Likelihood of victim co-operation
Legal Variables	
Victim statement	
Witness statement	
Photos	
Videotaped statement	+ *
Emergency tape	
Medical evidence	
Other evidence	
Child witness	
Adult witness	
Process Variables	
Victim met with VWAP	+
Victim met with Crown	

* A positive sign indicates that the variable being examined increases the likelihood of the outcome. The full table is shown in Appendix 6.A.

Sentencing Outcomes

This final section considers the factors that were associated with two types of sentencing outcomes: first, whether or not offenders were sentenced to jail, and second, for the 97 offenders who did receive a jail sentence, the determinants of sentence length (see Table 6.9). Relying again on multi-variate techniques, our next analysis controlled for the full range of factors that could be associated with the likelihood of being sentenced to jail. We again proceeded in two steps so that we could isolate the effect of relationship type.

In the first step (Table 6.9, Model 1), we found that two offender characteristics were significantly related to the likelihood of being sentenced to jail. First, being employed reduced the odds of an offender being sentenced to jail compared with those who were unemployed. Second, an offender who had a prior domestic violence conviction was more likely to be sentenced to jail than an offender without a previous conviction in domestic violence. In the second step (Table 6.9, Model 2), we introduced a variable representing both relationship type (i.e., estranged versus intact) *and* level of injury (see Injury*Intact in Table 6.9). The results indicated that type of relationship did matter, but only when the victim suffered serious injury. In short, we found that for cases in which the relationship between the victim and the offender was intact and in which the victim suffered serious injury, the odds of an offender being sentenced to jail increased by a factor of 10.7 compared with other cases (see full results, Table 6.A3, Appendix 6.A).

Table 6.9: Significant effects of factors predicting the likelihood of being sentenced to jail and length of jail sentence

	Likelihood of Jail		Sentence Length
Model 1	Model 2	Model 1	
Family status			
Relationship Intact			-†
Children			+
Offence characteristics			
Serious injury			+
Aggravated sexual assault			
Offender characteristics			
Offender employed	-	-	-
Domestic prior	+	+	+
Injury*Intact		+	n/a

†A positive sign indicates that the variable being examined increases the likelihood of the outcome whereas a negative sign indicates a decrease in the likelihood of the outcome. The full tables for all the multivariate results are shown in Appendix 6.A.

For the 96 offenders sentenced to jail, our final analysis considered the range of factors that might have determined the length of their incarceration.[15] Recall that, on average, offenders were sentenced to jail for 111 days. Below, we parcel out the specific factors that might have mitigated or aggravated sentences in cases of domestic violence. The results, also shown in the last column of Table 6.9, indicate that two family status measures had diverging effects on sentence length. When an offender's relationship with the victim was intact (compared with an estranged relationship), sentences were shorter by 17 days. However, when the offender and victim had children together, sentence lengths increased by slightly more than nine days, compared with couples without children. We also found that being employed had a mitigating effect on sentence length with employed offenders receiving sentences that were about 63 days shorter than the sentences received by those who were unemployed. In contrast, and as expected, offenders with a prior record for domestic violence were sentenced to jail for an additional 97 days compared with offenders with no prior record (see full results, Model 1, Table 6.A4, Appendix 6.A).

While our results display an intuitive pattern regarding the factors that mitigated and aggravated sentences, the results with respect to family status were somewhat surprising. That is, our analysis indicated that being in an intact relationship increased the likelihood that offenders would be sentenced to jail — but only in cases where the victim had suffered serious injuries. However, in cases where the victim and offender were in an intact relationship, jail sentences were shorter. Taken together, these two findings suggest that the relationship between the victim and the offender is integral to understanding court outcomes in cases of domestic violence. Below, we reflect on our major findings and highlight how these issues should be considered priorities for future research in the area of specialized courts, criminal justice and public policy.

Discussion

The Continuing Emphasis on Victim Co-operation

Based on our sample of cases from K Court in Toronto, we found that despite the court's objectives to reduce prosecutorial reliance on victims, victim co-operation continued to be a significant predictor of whether or not a case proceeded to prosecution. Specifically, when victims co-operated, we found that prosecutors were significantly more likely to pursue charges even after taking into account the effects of defendant characteristics, the victim-defendant relationship, type of evidence and the presence of witnesses. One might argue that these findings merely reflect the relative newness of the specialized court initiative under study and the period of time being examined; alternatively, however, one might also argue that often these programs run more closely to best practice guidelines when first implemented compared with later in their institutional life, when political and social attention on them has diminished.

It is, therefore, imperative that future research examine the current role of victim co-operation and other predictors of prosecutorial decision-making in the specialized court setting in Ontario and elsewhere. In such work, comparing how these specialized settings differ from or are similar to the processing of domestic violence cases in regular court settings (and even to the processing of other types of cases) should be a key research concern.

Understanding Victim Co-operation

Given the importance of victim co-operation in our sample, we also investigated the factors that were associated with the victim's decision to co-operate. Our findings demonstrated that neither demographic nor situational correlates of the incident were associated with victim co-operation. Rather, the two most important determinants of victim co-operation were the availability of their videotaped testimony and whether meetings were held between the victim and victim/witness assistance workers.

How might we explain the positive effects of videotaped statements and meetings with victim/witness assistance workers on victim co-operation? The significance of videotaped testimony in predicting victim co-operation might stem from the often complex interactions between prosecutors and victims of domestic violence. Some argue that the road to victim non-co-operation begins with the actions and attitudes of prosecutors and other criminal justice officials that lead to a self-fulfilling prophecy (Buzawa & Buzawa, 1996; Ellis, 1984; Ford & Regoli, 1993). Simply put, prosecutors' assumptions that some victims of domestic violence are not committed to participating fully in the process serve to reinforce negative impressions and a general distrust of the criminal justice system already held by victims. As a result, victims become discouraged and cease to engage with the process and with those criminal justice actors involved in that process. Research has consistently shown that many victims are frightened and intimidated by the criminal justice system and unsure about what they are expected to do (Erez & Belknap, 1998; Can-navale, 1976). When faced with a prosecutor whose assumptions may colour their interaction, victims may decide, in turn, that the prosecutor is not committed to their case and, as a result, disengage from the process. Our interviews with victims support this interpretation, as shown in the quotes below:

> I didn't find her [the prosecutor] very helpful. I provided names of witnesses and told her about the doctor's report, but she never followed up. (Case 98)

> I never got the information I wanted from him [the prosecutor]. I
> had to go to go elsewhere [victim/witness office] for information.
> In fact, I cornered him one day to ask him a question and he still
> didn't have time to speak with me. (Case 85)

If, on the other hand, the victim has already provided videotaped testimony, a prosecutor may perceive the videotape as one indicator of a victim's
commitment to the process; alternatively, prosecutors may be less inclined
to question the victim's commitment because the videotaped evidence
minimizes prosecutorial reliance on the victim. As a result, the victim is not
perceived as an obstacle in the process and the interactions that occur
between prosecutor and victim may be more positive throughout.[16]

Our analyses also demonstrated that meeting with VWAP workers
encourages victim co-operation. It may be simply that, through these interactions, victims gain the support they need to negotiate their way through
an unfamiliar system. Research has demonstrated that victims are often
afraid and anxious about criminal justice proceedings, particularly in cases
of domestic violence, and the support of victim advocates can help them
move through the system with less difficulty (Tomz & McGillis, 1997). For
this reason, advocacy programs have been implemented in various jurisdictions as a resource that seeks to help victims understand their options
and make informed decisions about their own safety (Tomz & McGillis,
1997; U.S. Department of Justice, 1998). Meetings with victim/witness
advocates, then, may foster an environment in which victims are more
likely to continue co-operating with the prosecution, leading to fewer
dismissals for lack of "prosecutability" (Tomz & McGillis, 1997). This
interpretation is supported by the following statements from victims interviewed as part of the evaluation of K Court:

> They [victim/witness workers] made me feel comfortable and were
> encouraging. If not for the victim/witness people, I wouldn't have
> gone through with it. I had a hard time understanding what was
> going on. They were patient and explained everything to me. The
> experience was not as bad as I thought it was going to be because
> of the support I got from them. (Case 146)

> I did not want to testify on the date of the trial. They convinced me
> that he [her abuser] needed help and would only get that help if I
> testified against him. (Case 99)

> The victim/witness people were very nice and accommodating ...
> having a victim/witness worker there made it easier for me to face
> him ... they made the process less intimidating. (Case 313)

> She [victim/witness person] was very helpful the day of the trial. She
> stayed with me through the whole thing and I found this calming.
> (Case 446)

Finally, for women who have come to believe that their lives will
always be filled with violence because there are no other options, advocacy
programs such as the Victim/Witness Assistance Program may be able to
inform victims about the choices they do have. The following portrays the
message given to one woman by VWAP workers:

> The victim/witness people explained to me that I have rights and
> that I don't have to put up with being abused. I always thought that
> it was my fault ... that I asked for it somehow. I have been beaten
> my whole life ... I didn't know any better. (Case 166)

Given the importance of victim co-operation in the prosecution of cases
of domestic violence shown in this study, future research should continue
to explore the ways in which various policies and practices affect victims.
In-depth interviews with victims across various research sites, for example,
can help shed light on the experiences of victims, allowing us to better
understand their goals and needs in the process.

Understanding the Sentencing of Domestic Violence Offenders

Finally, our examination of the data revealed that despite the rise of specialized domestic violence courts in which individuals are trained to recognize
the complexities of families, conceptions of what is "good" for families may
still be motivating sentencing decisions. For example, we find that judges
are more likely to incarcerate offenders who are still intimately involved

with the victim if the victim has suffered serious injuries (see Kingsnorth, MacIntosh & Sutherland, 2002). At the same time, however, there appears to be a reluctance to break apart these families for too long: our data indicate that offenders who are still in a relationship with their victims receive shorter sentences than those who are estranged from their victims. This finding underscores the continued importance of the victim-offender relationship in the sentencing of these cases and, in particular, the importance of relationship status (i.e,. estranged or intact) when a violent incident occurs.

A second finding demonstrates that the presence of children increases sentence lengths for male offenders; this pattern stands in contrast to the finding of prior studies that the presence of children *mitigates* sentences for female offenders (e.g., Daly 1987; 1989; Hedderman & Gelsthorpe, 1997). The data suggest, therefore, that being a parent works in different ways for men and women. We speculate that judges might sentence fathers more harshly in cases of domestic violence because of assumptions about the detrimental effects that violence in the home poses for children. This finding may also reflect the differing perceptions of the importance of gender-based roles in child-rearing, with the role of mothers considered more important than the role of fathers. Since our study did not examine judicial motivations for sentencing, future research is needed to shed light on the role of relationships — whether between the victim and offender, or the offender and his/her children — in the sanctioning of domestic violence cases.

Conclusion

In this chapter we discussed the evolution of specialized domestic violence courts in Ontario. Focusing on the first two courts implemented, we described the structure and process of two different specialized court models. Drawing on the data we collected in one specialized court, we then provided an overview of the types of cases heard in this setting and examined the court's efficacy with respect to various goals. It is important to emphasize here that our findings are based on cases processed in one jurisdiction at one point in time. Since the implementation of this court, most other jurisdictions in Ontario have now implemented a specialized domestic violence court program and it is therefore important to recognize that the findings discussed here may not necessarily reflect the dynamics in other jurisdictions. Similarly, the structure and process of these courts vary across the province and will differ from each other as well as from those in other parts of the country and beyond.

Our findings do, however, have general implications beyond this particular context. Regardless of locale, many specialized domestic violence courts share the same goals and face similar challenges and difficulties in responding to these cases. Our three analyses in this chapter focused on some common concerns in these courts; specifically, the role of victim co-operation in the decision to prosecute, the factors that determine the likelihood that a victim will co-operate with the prosecution and the role of familial and other determinants in predicting the type and length of sentences imposed in these cases.

Our findings also have important policy implications. Given the continuing importance of victim co-operation in prosecutorial decision-making demonstrated here, on a policy level we must begin to pay special attention to the determinants and correlates of co-operation in these settings. As such, two public policy and resource implications flow from these findings that bear repeating. First, our data demonstrate the importance of Victim/Witness Assistance Programs for victim co-operation. Continued evaluations of these programs are, therefore, needed to further specify the relationship between such programs and victims' willingness to co-operate (Sebba, 1996). If these programs are indeed successful in making the criminal justice process less intimidating for victims, it would be logical to increase funding to these and other community-based advocacy agencies that are available to victims. Second, if the availability of videotaped statements has, as we have found, a positive influence on the interaction between prosecutors and victims, then continued and increased use of this procedure in courts would be beneficial. Where this practice has not been instituted, training for police and prosecutors regarding the uses and procedures for such evidence should be undertaken, as well as judicial education on the importance of different types of evidence in the prosecution of domestic violence cases.

To be effective, public policy initiatives and research agendas that seek to improve the criminal justice response to domestic violence and its victims need to listen to the experiences of those who have been through the process.

But first we have to ask what those experiences have been. A key goal for future research is, therefore, a more concerted effort by researchers and policy-makers to seek out and encourage victims to voice their concerns, speak out about their experiences and identify what they see as needed improvements in a system that is, in part, designed to serve their interests as well as the interests of society.

Notes

1   A "successful prosecution" refers to those cases in which charges were not withdrawn, even if the victim chose not to testify and where convictions were secured either through a trial or a guilty plea. This is the language used by those involved in the K Court initiative.

2   At any given time, there were four prosecutors assigned to K Court in the period of time examined. However, over the course of the year of the evaluation, 13 different prosecutors were assigned to K Court. The court itself was presided over by judges assigned to K Court on a rotational basis for one week each month for a period of three months. This approach is intended to keep the same judges involved in K Court for the length of any one case thereby keeping the case wholly within K Court. At the same time, rotating judges out of K Court during this time avoids identifying them as part of a court designed to successfully prosecute such cases and allows judges to deal with cases other than domestic violence during this period.

3   Some of the practices were in place in some or all of the participating police divisions prior to the implementation of K Court, but they were confirmed as priorities for this project.

4   For example, in one case, the police videotaped the victim's statement in her hospital room where she was taken as a result of the violent incident and where she was expected to remain for several days.

5   This program is funded by the Attorney General of Ontario and is separate and independent of the prosecutors' office. Its mandate is to provide support to victims of crime.

6   The only exception to this is cases in which a guilty plea is entered at the bail hearing.

7   While operation of K Court actually began in mid-January 1997, it was hoped that a delayed start in case tracking would provide an opportunity for participants in the project to become accustomed to their responsibilities

so that the general principles and operational goals were more likely adhered to by the time case tracking began. We acknowledge that the case outcome data may still reflect, to some degree, the early evolution of the project. However, the first year of operation of any innovative program may be optimal in terms of performance. In other words, people that staff the program may be more highly committed. Over time, it is possible that people become less committed or high turnover means staff members are less well-trained or overwhelmed by workloads. Alternatively, it may be that staff members do not get up to speed on the objectives of the new program until it has been running for some time. Regardless of the situation, it should be noted that the external validity of analysis may be weakened somewhat. Our current research is examining the operation of this court since 2004, but this project is still ongoing.

8   Since data collection relied on notations in the case files, these are conservative estimates of the types of evidence that were collected. For example, the victim's statement may have been collected as evidence but the information was not recorded in the files that were examined.

9   As part of the VWAP's mandate to meet with all victims willing to do so, all K Court victims were contacted by mail or telephone to arrange a meeting with program workers. However, since some victims declined to meet and others could not be located by the VWAP, program workers only met with half the victims in this sample.

10   This variable was missing information in approximately 30% of cases. The procedures used to deal with this missing data and the implications of this are discussed below.

11   It may seem counterintuitive that the average number of days between arrest and trial was longer than between arrest and sentence; however, the latter also includes sentences that resulted from guilty pleas which usually occur much faster than sentences from trial proceedings.

12   In the early intervention courts, emphasis was on the treatment of the offender more so than on vigorous prosecution, however, treatment still involves a guilty plea from the offender and a prosecutorial resolution to the case.

13   We use logistic regression, a technique commonly used for dichotomous and highly skewed outcome variables, which allows us to predict the

odds of an event occurring (Demaris, 1992). For the full paper, please see Dawson and Dinovitzer (2001).

14 The cases for which data were missing on victim co-operation were dropped from the analysis. In this analysis, the variable representing victim co-operation is dichotomized because we are interested in the determinants of any victim co-operation rather than the quality of that co-operation. Victim age (measured in years) and victim sex (female = 1) replace the variables for offender age and offender sex included in the first analysis. All other variables remain identical to the first analysis.

15 As described above, we use OLS regression with a Heckman correction for sample selection bias; the correction model includes those variables that were significant in predicting the likelihood of being sentenced to jail, namely having domestic priors and the offender's employment status. The first equation enters all independent variables used in the model predicting the likelihood of being sentenced to jail.

16 To verify this interpretation, one would need to hear from the prosecutors themselves. While interviews were conducted with prosecutors involved in K Court as part of the larger evaluation, this information was not systematically recorded and, thus, is not available for analysis.

APPENDIX 6.A

Table 6.A1: Logit Estimates of the Effects of Legal, Background Variables and Victim Co-operation on the Likelihood of Prosecution in Cases of Domestic Violence

Variable	Model 1		Model 2	
	Coefficient	Odds	Coefficient	Odds
Def. Characteristics				
Defendant age	-.04** (.01)	.96	-.04** (.01)	.96
Male	1.32** (.43)	3.74	1.34** (.44)	3.81
Case Characteristics				
Weapon used	.06 (.37)	1.06	.20 (.38)	1.22
Domestic prior record	.46 (.40)	1.59	.54 (.42)	1.72
Violent prior record	.53 (.46)	1.70	.46 (.47)	1.59
Non-violent record	-.05 (.35)	.96	.07 (.36)	1.08
Injury	-.08 (.31)	.92	-.03 (.32)	.97
Relationship Type				
Ex-spouse	.22 (.61)	1.25	-.03 (.62)	.97
Common law	-.37 (.36)	.69	-.42 (.37)	.66
Ex-common law	-.99* (.50)	.37	-1.36** (.52)	.26
Boyfriend-girlfriend	-1.20** (.46)	.30	-1.30** (.48)	.27
Ex-boyfriend-girlfriend	-.46 (.60)	.64	-.56 (.62)	.57
Legal Variables				
Victim statement	-.16 (.34)	.85	-.22 (.36)	.81
Witness statement	.55 (.46)	1.74	.49 (.46)	1.63
Photos	.01 (.34)	1.01	-.03 (.35)	.97
Video	.90* (.38)	2.47	.75* (.39)	2.11
Emergency tape	-.23 (.32)	.79	-.34 (.33)	.71
Medical evidence	-.10 (.51)	.90	-.11 (.53)	.89
Other evidence	.19 (.33)	1.20	-.01 (.34)	.99
Missing evidence	.13 (.45)	1.14	.18 (.46)	1.20
Child witness	.26 (.46)	1.29	.26 (.47)	1.29
Adult witness	-.29 (.32)	.75	-.38 (.33)	.69
Missing witness	.17 (.35)	1.22	.19 (.36)	1.27
Process Variables				
Victim met with VWAP	.77* (.37)	2.15	.53 (.39)	1.69
Victim met with Crown	.01 (.41)	1.01	-.01 (.43)	.98
Victim Co-operation				
Fully co-operated		2.01***	(.50)	7.48
Reluctantly co-operated		.81	(.57)	2.25
Missing co-operation		.22	(.32)	1.25
Constant	1.39 (.71)		1.21 (.73)	
-2 Log Likelihood	379.38		356.26	

*Denotes $p < .05$; **$p < .01$; ***$p < .001$.
Note: Number in parentheses are standard errors.

Table 6.A2: Logit Estimates of Legal, Background and Victim/Court Process Variables on Victim Co-operation

Variable	Model 1		
	Coefficient		Odds
Victim Characteristics			
Victim age	.02	(.01)	1.02
Female	-.18	(.53)	.84
Case Characteristics			
Weapon used	-.24	(.36)	.79
Domestic prior record	-.68	(.39)	.51
Violent prior record	.23	(.43)	1.25
Non-violent record	-.43	(.35)	.65
Injury	-.38	(.30)	.68
Relationship Type			
Ex-spouse	.95	(.55)	2.59
Common law	.22	(.35)	1.25
Ex-common law	.84	(.58)	2.31
Boyfriend-girlfriend	.03	(.47)	1.03
Ex-boyfriend-girlfriend	.31	(.56)	1.37
Legal Variables			
Victim statement	.27	(.35)	1.31
Witness statement	.65	(.43)	1.91
Photos	.29	(.32)	1.34
Video	.97**	(.34)	2.63
Emergency tape	.48	(.32)	1.61
Medical evidence	.37	(.50)	1.45
Other evidence	.38	(.32)	1.46
Missing evidence	.44	(.46)	1.55
Child witness	.10	(.42)	1.11
Adult witness	.05	(.32)	1.05
Missing witness	.26	(.33)	1.11
Process Variables			
Victim met with VWAP	1.16***	(.34)	3.20
Victim met with Crown	-.01	(.35)	.99
Constant	-1.71	(.79)	
-2 Log Likelihood	360.82		

* Denotes $p < .05$; **$p < .01$; ***$p < .001$
Note: Number in parentheses are standard errors

Table 6.A3: Logistic regression predicting the likelihood of being sentenced to jail

	Model 1			Model 2		
	Coef.	Std. Err.	Odds Ratio	Coef.	Std. Err.	Odds Ratio
Relationship Intact	-0.193	0.324	0.825	-0.501	0.351	0.606
Children	0.617	0.391	1.854	0.639	0.397	1.895
Offence Characteristics						
Serious injury	0.829	0.438	2.292	-1.115	1.021	0.328
Aggravated sexual assault	0.599	0.427	1.820	0.648	0.432	1.911
Weapons present	0.073	0.466	1.075	0.052	0.470	1.053
Corroborating evidence	0.425	0.482	1.530	0.564	0.489	1.757
Offender Characteristics						
Offender age	-0.006	0.014	0.994	-0.004	0.015	0.996
Offender employed	-0.876	0.305**	0.416	-0.910	0.309**	0.403
Domestic prior	1.289	0.355***	3.629	1.257	0.356***	3.515
Guilty plea	-0.238	0.342	0.788	-0.196	0.346	0.822
Victim Co-operated	-0.099	0.371	0.906	-0.209	0.379	0.811
Injury*Intact				2.371	1.089*	10.703
Constant	-0.991	0.865	0.371	-0.880	0.874	0.415
-2 log likelihood	-164.126			-161.464		
Pseudo R²	0.126			0.140		

*p <.05; ** p <.01; *** p <.001 (two-tailed)

Table 6.A4: Heckman selection model predicting sentence length, correcting for those who were not sentenced to jail (jail sentence N = 96; Full model N = 299)

	Model 1		Model 2	
	Coef.	Std. Err.	Coef.	Std. Err.
Relationship Intact	-16.990	4.097***	-55.847	23.325*
Children	9.271	0.576***	-4.522	29.214
Offence Characteristics				
Serious injury	51.228	18.987**	-52.885	71.468
Aggravated sexual assault	0.405	17.684	56.720	27.126*
Weapons present	1.152	12.659	-34.278	30.294
Corroborating evidence	-14.242	12.845	7.910	37.863
Offender Characteristics				
Offender age	-1.543	1.117	-1.169	1.321
Offender employed	-62.588	26.534*	-3.003	29.263
Domestic prior	96.615	36.146**	0.902	37.671
Guilty plea	-0.818	19.173	-12.626	23.995
Victim Co-operated	-4.214	5.587	3.034	25.885
Missing Data Dummy Variables				
Missing data co-operation	-3.114	9.494	-43.993	26.487
Missing data employed	-47.789	31.459	-33.341	31.619
Missing data domestic prior	66.213	25.131**	134.893	44.667**
Missing data evidence	-20.743	37.673	22.281	41.035
Missing data kids	40.747	10.797***	15.949	31.944
Injury*Intact			79.000	
Constant	18.213	85.714	203.569	99.774*
Correction Factor	14.695	147.320	-0.232	0.604
-2 log likelihood	-711.6294		-734.2123	

* p <.05; ** p <.01; *** p <.001 (two-tailed)

CHAPTER SEVEN

Calgary's HomeFront Specialized Domestic Violence Court

Leslie M. Tutty, Kevin McNichol and Janie Christensen

In 1999, HomeFront, the dedicated domestic violence court process in Calgary, came into operation. This unique specialization was originally only in the "docket" or "first appearance" court,[1] in which the accused make their first court appearance following charges related to domestic violence. The court can perform all functions up to but excluding trial. Those functions include bail hearings, acceptance of pleas and sentencing. The specialized court hears all domestic violence-related cases charged in the City of Calgary, including violence by heterosexual or same-sex couples who are in either cohabitating or non-cohabitating relationships, interfamilial violence, child abuse and elder abuse. The most common offences seen in the court include assault, uttering threats and breach of court orders, and can include attempted murder and homicide.

What makes the HomeFront model unique is its focus on the first-appearance court in which low-risk accused can have their charges stayed with a peace bond if they acknowledge responsibility for their behaviour and are willing to participate in court-mandated domestic violence counselling. Its goals are to hold offenders accountable within the justice system and increase the likelihood that a meaningful intervention will be imposed on the offender through treatment. It is based on the premise that a more efficient court process can take advantage of the accused's guilt and shame that is usually present close to the time of the offence. It is hoped that the speedy access to treatment and tight monitoring of offenders will increase compliance with court orders and maximize the effects of treatment programs.

Additionally, victim safety is prioritized in the specialized court. Risk assessments and the victim's wishes are presented to the court team prior to docket court and are used to support and refine submissions made to the court by the Crown and defence attorneys. The addition of "real time" information improves the quality of submissions made in court and, ultimately, the decisions improve the response of the justice system to victims' safety and needs. Further, the more efficient process minimizes factors related to the dynamic of abuse and violence that impede or impair court processes, such as victims recanting their testimony or being reluctant witnesses.

Calgary is a city of one million citizens and is home to many specialized domestic violence agencies including a specialized police unit (domestic conflict unit or DCU), specialized probation officers and a community coordinating body (Action Committee Against Violence). An extensive protocol network promotes collaboration and the sharing of information across agencies, including the police, Crown prosecutors, legal aid, victim advocates, shelters, probation, and treatment programs.

Additionally, victims are supported by a non-profit law office (Calgary Legal Guidance), which provides the joint services of a lawyer and social worker and specializes in restraining and emergency protection orders along with various other matters related to family law. Victims and their children have access to a range of counselling and treatment options and a safe visitation and access centre. Further, while their partners are under community supervision through probation, victims are contacted and offered support through the Partner Support Program, a partnership between a volunteer victim support staff and probation services.

The accused have the benefit of a fast-tracked legal aid appointment process and a dedicated legal aid lawyer attached to the specialized court. Calgary Police Services follow a mandatory charge policy and undergo extensive training on dominant aggressors and domestic violence investigations. Dominant or primary aggressor policies are guidelines for the police in deciding who to charge in circumstances in which it is difficult to determine who is the victim because of ambiguity, such as when both parties are injured or accuse the other of assault. The dominant aggressor is the individual who has been the most significant aggressor throughout the relationship (Strack, n.d.).

This chapter describes the critical elements of the HomeFront first-appearance court, including the court team that consists of domestic court caseworkers, specialized Crown attorneys, police, probation and duty counsel officers. In addition, we present data with respect to the nature and disposition of domestic violence cases in HomeFront's first three full years in operation (2001–03). In 2004, Calgary created a specialized domestic violence trial court; however, court data are not yet available to assess this important additional development.

The HomeFront Court Team

One of the key elements of the HomeFront process is the court "team," perceived by many as the "backbone" of the process. The team includes specialists from the Crown prosecutor's office and probation office, a member of the Domestic Conflict Unit of Calgary Police Services and domestic court caseworkers from HomeFront. Currently, four Crown prosecutors are specialized in domestic violence and appear in the court on a rotating basis. Two representatives from the specialized probation office rotate daily in the docket court, while their seven other colleagues manage the majority of domestic violence offenders at a central location. Likewise, one member of the Domestic Conflict Unit sits in the court. The Domestic Conflict Unit consists of 10 investigators, a sergeant and staff sergeant. The unit reviews all domestic violence calls responded to by the Calgary Police Service and directly handles approximately 400 high-risk and/or chronic files per year, while offering support to frontline police officers. Four court caseworkers from HomeFront cover docket court on a rotating basis.

A major undertaking of the court team is to assess risk in order to attain or maintain the safety of victims and their children. The specialized domestic violence team exists to bring to the justice system a greater understanding of the nature of domestic violence and to bring about the best and most expedient response. The Crown prosecutors assess risk and recommend to the judge and defence counsel the directions that they consider most appropriate in each case. Their recommendations are based upon information and assessments provided to them during "pre-court conferences" that occur prior to case resolutions or bail hearings each day and for every file. The pre-court conferences involve all the court team members to ensure that relevant information is provided or confirmed regarding victim concerns/wishes and the conditions requested. For example, the accused may be given no contact orders, orders not to drink, orders to attend counselling within a specified time period, and may have their weapons confiscated.

The Domestic Court Caseworkers

The HomeFront court caseworkers provide two essential services. The first is victim support. Each morning they review the police 24-hour incident reports to collect new offence information and begin contacting the victims in those cases within a day of the police laying charges. Further, they review each case before every court appearance and ensure that victims' wishes are up to date and that victims are aware of the status of the case against their partners. The workers typically inquire about a past history of abuse, current relationship status with the accused, perceived level of danger, as well as the victims' wishes with respect to what they would like to happen at court. In addition, the clinical interview is supplemented with standardized risk assessment tools such as the Danger Assessment (Campbell, Sharps & Glass, 2001).

Safety planning for victims is an essential component of the court caseworker's role. Safety is ensured by connecting the victim to other community or legal resources: counselling programs for victims or children exposed to domestic violence, immigrant serving agencies, shelters and the Court Preparation and Restraining Order programs at Calgary Legal Guidance. The court caseworkers also keep victims updated about the progress of their partner/ex-partner's case within the justice system, including such information as the date of the next court appearance and the plea entered. Court caseworkers, by necessity, may also liaise with other agency representatives in the City of Calgary, including the Child and Family Services Authority (child welfare).

The second essential service is conducting risk assessments and providing the victim's wishes to the court team. This information is often vital in supporting and guiding the decisions of the court and supplementing/

balancing information provided by other sources, including the police and defence representatives.

Probation Services

Probation officers are key stakeholders in the specialized court process as they can provide considerable information about an accused's past history of criminal offences. Further, the court probation officer acts as an information conduit between the court and the accused's supervising probation officer.

In addition to case conferencing, probation officers are officers of the court and may answer questions posed by counsel, the accused or the court. The information requested often includes past involvement with probation, current orders against the accused (including pre-trial), compliance history, as well as possible treatment options and suggested conditions. To prepare for court, the probation officers preview the docket list to assess what information might be needed during the daily docket, including checking databases and talking to any assigned probation officers about whether the accused is complying with community supervision.

An advantage of having a probation officer in court is that the accused makes immediate contact with the probation officer and is directly referred to treatment services from court. This significantly decreases the delay of an offender entering into treatment. The probation offices are located on the ground floor of the provincial court building and are easily accessible. Once an accused has been sentenced, he/she meets with the probation officer to review the court order with the officer, signs it to signify compliance and receives reporting instructions about when he/she must reconnect with the supervising probation officer.

Common probation conditions include immediate monitoring of the accused and ensuring that the accused follow court orders. At this time, probation officers also complete a preliminary intake with the accused to screen for any mental health, medical or treatment related issues such as language fluency to better direct accused into appropriate programming.

Within the HomeFront court, the accused are given a shorter time frame to contact their probation officer and treatment agencies than if they were to appear in a non-specialized court. The accused are generally given seven to ten days to contact their supervising probation officer in a non-specialized court, whereas in the HomeFront setting, they are given, on average, four days.

The HomeFront Court Process

The HomeFront docket court is in session from 9 a.m., Monday to Friday, and runs until the cases on the docket are heard that day, usually ending at noon or 1 p.m. The judiciary was initially specialized in domestic violence, though now all Calgary provincial criminal court judges rotate into the specialized court.

The court team meets before court is in session each day and again during breaks. The team reviews the particulars of each case with the defence or duty counsel and determines what course they will pursue. At this time new information from any team member can be introduced. As well, members have the opportunity to request additional information they may need from other members before meeting again. Examples of information shared include: letters from victims asking that no contact orders be lifted, or that the victim is fearful and pursuing a restraining order; address and employment updates from probation and police officers; verification of treatment attendance and compliance; or any changes in the perceived level of risk for the accused or the victim. The goal is to provide the court with as much information as possible in order to allow it to make appropriate and efficient decisions.

Docket court is the first opportunity for an accused to enter a plea; however, many other steps and procedures often need to take place before a plea is accepted. These procedures can include adjournments to allow an accused to make application for legal aid coverage and retain a lawyer; to allow information or paperwork to catch up to the court; or until an interpreter can be made available. Some adjournments are made for tactical reasons such as if other charges or court decisions are pending for an accused. Duty counsel, the defence or the Crown may request that the case be heard at a later time because they do not yet have all the necessary information.

About one-third of all cases are stayed with a peace bond whereby an accused enters into an agreement with the court to abide by conditions to keep the peace, report to a probation officer, attend and complete mandated treatment for either domestic violence or substance abuse, or attend a parenting course. Often peace bonds include conditions of no contact, geographic restrictions and abstinence from drugs and/or alcohol. In all cases, the accused are required to acknowledge before the court the substance of their actions that led to the criminal charges being laid and express a willingness to participate in domestic violence or other appropriate treatment programs.

The bulk of cases seen by the court and mandated to treatment are referred primarily to the Calgary Counselling Centre, YWCA Sheriff King Home, and the Alberta Alcohol and Drug Abuse Commission, with a smaller percentage going to Forensic Assessment Outpatient Services at the Peter Lougheed Hospital. Additional referrals would also be given, depending on case circumstances, to immigrant serving agencies or first-language counsellors that can address cultural and settlement issues, First Nations counselling or culturally based services, mental health resources, brain injury resources, and others.

Key Points in the Court Process

Fast and efficient resolution of domestic violence cases is considered a central goal in the coordinated justice response. This is because the longer the delay until the court intervenes, the greater the likelihood that the evidence, usually hinging on victims' willingness to testify, will be lost. Further, offenders' remorse and willingness to acknowledge a problem in their lives wanes the more time passes between intervention and the original offence. Delays also play significantly into the cycle of violence and can exacerbate victims' feelings of helplessness.

Treatment is an integral and effective response to domestic violence and every effort is made to direct the accused into treatment as soon as possible following police charges and fast-tracked court dispositions. Being fast-tracked into counselling, which is monitored by probation, is believed to be an effective means of maintaining the safety of victims and families and breaking the cycle of violence. Holding offenders accountable is essential to an effective domestic violence intervention because offenders need to know that there are consequences unless they better regulate their behaviour. Monitoring helps ensure the victim's safety and reassures victims that they are not solely responsible for supervising the offenders' behaviour.

Immediate screening and regular contact with victims throughout the justice process is a further means of checking on safety and offering needed support to victims of violence, thereby increasing the likelihood that they will seek support in the future.

Characteristics of the Accused and Victims of HomeFront Spousal Assault Cases

The first three years of data on the HomeFront specialized Domestic Violence Court were collected by Hoffart and Clarke (2004) with funding from the National Crime Prevention Centre and RESOLVE Alberta's SSHRC CURA grant, the Alberta Mental Health Board, the Alberta Law Foundation and the Prairie*action* Foundation. This section documents the results of analysis of the first three years of the HomeFront process that focused only on spousal assault cases,[2] first presenting information on the characteristics of the accused and victims, then the characteristics of the incident and police charges. The final segment presents the outcomes of the court processes, including sentencing and recidivism. Because gender is central to domestic violence assaults, with women generally being victimized more often and suffering more severe consequences (Johnson, 2006), a number of the analyses compare data about the male and female accused and the victims.

With respect to the sex of the accused, the majority were men, while women represented less than 15% of the total. As can be seen in Table 7.1, the victims were primarily women and the accused mostly men.

Table 7.1: Sex of Accused and Victims

	Men		Women		Total*
Accused	1,931	86.0%	315	14.0%	2,246
Victim	317	14.1%	1,928	85.9%	2,245

* The numbers are not equal because of missing data on the gender of the victim.

The accused were an average age of 34 years when first charged (range of 18 to 81 years). The average age of victims was 33 years with a range of from 15 to 76 years. As highlighted in Table 7.2, over four-fifths of both accused

(86.7%) and victims (86.8%) were under age 44. Relatively high proportions were young adults aged 24 or younger.

Table 7.2: Ages of Accused and Victims

Age Category	Accused		Victim	
15–24 years	376	16.8%	482	24.4%
25–34 years	814	36.3%	659	33.4%
35–44 years	753	33.6%	573	29.0%
45–54 years	225	10.0%	210	10.6%
55–64 years	61	2.7%	40	2.0%
65 years and above	13	0.6%	12	0.6%
TOTAL	2,242		1,976	

The types of relationships between the accused and the victims are displayed in Table 7.3. Nineteen victim-accused couples were both male and 19 were both female. The high proportion of common-law relationships is interesting given that these make up only 12% of the spousal population in Canada, much smaller than the proportion of married couples (74%) (Johnson, 2006, p.38). Further, that about 20% of the assaults involved past partners reminds us that abuse often continues past the point of couple separation and, according to several researchers, the risk of homicide post-separation rises (Campbell, 2001; Ellis, 1992).

Table 7.3: Victim-Accused Relationships

Type of Relationship	Frequency/Percent	
Common-law husband or wife	750	33.8%
Married	643	29.0%
Boyfriend-girlfriend	299	13.5%
Ex-boyfriend-girlfriend	206	9.3%
Ex-common-law partners	121	5.5%
Ex-spouse/Legally separated	113	5.1%
Same-sex/ex-same-sex relationship	38	1.7%
Divorced	15	0.7%
Other	34	1.5%
TOTAL	2,219	

Of the total cases, 9.8% (217) represent dual charges in which both members of the couple were charged by the police. Of the 315 women charged, 205 (65.1%) were solely charged, while 110 (34.9%) were charged as well as their male partners.

Of the 2,150 accused files that specified racial background, the majority were of Caucasian background, one-tenth were Aboriginal and two-tenths were from visible minority groups (see Table 7.4).

Table 7.4: Racial Background of Accused and Victims

Racial Group	Accused		Victim	
Caucasian	1,460	67.9%	962	67.1%
Aboriginal	219	10.2%	158	11.0%
Visible minority groups	471	21.9%	313	21.8%
TOTAL	2,150		1,433	

Of the accused from other ethic minority groups, the largest group were South Asian (5.7%) and East and Southeast Asian (5.0%). The 22% of accused from visible minority groups was slightly higher than the estimate for Calgary from the 2002 Canada Census (21%). The proportion of accused from an Aboriginal background was higher than the approximately 3% among the City of Calgary population, indicating that they were overrepresented in the justice system with respect to spousal abuse.

The racial backgrounds of the 1,433 victim files that included that information were very similar to that of the accused: about two-thirds were Caucasian, one-tenth were Aboriginal and two-tenths were from visible minority groups.

As can be seen in Table 7.5, there were significant differences in the racial background of the accused based on gender (chi-square = 13.6, p = .001, phi coefficient = .07 which indicates a weak effect). In comparison to the male accused, women accused were more likely to be Caucasian and less likely to be from an ethnic minority group.

Less complete information is available with respect to the education levels of the accused and victims (see Table 7.6). Of the accused for whom this data were available, 37.1% had not completed high school (28.0% of victims), another 32.7% were high-school graduates (25.5% of victims), and a final 30.3% had some post-secondary education or training (46.5% of victims). In summary, the education levels of victims were higher than those of the accused, consistent with other research on abused women and their abusive intimate partners (Tutty, 2006).

Table 7.5: Racial Background of Accused Based on Gender

	Male		Female		Totals
Caucasian	1238	84.7%	224	15.3%	1462
Aboriginal	182	83.1%	37	16.9%	219
Ethnic Minority	428	90.9%	43	9.1%	471
Total	1848	85.9%	304	14.1%	2152

Table 7.6: Education Levels of Accused and Victims

	Accused		Victim	
No high school	102	8.3%	49	3.7%
Some high school	354	28.8%	319	24.3%
Completed high school	402	32.7%	335	25.5%
Some post-secondary (technical)	40	3.3%	35	2.7%
Completed post-secondary (technical)	52	4.2%	34	2.6%
Some post-secondary/university	119	9.7%	186	14.1%
Completed post-secondary/university	161	13.1%	357	27.1%
Total	1,230		1,315	

With respect to current employment status (see Table 7.7), almost two-thirds of the accused were employed in some manner (55.9% were employed full-time) and almost one-quarter were unemployed.

Table 7.7: Employment of Accused and Victims

	Accused		Victim	
Employed full-time	916	55.9%	671	49.3%
Employed part-time/ Casual/Self-employed	154	9.4%	186	13.7%
Welfare/Disability	64	3.9%	96	7.1%
Unemployed	396	24.2%	267	19.6%
Other*	109	6.7%	140	10.3%
Total	1,639		1,360	

* Includes students and retirees.

Of the 1,901 individuals accused for whom this information was available, 1,098 had children under age 18 (57.8%) and 738 (38.8%) had no children. Of the 1,214 cases that catalogued whether the children had witnessed the assault, 46.9% (569) of the children had been exposed to the violence.

Criminal Background and Characteristics of the Incident

With respect to prior criminal convictions, more than half of the accused (57.3% or 1,253 of 2,186) had such a record, whereas about four-tenths (42.7% or 933 of 2,186) did not. Information about the type of past record was collected only for accused who went to trial. As can be seen in Table 7.8, of those cases, about one-quarter had no record and four-tenths had convictions for charges other than assault, including sexual assault (11 cases) and child abuse (one case). Almost one-third had previous assault convictions, 40% of which were specifically identified as domestic assaults and the other 60% were labelled simply as general assaults.

Table 7.8: Prior Criminal Convictions of Accused Persons for Trial Cases Only

Prior Criminal Convictions	Accused	Percentage
Assault convictions	228	32.9%
Domestic assaults	92	40.4%
General assaults	136	59.6%
Charges other than assault	297	42.9%
No prior record	167	24.1%
TOTAL	692	

In the 1,131 cases for which information about breaches of court orders or peace bonds prior to the first incident was available, only a minority (21 cases or 1.9%), had breached orders, the majority of these only once before (15 cases).

The characteristics of the first incident for each accused are provided to portray the nature of the situations to which the police responded by laying criminal charges.

Table 7.9 identifies who reported the incident to the police. The vast majority of incidents were reported by the victim. Interestingly, the accused reported about 5% of cases and children under 18 called for assistance almost 4% of the time.

Table 7.9: Who Reported Incident to the Police

Who Reported	Frequency	Percentage
Victim	1,313	70.7%
Neighbour/Friend	200	10.8%
Accused	88	4.7%
Child under 18	72	3.9%
Passersby	61	3.3%
Other	123	6.6%
TOTAL	1,857	

Table 7.10 displays data on the presence of either alcohol or other sub-stances in the accused or the victim when the police attended the domestic violence incident. In cases for which this information is available, a relatively high proportion of accused persons (78.3%) were identified as having used substances in comparison to about 35.2% of victims.

Table 7.10: Alcohol/Drugs Present at Incident One

Alcohol/Drugs Present	Frequency/Percentage	
Present in both victim and accused	356	30.8%
Present in accused but no information for victim	285	24.6%
Present in accused but not victim	265	22.9%
Not present in either	171	14.8%
Present in victim but no information for accused	35	3.0%
Present in environment	29	2.5%
Present in victim but not accused	16	1.4%
TOTAL	1,157	

Table 7.11 displays the most serious police charges that were seen in the HomeFront first-appearance court. There was a different pattern of charges for male and female accused such that only men were charged with sexual assaults, and men were more likely to be charged with uttering threats and aggravated assault (chi-square = 56.7; $p < .000$; phi coefficient is .16, indicating a weak to moderate effect). Further, a relatively higher

proportion of women were charged with assault with a weapon as compared with the other charges, the percentages of which were more equal.

Table 7.11: Most Serious Charge to HomeFront Court

Charge	Male Accused		Female Accused		Total Accused	
Common assault	1,356	70.7%	214	68.6%	1,570	70.4%
Assault with a weapon	97	5.1%	48	15.4%	145	6.5%
Uttering threats	132	6.9%	12	3.8%	144	6.5%
Aggravated assault/ Assault causing bodily harm	99	5.2%	8	2.6%	107	4.8%
Mischief	72	3.8%	13	4.2%	85	3.8%
Criminal harassment	36	1.9%	5	1.6%	41	1.8%
Breaches of court orders	32	1.7%	5	1.6%	37	1.7%
Sexual assaults	13	0.7%	0	0%	13	0.6%
Other	80	4.2%	7	2.2%	87	3.9%
TOTAL	1,917		312		2,229	

Information with respect to the outcomes from those appearing in the HomeFront specialized domestic violence first-appearance court is presented in Table 7.12.

Table 7.12: Dispositions from the HomeFront First-Appearance Court

	Male Accused		Female Accused		Total Accused	
Stay with peace bond	629	32.7%	165	52.4%	794	35.5%
Not guilty plea	685	35.6%	76	24.1%	761	34.0%
Guilty plea	461	24.0%	24	7.6%	485	21.7%
Withdrawn/Stay of Proceedings/Dismissed	74	3.8%	41	13.0%	115	5.1%
Not guilty plea & early resolution	74	3.8%	9	2.9%	83	3.7%
TOTAL	1,923		315		2,238	

As can be seen, the most common disposition from the HomeFront specialized first-appearance court was that charges were stayed with a peace bond (a little more than one-third of cases). As mentioned previously, this disposition may be offered to low-risk accused who do not have a criminal record or have a minor unrelated criminal record and who have expressed a willingness to take responsibility for the incident. This sentence also takes into consideration the wishes of the victim. The conditions of the peace bond usually entail being mandated to offender treatment and/ or substance abuse interventions. The second most common outcome was a not guilty plea (34.0%), in which the case typically proceeds to trial. A further one-fifth (21.7%) of cases were concluded with a guilty plea at first-appearance court.

There were significant differences in the dispositions of the HomeFront court based on the gender of the accused (chi-square = 118.4; p < .000; phi-coefficient = .23, indicating a weak to moderate effect). Women were more likely to have cases withdrawn/dismissed for want of prosecution. This is likely due to the higher proportion of dual charges, which are difficult to prosecute. Further, males are less credible as victims and can be reluctant to participate in court proceedings. Women are less credible as accused and therefore more likely to have charges dismissed. They are also more likely to engage and maintain themselves in counselling and support programs, which can mitigate the need to prosecute their offences.

Table 7.13: Resolutions at Trial

Resolution	Male Accused		Female Accused		Total Accused	
Dismissed for want of prosecution	289	41.5%	34	46.6%	323	41.9%
Stay with peace bond	143	20.5%	17	23.3%	160	20.8%
Guilty plea	118	16.9%	10	13.7%	128	16.6%
Trial found guilty	74	10.6%	7	9.6%	81	10.5%
Stay of proceedings/ Other	39	5.6%	3	4.1%	42	5.5%
Trial found not guilty	32	4.6%	2	2.7%	34	4.4%
Accused deceased	2	0.3%	0	0%	2	0.3%
TOTAL	697		73		770	

Perusing the resolutions at trial is also integral in assessing the effectiveness of the justice system response to domestic assaults. At the time that this data were collected, Calgary had no specialized domestic violence trial court. As can be seen in Table 7.13, only 14.9% (115) of the 770 cases that proceeded from the HomeFront first-appearance court were actually tried in court, of which 70.4% were found guilty. Most cases were dealt with before reaching trial: over one-third of the cases were dismissed for want of prosecution and another one-fifth were stayed with peace bonds. Another one-fifth changed their plea to guilty. There were no significant differences between the resolutions of men and women accused in the trial court (chi-square = 4.7, $p < .58$).

Table 7.14: Dispositions from Trial

Disposition	Frequency / Percentage	
Peace bond	162	47.4%
Suspended sentence	58	17.0%
Supervised probation	38	11.1%
Fine	19	5.6%
Incarceration	18	5.3%
Other	47	13.7%
TOTAL	342	

The most common dispositions from trial are provided in Table 7.14 and the most common conditions are documented in Table 7.15. Notably, a high proportion of spousal abuse cases that went to trial resulted in the accused being mandated to batterers' treatment or other counselling.

Table 7.15: Conditions from Trial

Condition	Frequency / Percentage	
Batterer treatment	122	40.3%
No contact/Communication with complainant	86	28.4%
Other counselling as directed	32	10.6%
Alcohol/Substance abuse treatment	24	7.9%
Abstain from alcohol	21	6.9%
Other	18	5.9%
TOTAL	303	

Recidivism

Recidivism is one of the major indicators that a specialized justice approach to domestic violence is more effective than non-specialization (Gondolf, 2002). With respect to all cases in the HomeFront court (including other forms of family violence as well as spousal assaults), Hoffart and Clarke (2004) looked at recidivism in 757 HomeFront files as compared with 820 files in a baseline sample of cases before the HomeFront court was established. Using data that included police investigations with no charges, the HomeFront cases had lower recidivism in most categories. Hoffart and Clarke reported fewer investigations with no charges (31.4% HomeFront versus 48.9% baseline), new offences only (12.2% HomeFront versus 34.1 % in the baseline), breaches only (15.2% HomeFront versus 20.7% baseline) and breaches plus new offences (21.4% HomeFront versus 38.8% baseline). In summary, accused that went through the HomeFront court were much less likely to commit new offences compared with those who were charged in the years preceding HomeFront's implementation.

To assess recidivism rates for spousal assault cases dealt within the HomeFront court, we chose only cases from 2001 and 2002. Since data were collected until the end of 2003, this allowed a time period of 12 months to 36 months in which accused could have committed further criminal acts or breached court or civil orders.

As is apparent from Table 7.16, the overall recidivism rate for new criminal charges was 7.9%, with breaches of orders at 10.9%. Of the 320 cases in which the accused were charged with additional offences, the majority (86.9% or 278 cases) noted only one additional event in which charges were laid, 12.2% (39 cases) listed two further events and 2.2% (three and four individuals that were accused) were charged with additional offences three or four times respectively.

Table 7.16: Recidivism Rates for Trial Compared with HomeFront Cases

Case Proceeded to Trial	No Recidivism		Breaches		New Criminal Charges		Totals
No	939	84.3%	135	12.1%	40	3.6%	1,114
Yes	447	75.5%	51	8.6%	94	15.9%	592
TOTAL	1,386	81.2%	186	10.9%	134	7.9%	1,706

There was a significantly greater number of new criminal charges for cases that proceeded to trial court as compared with those that were resolved in the HomeFront first-appearance court (chi-square = 82.4; $p > .000$; phi-coefficient = .22, which indicates a weak to moderate effect). This makes conceptual sense since cases stayed with peace bonds involve low-risk cases — that is, accused with no or minor criminal records who are willing to accept responsibility for their behaviour and recognize the need to address their actions through counselling. The analyses should also reassure victim advocates who have been concerned that the practice of using peace bonds decriminalizes the criminal behaviour and does not send a strong enough message to the accused that their behaviour is unacceptable.

Discussion and Conclusions

With its emphasis on the docket court, Calgary's HomeFront specialized response is a unique model, different from other specialized domestic violence courts across Canada (Tutty, Ursel & Douglas, chapter 4, and Dawson & Dinovitzer, chapter 6 in this volume). Much of the HomeFront emphasis has been on creating a speedier response to assaults in domestic violence cases: seeing the accused in a specialized docket court more quickly than previously, and having treatment available much more quickly than before. Further, crisis intervention theory has long posited that the sooner one receives intervention, the more likely the counselling will be effective (Roberts & Everly, 2006). Also, the safety and wishes of the victims are taken into consideration by the court team early on in the process, while the assault is still fresh in their minds and they are not influenced by the accused to the same extent as they might be later on.

The data from the HomeFront court validate that accused receiving the option of having their charges stayed by a peace bond (typically mandating them to treatment such as intervention for batterers or substance abuse) are less likely to have previous criminal records. This is not surprising since those who plead not guilty and proceed to trial are often more knowledgeable about the justice system and understand that long delays often result in dismissals. Further, pre-custody time is counted as double time and therefore substantially reduces the amount of actual jail time served in cases in which a long jail sentence may be imposed.

Even so, some advocates for victims and others have expressed concern about utilizing the outcome of stays with a peace bond (Hoffart & Clarke, 2004), since it gives the appearance of letting the accused off without a criminal record. While this remains a philosophical concern, results from the HomeFront evaluation indicate that accused who receive a peace bond reoffend at a much lower rate than those who receive other dispositions. . Further, an evaluation of the batterer treatment programs in Calgary (Cairns, 2005) concluded that those with peace bonds who attended and completed counselling had significantly lower new charge rates (6.1%) than those who did not show or complete treatment (23.7%). The lower recidivism rates for all cases concluded at the first-appearance court, whether stayed with a peace bond or entering a guilty plea, provide additional support for dealing with these cases in this manner.

While noting difficulties in comparing recidivism studies because of differing definitions of recidivism and time periods, HomeFront's recidivism rates of 7.9% for police charges for new offences and 10.9% of charges for breaches of court orders over an average of one to two years following the first offence (a total of 18.8 %) appear relatively low when compared with other research (in fact, this percentage is likely inflated because a number of accused both breach and are charged with new offences). In terms of official reports in which the police laid subsequent charges, three studies from the United States (Maxwell, Garner & Fagan, 2001; Thistlewaite, Wooldredge & Gibbs, 1998; Tolman & Weisz, 1995) reported recidivism rates of 30% (six months to three years), 17% (one year) and 23.6% (18 months) respectively. Further, the lower recidivism rates since the inception of the HomeFront court as compared with the baseline data conducted by Hoffart and Clarke (2004) provide additional support to the premise that specialization has contributed significant improvements in the justice system response to domestic violence in Calgary.

Following the early successes of the HomeFront first-appearance court, the Calgary justice community instituted a specialized domestic violence trial court in 2004. One rationale for this was the recognition that the domestic court caseworkers were not available to support victims in cases going to trial. The high number of cases withdrawn or dismissed for want of prosecution at trial is often because victims recant their testimony (Ursel, 2002), and providing ongoing support could decrease the number of withdrawals and possibly increase the number of cases found guilty or concluded with intervention conditions at trial.

If accused know that the trial court is also specialized, with Crown prosecutors and other staff that have a strong understanding of the serious nature and dynamics of intimate partner violence, some accused could be encouraged to plead guilty at first appearance or take the offer of the case being stayed by a peace bond.

In conclusion, a significant advantage of the HomeFront model is the extent to which the police and court systems are perceived by the general public, by accused persons and by victims as mobilizing significant resources to address family violence. The hope is that this specialized response will signal that these offences are taken seriously and will not be tolerated, thereby serving as a deterrent and preventing offences from occurring in the future.

Notes

1   Also called "plea" court in other jurisdictions.
2   Hoffart and Clarke (2004) evaluated all cases of family violence heard in the HomeFront court.

CHAPTER EIGHT

The Yukon's Domestic Violence Treatment Option: *An Evaluation*

Joseph P. Hornick, Michael Boyes, Leslie M. Tutty and Leah White

This chapter presents some key results from a comprehensive process and outcome evaluation designed to monitor and test the effectiveness of the Domestic Violence Treatment Option (DVTO) located in White-horse, Yukon. The DVTO program includes both a therapeutic treatment program, the Spousal Abuse Program (SAP) and an elaborate justice intervention system. The key component of the intervention system is a specialized DVTO court that deals only with spousal (partner) abuse cases. The system also includes the police, Probation Services, a special Crown prosecutor, Victim Services and non-governmental women's groups. The evaluation was designed to determine the effectiveness of both the SAP using a quasi-experimental pre-test/post-test group design (Tutty, Hornick, Boyes & White, in preparation) and the intervention system. This chapter focuses on the justice system response (the court outcomes) rather than on the outcomes from the treatment program for batterers.

Background and Rationale for the Domestic Violence Treatment Option

The inability of the formal adversarial court process to effectively address many spousal assault cases is known to anyone who practices in the criminal courts, and is well documented in the literature. These limitations were identified in the Final Report of the Committee to Assess the Responsiveness of Yukon Justice to Family Violence, September 1993 (Yukon Department of Justice). The report concluded with a number of salient points. First, the courts are not able to reduce or eliminate family violence because they do not to deal with the underlying issues or provide long-term protection to individuals. Perpetuating the myth that courts can solve the problem of family violence results in a misallocation of limited financial and human resources. Courts focus on laws and those who break them. As long as society expects courts to be punishment-oriented, it will be difficult to address the needs of a number of victims. Finally, at the trial stage and prior to a finding of guilt or a guilty plea, the system, governed by the Criminal Code and the Charter of Rights and Freedoms, is adversarial and is primarily concerned with the rights of the accused person.

As well, the Yukon Department of Justice highlighted the problem of high court-collapse rates in domestic assault cases, meaning that a large percentage of complainants fail to show up in court or, if they do, change their version of events in order to exculpate the accused. While high collapse rates disrupt court scheduling, it is of greater concern that many of these complainants continue to live with their abusive partners.

Further, the majority of victims choose not to contact the police and endure the violence in silence. Some fear retaliation from their partner and do not believe that the system can protect them. Some have already been through the formal justice system only to find that it did not respond to their needs or that the process "revictimized" them. For others, economic, family, cultural or social considerations act as barriers to accessing the formal justice system. Some want help and treatment for their abusers but know that once they initiate a call to the police for help, they lose control of the process and have little opportunity to influence the outcome. For these victims at this point in their lives, the formal justice system is not an appropriate alternative and no degree of fine-tuning, tinkering, or even modest improvement is going to make a difference. Victims are not a homogenous group and their needs and personal circumstances are varied. One should not be surprised, therefore, that an inflexible justice system is not responsive to the needs of all victims and, worse, excludes a significant proportion of them.

A logical response would be to make available a variety of alternatives that provide realistic choices for a greater number of victims of domestic violence. Some of these alternatives should be based in the criminal court while others should be established as civil law remedies. Most importantly, victims should be allowed a much greater role in choosing the response appropriate to their personal circumstances and state of mind. It is hoped that empowering victims through giving them greater control and responsibility over the process and remedy will encourage more timely disclosures of domestic violence. These considerations were of prime importance in developing the Domestic Violence Treatment Option program.

The Domestic Violence Treatment Option (DVTO)

In cases of spousal or partner abuse, the DVTO provides offenders, and, indirectly, victims, an opportunity to choose a therapeutic treatment alternative to traditional sentencing in criminal court. The goals of the program are to encourage more disclosures of domestic violence; provide early intervention; and provide a non-adversarial, court-based alternative to formal criminal court as a means of responding to domestic violence. Additional goals are to reduce the high collapse rate for domestic violence charges; hold offenders accountable in a meaningful way; provide a therapeutic option to offenders prior to sentencing under the close supervision of the court and treatment professionals; encourage the early acceptance of responsibility and guilty pleas by perpetrators of domestic violence; and provide protection, information and support for victims.

Cases in the DVTO system begin with a report to police (see Figure 8.1). Enhanced police investigations, management and reporting procedures support this initiative. The approach taken by officers when attending a complaint has a significant impact on both the victim's disclosure and willingness to follow through with a formal complaint. The evidence collected, including transcribed 911 calls, photographs, audio and video statements from the victim, statements from independent witnesses and medical records encourage early guilty pleas.

One goal for the DVTO specialization was the fast-tracking of cases by the police, Crown counsel and defence counsel, assessed by various protocols by the DVTO system. In the vast majority of situations, the first appearance occurs within the approximately two weeks after charges are laid by the police. In addition to fast-tracking the cases into the court, the DVTO system has encouraged offenders to accept responsibility earlier in the process by providing them with a viable alternative to proceeding to trial. Those who plead not guilty and proceed to trial often spend up to six months in the court system before final disposition and sentencing. Those found guilty are usually required to attend SAP as a condition of their sentence.

As part of the DVTO program, the Royal Canadian Mounted Police (RCMP) protocol was expanded to include a summary checklist of the Spousal Assault Risk Assessment (SARA) (Whittemore & Kropp, 2002), a measure designed to predict the risk of reassault in domestic violence cases. Risk assessment using SARA begins at the first contact with the RCMP, which assists the DVTO program in a number of ways. First, it helps the RCMP decide whether to detain or release the accused and, if they release, what conditions should be imposed. Second, it facilitates early contact with Family and Children's Services in cases involving children. Finally, it assists probation officers and SAP counsellors in obtaining more detailed information about the incident and level of risks earlier in the process.

Both Yukon Legal Services Society and the Crown's office assign specific lawyers to the DVTO court, allowing expertise to develop and providing continuity, as the same counsel manages all the case files in that court. Duty counsel (the specifically assigned defence counsel) treat this sitting of the court as a circuit point, meaning that he/she assesses the accused's eligibility for legal aid at the time of court appearance, avoiding further adjournment and delay.

All first court appearances for domestic violence are set for the Monday approximately two weeks after the incident. It is during the first appearance that the DVTO option is explained to the accused. If the accused accepts responsibility and volunteers for the SAP treatment option, then a detailed assessment is conducted by a SAP clinician to ensure the suitability of the offender. If the accused pleads not guilty, then they are referred to trial court.

This special Family Violence Territorial Court has specifically assigned judges and is in session every other week. This period is several weeks shorter than the normal time for first appearances, an essential aspect of fast-tracking domestic violence cases. The appearance schedule is adhered

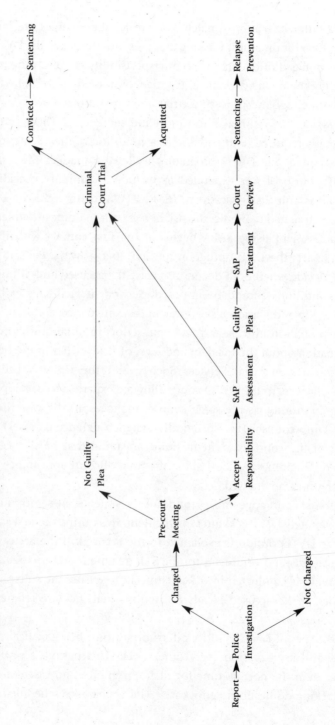

Figure 8.1: The Processing of Cases in the Domestic Violence Treatment Option Program

to whether the accused is detained or released on bail. The court also deals with judicial interim release (applications for bail), and other applications involving domestic violence that arose during the preceding two weeks.

Individuals charged with domestic violence are required to appear in the special court, which is held every other Monday afternoon. Holding court at the same time and in the same courtroom every other week facilitates attendance by resource persons, such as representatives from the Family Violence Prevention Unit of the Yukon Territorial Government consisting of Victim Services, Family and Children's Services and Probation Services. Prior to the commencement of court, a pre-court meeting is held in which all key justice system professionals attend to discuss cases that are on the court docket for the day. Information is shared about the accused, the victim and the offence, and issues are discussed or recommendations made amongst the parties. This assists the fast-tracking of cases because all parties are typically in agreement prior to court commencing.

Information about the DVTO, of which the SAP is one component, is provided to the defendant at the first court appearance. The DVTO is available if the accused chooses to take responsibility by pleading guilty at the first or second court appearance. When a DVTO application is received, the case is adjourned for two weeks for the SAP personnel to assess eligibility for the treatment program. If the defendant chooses to plead not guilty or is considered ineligible for the DVTO, he/she is returned to the regular mainstream court process. Ineligibility for the program, though infrequent, is typically due to serious mental health or substance abuse problems. Occasionally, the program gives conditional acceptance, meaning that the defendant must complete some other form of programming prior to entering SAP.

The treatment recommendations are presented to the court and may be incorporated in an undertaking or in a recognizance, which is an order that sets the conditions for the release of the accused. Modest modifications of the treatment plan may take place during subsequent court reviews. The defendant may have other needs besides treatment, which are addressed by Probation Services.

Once a defendant is accepted to the treatment program, a formal guilty plea must be entered into the court prior to commencing treatment. The major rationale for this is that treatment requires individuals to take responsibility for both the charges that brought them before the court and their violence. Treatment requires them to discuss their assaultive behaviour in a group.

When guilty pleas are entered, Crown counsel and defence counsel usually file a written agreed statement of facts setting out the details of the offence. Sentencing is then held off until treatment is completed. This ensures that the offender will complete treatment and permits the court to tailor the sentence to the unique circumstances of the case as well as to how the offender responded to treatment.

The Spousal Abuse Program, a core therapeutic component of the Domestic Violence Treatment Option, offers early intervention, information and therapeutic initiatives and programming to this multi-faceted, co-operative approach to ending domestic violence. For offenders who accept this component, the aim of SAP is to provide treatment to assist men (and, as of March 2002, women) in changing their abusive attitudes and behaviours. Usually there is a waiting period prior to beginning group sessions since the treatment program has to set up a waiting list until there are enough offenders to offer the group session. During this waiting period clients must "check in" with their assigned counsellors to ensure that safety plans are in place and that any emergency issues are dealt with.

The men's treatment program consists of 12 weeks of group therapy held twice a week for two hours, followed by six weeks of aftercare follow-up. Consistent with batterer intervention programs across North America (Gondolf, 2002; Tutty et al., 2001) — since abusers use violence and various forms of intimidation to control their victims' actions, thoughts and feelings — treatment focuses on examining the intent of the abuser's actions and looking at the underlying belief systems from which they operate. Group members are taught new skills for managing stresses, emotions and behaviours. The objective is to help batterers stop behaving abusively and violently toward their intimate partners. The SAP program also offers a cognitive group for men who have been diagnosed with FASD or have cognitive impairments (such as fetal alcohol syndrome) that leave them unable to manage the 12-week group. This option provides for a more individualized approach, including one-on-one counselling for the small number of offenders who would not be capable of participating in a group.

The SAP group for women offenders is quite different from the men's:

it is long-term and open-ended. Although many of the topics are identical, there are additional topics designed to respond to the fact that many of the women have been diagnosed with borderline personality disorder, alcohol/ drug abuse or post-traumatic stress disorder. Group completion is based on goal attainment, attendance and a case conference with the probation officer, client/offender and the SAP counsellor.

The SAP program serves as a link to various key players. It offers the legal process a specialized perspective derived from the specific knowledge and expertise required in the field of domestic violence intervention and treatment. The SAP also plays a role in defining how the process is shaped with regards to seeking the most efficient and concise application of both therapeutic and judicial roles and responsibilities. This is addressed through effective communication and understanding between the key professionals involved.

After the defendant has pled guilty, the SAP conducts a lengthy clinical assessment prior to commencing treatment. Once this has been completed, the defendant begins to attend the treatment group. While the defendant is attending treatment, the court undertakes regular monthly reviews of the defendant's progress, referred to as judicial reviews. Reviews may also be initiated by the assigned probation officer or by treatment personnel. A defendant may be returned to the formal court process and sentenced as a result of failing to follow the treatment plan, missing three treatment sessions or not participating in group sessions.

The safety of women and children is always of paramount concern and this is taken into consideration before any intervention with men occurs. Every effort is made to address the victim's needs and concerns while the defendant is participating in the treatment program. Victim Services can assist the victim and provide information about available services. Further, a counsellor in SAP invites the victim to participate in the defendant's assessment process through a partner assessment. The victim is also con-tacted throughout the offender's treatment to discuss any concerns that may arise. The court encourages the victim to be heard at all stages of its process and may direct that appropriate court documents be made available to her/ him.

Probation Services identifies other programming needs and normally prepares a report for the court to assist with sentencing. Victim Services, defence counsel and Crown counsel provide their recommendations to Probation Services. Effective communication among all interested parties ensures that the "fast-track" is maintained.

As indicated above, the court normally imposes the sentence after the defendant has completed the SAP treatment and other recommended programming has been identified or initiated. The court encourages and places significant weight on joint submissions from counsel but, as in any case, reserves the right to impose the appropriate disposition based on all of the relevant information. After completion of the SAP program, court sentences can include absolute discharges, conditional sentences, probation with the condition to continue with treatment and, on occasion, incarceration.

Research Method and Results

As part of the assessment, data were collected from both offenders and victims that served as a baseline for later comparisons with post-test data. Follow-up reports of reoffending for the offenders, using various police information systems, continued until the end of the project.

Data collected during the assessment were entered into the SAP Management Information System (MIS), a database developed specifically to manage case notes, measures and treatment statistics, between June 2002 and November 2004. Prior to June 2002 (from May 2000 to May 2002), 238 clients were processed through intake but were not included in the evaluation data set. During the evaluation (June 2002 to November 2004), data were collected on 318 additional clients. Thus, the total number of clients involved with the SAP since the DVTO was implemented in May 2000 until December 2004 was approximately 550.

The Demographic Characteristics of SAP Clients

As mentioned previously, the Spousal Abuse Program clientele include three groups from three different referral sources: DVTO, sentencing requirements (for those that pled not guilty but were found guilty at trial) and other (self-referred and referred by Family and Children's Services, private therapists, the Sex Offender Program and Victim Services).

It was of interest to compare the background information with respect to these three groups. A breakdown of the clients included in the SAP-MIS by race and initial referral source is pictured in Table 8.1, which includes all clients, active/in-process and closed cases, involved with SAP and entered into the MIS from June 2002 to November 2004. As indicated in Table 8.1, the total number of clients for this period was 318 and approximately 40% of all cases were initially referred by the DVTO, approximately 70% of whom were First Nations clients.

Table 8.1: SAP Clients by Initial Referral Source and Race

	N	Caucasian		First Nations	
DVTO	129	43	33.3%	86	66.7%
Sentencing requirement	103	14	13.6%	89	86.4%
Self-referral	56	27	48.2%	29	51.8%
Family and Children's Service	27	12	44.4%	15	55.6%
Private therapist/other	3	1	33.3%	2	66.7%
TOTAL	318	97	30.5%	221	69.5%

As is clear from Table 8.2, approximately 20% of the total number of offenders were women. The only referral source in which women outnumbered men was Family and Children's Services (child welfare). Of note, of the 64 female offenders in the SAP, 11 (17.2%) also had partners in the program.

Table 8.2: SAP Clients by Initial Referral Source and Sex

	N	Male		Female	
DVTO	129	114	88.4%	15	11.6%
Sentencing requirement	103	80	77.7%	23	22.3%
Self-referred	56	46	82.1%	10	17.9%
Family and Children's Service	27	11	40.7%	16	59.3%
Private therapist	3	3	100%	0	0%
TOTAL	318	254	79.9%	64	20.1%

Further, in the first two years of the evaluation, seven were cases of "dual charges" (i.e., charging both partners at the same occurrence). In the last year, 11 new cases involved dual charges, half of which concluded in a stay of proceedings. In a dual charge situation, it is difficult to circumvent the adversarial nature of an accused-accuser scenario when the individuals involved are considered by police to be both accused and victim. As such, stays are more common due to an unwillingness on the part of the either accused to either plead guilty or testify.

The second largest proportion of SAP clients were those who were involved because of a sentence requirement (32.4%). Note also that over 17% of cases were self-referred and approximately 9% were referred by Family and Children's Services (the majority of whom were women referred because of child welfare concerns).

Criminal Conviction Histories of SAP Clients

The conviction data on the clients' criminal histories was grouped into three broad categories: (1) assaults, which include all assaultive types of behaviour against a person; (2) failure to comply/breaches, which include all breaches of recognizance and probation, as well as failure to appear; and (3) all other offences, such as property crimes and drug and alcohol offences. Unfortunately, because the Criminal Code of Canada does not distinguish whether assaults are domestic or not, it was not possible to discern whether prior assault histories indicated spousal assaults or the assaults of others.

Table 8.3: Prior Conviction Histories

	N	Assaults		Breaches		Other Offences	
DVTO	129	77	59.7%	54	41.9%	78	60.5%
Sentencing requirement	100	65	65.0%	57	57.0%	61	61.0%
Other	85	10	11.8%	4	4.7%	12	14.1%
TOTAL	314	152	48.4%	115	36.6%	151	48.1%

As can be seen in Table 8.3, the "other" group of offenders, those referred from sources other than the court, had significantly lower rates of prior convictions across categories. The DVTO clients had lower convictions on assaults and breaches than the sentencing requirement clients, but at still relatively high rates. With respect to assaults, many had been convicted of three or more assaults: 21% of the DVTO clients and 31% of the sentencing requirement cases. The high level of conviction for prior assaults with this client group is consistent with other research on specialized domestic violence courts: 73% in Winnipeg (Ursel, 2000) and 56% in Calgary's HomeFront specialized first-appearance court (Hoffart & Clark, 2004). Further, prior to intake to SAP, many had also been convicted of three or more failure to comply/breaches: 27% of DVTO clients, 35% for the sentencing requirement cases, but only 5% of the "other" clients.

Prior to SAP, the number of other convictions (including alcohol and property offences) was also high for the DVTO and sentencing requirement clientele. Those convicted of three or more offences included 43% of the DVTO clients and 48% of the sentencing requirement cases.

Spousal Assault Risk Assessment (SARA)

The full Spousal Assault Risk Assessment (Whittemore & Kropp, 2002) is completed by SAP staff and acts as a means for systematically reflecting upon and reviewing key issues that contribute to an overall assessment of the extent to which the targeted client is likely to place him- or herself or others at risk. The SARA has four subscales each consisting of different numbers of items and each rated on a 0 to 2 point scale. Scores are totalled and an overall percentile rank is calculated. The four subscales are:

1. Criminal History: asks about past assaults of family members or strangers, and past violations of court orders.
2. Psychosocial Adjustment: asks about the presence of recent problems with relationships, employment, substance abuse, psychological control and past exposure to family violence.
3. Spousal Assault History: asks about past abusive behaviours.
4. Current Offence: asks about the nature and severity of the current offence.

As indicated in Table 8.4, all of the study groups — those referred by DVTO, sentencing requirement and "other" — were comparably high risk at intake. Further, the Psychosocial adjustment and spousal assault history subscales were particularly high, pointing to the complex and long-term etiology behind the clients' situations.

Table 8.4: SAP Clients' Average SARA Profiles by Referral Source at Intake

Referral Source	N	Criminal History (range of 0–9)	Psychosocial Adjustment (range of 0–14)	Spousal Assault History (range of 0–14)	Current Offence (range of 0–9)
DVTO	62	2.4	6.0	6.2	1.7
Sentencing requirement	42	3.3	6.5	7.2	2.0
Other	12	3.4	7.1	5.7	1.6

Client Flow Through the Spousal Abuse Program (SAP)

While the overall DVTO process described above suggests a stepwise process that begins with assessment and progresses to 12 weeks of group treatment and six weeks of relapse prevention, the progression of real cases through the system is far more complex. First, some cases may not be appropriate for SAP initially and may be referred to other treatment (e.g., one-on-one counselling or other agencies). Secondly, a group may not be available immediately and the client may go on a waiting list that involves "checking in" with the program until a group space is available.

While group treatment ideally lasts 12 weeks, individuals may be referred out of group to other treatments such as one-on-one or substance abuse counselling, and return to group treatment later. Alternatively, clients could drop out of group (i.e., miss three sessions). Dropping out can result in a breach if the treatment was a sentence requirement of DVTO.

As mentioned previously, once group is completed the DVTO clients are sent back to court for sentencing. They are also encouraged to attend a relapse prevention group and, quite often, this is included as a condition of their probation at sentencing.

An analysis of client flow data for clients who entered the program from June 2002 to November 2004 indicated that pre-group collapse rates were highest for "other" cases at 45% and the DVTO cases were the lowest at just 13%. Twenty-four percent of cases in the sentencing requirement group collapsed before group, suggesting the importance of the court process in encouraging clients to actually attend group intervention. In-group collapse was approximately 13% for both DVTO clients and sentencing requirement cases, and 25% for "other." These percentages suggest that once group treatment has started, most group members complete the program, although those mandated to treatment have higher completion rates than those who self-refer.

The highest overall completion rates, approximately 67%, were achieved by DVTO clients. The next highest rate, approximately 56%, was for cases in the sentencing requirement category, followed by 22% for "other" cases (which included the self-referral group with only a 12.8% completion rate). Both the DVTO and sentencing requirement cases had approximately 26% who finished the first-time-through group. However, more of the DVTO clients (27%) completed with restarts compared with sentencing requirement cases (21%).

Referrals out of group for other treatment (not a collapse) were similar for these three groups of clients: 7% of both DVTO cases and sentenced cases were referred out compared with 6% of "other" cases.

The average number of months in the SAP indicated that "other" cases were in the program for the shortest period of time (an average of 10.9 months); these cases had the highest collapse rates and few had completed the program — thus, the lower number of days. The overall average time in the program for DVTO cases was 13.6 months compared with 13.4 months for the sentenced cases, but many more of the DVTO cases actually completed group treatment.

It should be noted that the amount of time for which the DVTO client's case was open corresponded closely to the time the DVTO court file was active (i.e., from first appearance — usually two weeks after the assault occurred — until date of sentencing). The sentencing requirement clients, however, came to the SAP after their trial and sometimes after jail time. Thus, their "contact" with the legal system was actually, on average, at least six months longer than the DVTO clients. This, of course, also meant that the time between their offence and commencing treatment was at least six months compared with a few weeks for DVTO clients.

The time spent in the relapse prevention group was not included in the data with respect to the length of case time. This decision was made because very few clients actually attended the relapse prevention group even when it was a condition of their probation sentence. Further, evidence on the SAP client files indicated that a number of these cases were reported to the probation officers as breaches, but no further action was taken. This problem was isolated as opposed to systemic and follow-up indicated that the issue had been recognized and dealt with by probation services.

To add to the confusion about when a case was opened or closed, over the 30 months that clients were followed, 15% of the cases (n=48) were closed and reopened, and 1% (n=4) were closed and reopened three times. In 44% of the reopened cases, a reassault had occurred. Further, of those who re-entered SAP, only 26% (n=14) had completed group the first time round. Interestingly, after returning to the program, most of those who had completed it the first time (n=9), dropped out the second time. Only one completed it the second time and four were referred to one-on-one counselling.

Contact with the Police During and After SAP

The number of convictions during and after the program were significantly fewer than prior to program involvement due to two factors. First, the time frame during and after the program was short compared with the historical time frame prior to intake. Second, once in the program, all clients were monitored more closely and thus were less likely to reoffend. The one exception was the number of convictions for breaches: during the program, 16% of the DVTO clients and 19% of the sentencing requirement clients were convicted of a failure to comply/breach.

The occurrence data measuring the type of contact with police were tracked both during the clients' involvement with the program and after the clients' files were completed/closed up to May 2005. The most common categories included occurrences in which the client was (1) a complainant, (2) intoxicated, (3) subject chargeable, (4) charged, and (5) a victim. These categories were not mutually exclusive (i.e., intoxicated was the most common multiple category). One incident could involve more than one occurrence-category.

Overall, 54% of the DVTO clients, 48% of the sentencing requirement clients and 16% of the "other" clients had at least one official contact with police during their involvement with the program. Many of those had more than three contacts: 37% of DVTO clients, 40% of sentencing requirement clients and 10% of "other" clients.

After the program was completed/closed, 30% of DVTO clients had additional contacts with the police compared with 32% of sentencing requirement clients and 1% of "other" clients. This drop-off in contacts is to some extent a function of the length of time since the program was completed/close. Overall, the data indicate that a significant proportion of both DVTO and sentencing requirement clients (approximately 20%) continued to have numerous contacts with the police. In part, this may be because of the increased monitoring provided by the DVTO system.

An analysis was conducted of the differences between the three referral groups for additional incidents (intoxicated, subject chargeable, charged, etc.) during and after program completion/closed. During the program, the occurrence patterns were very similar for the DVTO clients and the sentencing requirement clients and these two groups had much higher rates of contact than the "other" clients. For all groups, "intoxicated" was the most common occurrence (DVTO average number of new incidents was 1.4; sentencing requirement average number of new incidents was 2; and for those referred by "other" sources, the average number of new incidents was 0.5).

With respect to post-program occurrences, there was a decrease in the number of police contacts for the DVTO and sentencing requirement groups when compared with the program period. The most notable change was that the DVTO group rates of contact for "intoxicated" and "subject chargeable" were significantly lower than the sentencing requirement group (an average of 0.4 instances of intoxication for DVTO clients compared to 1 for sentencing requirement, and 0.3 instances of subject chargeable for DVTO compared to 0.9 incidents for sentencing requirement, respectively). The occurrences for both groups remained significantly higher than for the "other" group.

Spousal Reassaults

Choosing a strategy to measure spousal reassaults is both complex and controversial. While "convictions" would seem the most reliable measure, there are a number of reasons, including underreporting, that reassaults may not necessarily result in a conviction. Further, the time between an incident and a conviction can be considerable, thus making convictions an inappropriate measure in a shorter-term evaluation.

Victims' reports on their partners are also used, but maintaining contact and conducting interviews with victims is problematic and few researchers have successfully accomplished this. Probably the most common and reliable approach to operationalize reassaults is by using police records of arrests or charges, which is the approach used in this evaluation.

The police occurrence file data were searched to identify the presence of charges relating to occurrences both during and after SAP. After identifying whether assault charges were present, we inspected the Crown paper files to ensure that the assault charges were spousal, since this could not always be determined from the occurrence data. Interestingly, of all the assault charges searched, 90% were spousal assaults, indicating that the offenders had once again targeted their partners.

We first examined the group of SAP clients who had either completed or had their case closed for 12 months before May 2005 (n=174) and identified the percentage of reassaults within this group (see Table 8.5). Secondly, we used procedures used by Gondolf (2002) and Palmer, Brown and Barrera (1992), based on the victims' reports on their partners and confirmed with an analysis of police reports and offenders' self-reports.

Table 8.5: Rate of Reassaults by Referral Source

Rate of Reassault	Total	N	%
12 months after intake			
DVTO	65	6	9.2%
Sentencing requirement	50	5	10.0%
Other	59	0	0%
TOTAL	174	11	6.3%
15 months after intake			
DVTO	100	18	18.0%
Sentencing requirement	74	12	16.2%
Other	72	2	2.8%
TOTAL	246	32	13.0%

As indicated by Table 8.5, the rate of reassaults 12 months after the case was completed/closed was 9.2% for DVTO clients compared with 10.0% of the sentencing requirement cases and none of the "other" cases. Almost half (45.5%) of these reassaults occurred within two months of the case having been completed/closed.

The rate of reassaults 15 months after intake were also relatively low. As indicated by Table 8.5, the rates of reassaults were very similar for the DVTO group, with 18.0, and the sentencing requirement group, with 16.2%. The "other" group was very low at 2.8%. These rates compare well with Gondolf's rate of 32%, which included a component of victim reporting that could account for some of the differences. Interestingly, almost half of the reassaults occurred within two months after program intake. It is also interesting to note that the assault rates for the "other" group were very low (i.e., 0.0% at 12 months and 2.8% at 15 months). The program may be having a preventative effect on these clients, although their risk was lower to begin with.

Within the total time frame of the evaluation, six clients (15%) reassaulted at least twice. An assessment of the file data for these cases suggested that they were very similar to the group that reassaulted only once.

In an attempt to identify the significant predictors for reassaults, correlations were calculated for 314 individuals. As suggested by previous research, prior criminal behaviour is the strongest predictor. Pre-program assaults ($r = .27$), failures to comply/breaches ($r = .28$), and other convictions ($r = .30$) were all significantly correlated to reassaults at or above the $p < .01$ level). The number of weapons convictions was low and thus it was not a significant predictor ($r = .08$). However, being male ($r = .12$) and being First Nations ($r = .10$) were positively correlated to reassaults at or above the $p < .05$ level.

Interestingly, neither initial referral source ($r = .01$) nor whether the program was completed ($r = .04$) were significantly correlated with reassaults. The lack of predictive power with these variables could be a result of what researchers in this area refer to as the "difficulty in distinguishing the effects of the treatment program from the system effects or context of the program" (see Gondolf, 2002; Bennett & Williams, 2001., p. 15). In other words, the relatively low reassault rates using both ways of conceptualizing recidivism strongly suggest an overall positive effect in reducing reassault rates regardless of the initial source of referral and whether the clients had a "high or low dose" (i.e., completed or did not complete the program).

The comparably low reassault rate is a reassuring finding, particularly given the extensive prior criminal histories of clients and the overall high levels of assaultive behaviour in the Yukon as reported in Statistics Canada's *Crime Statistics in Canada* (2004a).

Case Collapse Rates

As is discussed earlier, the rate of domestic assault cases collapsing because the complainant failed to show or changed his/her view of what happened in order to excuse the accused has been a significant issue. These collapses have disrupted court scheduling and wasted valuable resources. Worse yet, complainants may have reconciled with their partners, becoming vulnerable once again to assault. Thus, one of the objectives of the DVTO court was to reduce the collapse rate for spousal assault cases. Another important issue is to encourage offenders to accept responsibility/guilt early in the process, thus taking the pressure off the victim to testify. In order to examine the effect the DVTO court has had on these two issues, a comparison of initial court dispositions was conducted. Cases of spousal assault for the year 1999 (prior to launching the DVTO court) were compared with spousal assault cases processed by the DVTO court in 2003.

First, as expected, there was a significant increase in the early guilty pleas from 35% pre-DVTO to 53% after DVTO was implemented. While there was a significant number of accused pre-DVTO that changed pleas to guilty (26%), the overall rate of acceptance of responsibility was still significantly higher for the DVTO cases (72% compared with 63% for trial cases). In terms of collapse or dropout rates, the rate fell from 28% pre-DVTO to 20% after DVTO was implemented.

Only a small portion of cases proceeded to trial, both before and after DVTO was implemented (9%). Even though the number of these cases is small, it is interesting to note that the conviction rate has increased from 40% pre-DVTO to 66% after implementation of DVTO. Overall, 66% of the cases pre-DVTO proceeded to disposition compared with 78% after DVTO was implemented, all of which would have been referred to SAP as part of sentencing.

Summary and Conclusions

This chapter presents the results of a comprehensive process and outcome evaluation designed to monitor and test the effectiveness of the Domestic Violence Treatment Option (DVTO) located in Whitehorse, Yukon. We conclude by revisiting several key questions posed for the evaluation: whether the DVTO was implemented as planned and whether its outcomes with respect to the judicial process have been achieved.

One important goal was to reduce the number of victims of domestic violence who abandon or withdraw from the criminal justice system (referred to as the collapse rate). As the findings on pre-DVTO and DVTO comparisons on collapse rates show, the DVTO system has decreased collapse rates from 28% to 20%. Further, the specialization has also increased the rate of acceptance of responsibility by the offender early in the process.

Providing speedy access to counselling and treatment programs for offenders was another major hope in implementing the DVTO program. The protocols set in place by the DVTO system appear to result in speedy access to counselling for offenders. In most situations, intake into the program occurs within several weeks after the first appearance in court.

One method of holding offenders accountable is providing close court supervision throughout the therapeutic process: the average DVTO case is before the courts for just over 300 days. During this time, the court reviews and monitors the case every other week, if necessary. Thus, the average case could be required to appear in court up to 21 times during this 300-day period.

One hope of implementing the DVTO program was to encourage more victims of domestic violence to seek protection and help from the criminal justice system. Unfortunately, neither the evaluators nor the staff of the SAP were very successful at connecting with victims. Thus, it is not possible to identify whether the system is encouraging more victims to seek help and protection.

The relatively low reassault rates provide strong evidence that the DVTO system, most likely because of increased monitoring, does provide victims with protection against reassaults. The DVTO system also provides information and support for victims, as well as referrals to appropriate programs. However, while these services are available, the victims must choose to make use of the information and supports. As our findings indicate, victims for the most part were partly detached from the process and did not take advantage of the resources that were available to them. Just because this is recognized in the research literature as a general problem doesn't mean it can be ignored.

For the most part, the DVTO program has been implemented as planned and has achieved the majority of its objectives. The only process objectives that the DVTO program has not fully achieved are those that deal with motivating victims to become involved and to take advantage of the resources available to them.

The second major evaluation question is whether the DVTO system and the SAP treatment are effective in achieving their objectives. The data and findings of this chapter indicate that both the DVTO clients and sentencing requirement clients are generally difficult and challenging. Prior to their involvement with the DVTO, many had extensive histories of assaults as well as high levels of involvement in other criminal activities. Addiction and substance abuse problems were very prevalent, as indicated by the high number of contacts with police that involved intoxicated states as well as information from the SAP counsellors that documented the frequent need to suspend treatment in the program to deal with addiction issues.

Despite the fact that these clients were difficult, the rates of reassaults were quite low. For example, 12 months after the clients completed their contact with the program, only 9% of the DVTO clients and 10% of the sentencing requirement clients had reassaulted. These rates compare well with the rates identified by Palmer, Brown and Barrera (1992) of the 10% reassault rate for an experimental treatment group and 31% for a group of non-treatment offenders. Likewise, the rate of reassaults 15 months after intake into the program was also comparatively low. Of the DVTO clients, 18% had reassaulted and 16% of the sentencing requirement clients had reassaulted. These rates are relatively low when compared with the rate of 32% identified by Gondolf (2002).

While the overall DVTO system and SAP together appear to be effective in terms of preventing reassaults, it is difficult to distinguish the effects of the treatment program from the system effects, a common problem in this area of research (see Gondolf, 2002; Bennett & Williams, (2001). However, as indicated above, the DVTO process has been successful in achieving many of its stated goals. Further, SAP has also achieved relatively high rates of program completion for the DVTO clients at 69%.

In conclusion, we suggest that the DVTO system and SAP as a whole are effective, at least in the short term. While each of these components of the overall system has some claim to achieving individual objectives, the interactive effect seems to be the strongest in preventing reassaults with a very difficult client group. The DVTO model, which combines a comprehensive justice system approach with a treatment program for batterers, provides a promising model for dealing with spousal assault and abuse.

PART III

Civil Justice: New Programs and New Challenges

Civil Domestic Violence Legislation in the Prairie Provinces: *A Comparative Legal Analysis*

Karen Busby, Jennifer Koshan and Wanda Wiegers

Introduction

In the 1980s and 1990s, a dominant goal of the criminal justice system was improving the legal response to domestic violence complaints and prosecutions. The focus on criminal law had been harshly criticized and many women, particularly marginalized and disadvantaged women, resisted co-operating (Martin & Mosher, 1995; Koshan, 1998; but see McGillivray & Comaskey, 1999). According to Turner (1995, p. 184), one significant criticism was that "sole reliance on *Criminal Code* charging in response to situations of domestic violence often meant that the point of intervention was delayed, reactive and under-utilized." As well, the forms of relief provided through the criminal system, a simple no-contact order for example, did not address fully the needs of victims in domestic violence situations (Turner, 1995; Rigakos, 2002). Civil family law remedies were also believed to be procedurally deficient in volatile domestic violence situations because they were time-consuming to obtain, required notice to the respondent and usually required the assistance of a lawyer. In short, neither the criminal justice nor the civil family law systems were considered capable of providing effective immediate or short-term protection to victims.

In the 1990s, each Prairie province passed laws to improve access to civil legal remedies for domestic violence victims. The *Victims of Domestic Violence Act (Saskatchewan VDVA)* came into effect in Saskatchewan in 1995, and *The Domestic Violence and Stalking Protection, Prevention and Compensation Act (Manitoba DVSA)* and the *Protection Against Family Violence Act (Alberta PAFVA)* became the law in Manitoba and Alberta in 1999. Each of these acts created civil remedies for victims of domestic violence that were intended to be easier, faster and less costly to obtain and more comprehensive than the existing criminal or civil remedies. In particular, these acts permit victims (hereafter "applicants") to make immediate applications for emergency orders that, for example, prohibit abusers (hereafter "respondents") from contacting the applicant and others or attending places where the applicant may be. Emergency orders can also grant an applicant possession of the family home, amongst other remedies. These emergency orders are called "emergency protection orders," "emergency intervention orders" and "protection orders" in Alberta, Saskatchewan and Manitoba respectively, and will be referred to as "emergency orders" in this chapter. As will be discussed, the Manitoba act does not limit these orders to serious or urgent situations (as do the Saskatchewan and Alberta acts) but does currently require that specific relief be necessary or advisable for the immediate or imminent protection of the victim.

Emergency applications are usually made without notice to the respondent, who will only learn of an emergency order after it has been granted. As will be described, applicants can also apply, usually on notice to the respondents, for non-emergency orders.

The benefits of immediate intervention include that it can provide a "cooling-off" period to help prevent an escalation of violence. If the intervention occurs at a point when the respondent is repentant (as often occurs after a significant assault), it reinforces the message to both the respondent and the applicant that the abuse is significant. Immediate removal of the respondent from the home means that the victims (including children) typically experience less disruption. A significant benefit of an emergency order is that once it has been issued, police should have better information on potentially volatile situations and therefore improve subsequent crisis responses.

Some aspects of the legislation have been controversial. As will be discussed, the attempt to provide immediate and comprehensive relief without notice to the respondent has raised concerns as to whether the procedures are fair to respondents and whether the constitutional division of powers may undermine the application of the legislation on First Nations reserves. Some critics have also worried that the legislation could be abused and used strategically to gain an upper hand in property and custody disputes (Alberta Law Reform Institute, 1997; Trobert, 2001).

Our primary intention in this chapter is to identify inter-provincial differences between the text of the three acts and their interpretation and application that may help explain the different rates and patterns of usage for protection orders that have been observed across the Prairie provinces. We focus in particular on the provisions in force in 2002, as that is the base year for most of the research in the broader project of which this study is a part ("Evaluating the Justice and Community Response to Domestic Violence Across the Prairie Provinces," L. Tutty and J. Ursel, co-primary investigators, funded by the Community University Research Alliance of the Social Sciences and Humanities Research Council).

In 2002, usage rates for emergency orders made without notice to the respondent were highest in Manitoba, then Saskatchewan, and lowest in Alberta. Per 100,000 population in 2002, the rates for applications made and orders granted were respectively about 73.8 and 36.0 in Manitoba, 18.2 and 15.5 in Saskatchewan and 9.8 and 8.2 in Alberta. Expressed in percentage terms, the grant rates for applications made within each province in 2002 were as follows: Manitoba, 48.8%, Saskatchewan, 85.2% and Alberta, 83.7%. Usage rates also varied within provinces. For example, 187 emergency applications were made in Edmonton, Alberta (population 750,000), in 2002, but only 30 such applications were made in Calgary, Alberta (population 1,000,000). In Manitoba, there were significant differences between the number of applications made in Winnipeg (population 650,000) and the rest of the province (population 400,000) during the one-year period of April 2002 to March 2003: 749 applications were made in Winnipeg compared with 184 in the rest of the province (Manitoba Justice-Judicial Support Services, 2003).

It is also notable that the number of emergency applications has been declining over time in Saskatchewan and Manitoba. For example, the number of emergency applications and orders granted has dropped off dramatically in Winnipeg. According to Manitoba Justice-Judicial Services, 1,208 emergency applications were made, and orders were granted in 65% of these cases in 2000. By 2003, only 640 emergency applications were made and orders were only granted in 36% of these cases. The number of applications in Saskatchewan declined from 410 in 1997 to 187 in 2002, with orders granted in about 80–85% of the cases in each year, respectively. In Alberta, the number of applications overall has been low but did significantly increase from 296 in 2002 to 393 in 2003 (the last full year for which data were collected) and was projected to increase to 581 in 2004, largely because of increased usage in Edmonton. The grant rate in Alberta has remained fairly steady with 84.5% of applications granted in 2002 and 80.4% in 2004 (Tutty et al., 2005).

This chapter first provides a brief overview of the essential features of the legislation in each province, highlighting both similarities and differences that may help explain the disparate and changing usage and grant rates identified above. Next, the threshold criteria for obtaining emergency orders is more closely examined, largely by reference to reported cases that have interpreted the statutory requirement of a need for immediate protection. Finally, we review several constitutional issues that arise with the legislation, including whether it provides sufficient procedural protections, particularly for respondents, to satisfy Charter requirements and to what extent, if any, the legislation can be used in First Nations territory. Throughout the chapter, we offer possible explanations for the differences in usage and grant rates.

Similarities and Differences in the Legislation

This section outlines similarities and differences in the three acts. A chart comparing the legislative provisions, including references to specific section numbers, is included as an appendix. For a more in-depth examination of the histories of the acts, see Tutty et al. (2005), Wiegers and Douglas (2007), the Lavoie Inquiry Implementation Committee (1998) and MacDonald (2001).

What Conduct is Covered?

In all three jurisdictions, the civil legislation applies to either "family violence" or "domestic violence" and the abuse experienced by the applicant must fit within these definitions to qualify for an emergency or non-emergency order. These terms include actual and threatened physical injury, property damage, sexual abuse and forced confinement. Manitoba is the only jurisdiction to explicitly include emotional and psychological abuse in its definition of domestic violence. The *Alberta PAFVA* refers to actual or threatened "injury," which was interpreted in *T.P.* v. *J.P.* (2005) as suggesting that emotional injury may be included. *The Saskatchewan VDVA* defines domestic violence to include actual or threatened "bodily harm," which seems to preclude an applicant from relying on evidence of psychological or emotional harm to establish grounds for an order. Prior to 2005, a Manitoba applicant had to establish that the violence would "continue," but after 2005, this requirement changed to "continue or resume." A similar requirement was added to the *Alberta PAFVA* when amendments took effect on November 1, 2006.

The *Manitoba DVSA* also applies to stalking even where there is no pre-existing familial relationship between the parties, thereby including dating and other acquaintance relationships. For example, in *Ballingal-Scotten* v. *Wayne* (2005) the parties were in a professional relationship and in *Baril* v. *Obelnicki* (2004) the parties were neighbours. The stalking provision, which mirrors the Criminal Code's criminal harassment provisions, requires the respondent to have "knowing[ly]" or "reckless[ly] ... repeatedly engaged in conduct that causes another person reasonably, in all the circumstances, to fear for his or her own safety." The inclusion of stalking is one explanation for the higher usage rate of Manitoba's legislation in 2002. According to Laurie (chapter 10 in this volume), 178 emergency applications (23%) were made on the basis of stalking alone in 2002. (For a more detailed examination of the applications made in Winnipeg that included evidence of stalking, see chapter 10 in this volume.) Alberta included protection against stalking in its recent amendments to the *Alberta PAFVA*, but the amendment only covers stalking between family members.

The *Alberta PAFVA* is narrower in some other key respects. First, Alberta's definition of "family violence" excludes reasonable force used by a parent toward a child for the purposes of correction. Second, in 2002, only Alberta required that respondents behave with the purpose of intimidating or harming a family member for their conduct to be captured in the definition of family violence. Unless this purpose could be established (which is difficult because it requires actual evidence of the respondent's intent and not simply, say, evidence of indifference or negligence), an emergency order could not be granted. While some judges questioned whether intent had to be established if the case involved physical injury (see for example *T.P.* v. *J.P.*, 2005), the evidence-of-intent requirement might explain the lower usage rate in Alberta in 2002. However, given the almost universal claim that more public education is required, most potential applicants would not be aware of this requirement, so it likely provides only a limited explanation for differences in usage rates. Importantly, the intent requirement was removed when the amendments to the *Alberta PAFVA* came into force in 2006.

What Relationships Are Covered?

All three acts focus on violence within families, including spousal, intimate and other familial relationships. In all three provinces, orders in 2002 were available only if the parties had cohabited or had a child together or, in Manitoba only, if the situation involved stalking. No act requires a minimum period of cohabitation, unlike some other family legislation.

Same-sex intimate relationships were included in Saskatchewan and Manitoba in the original legislation. While there were calls in Alberta for the inclusion of same-sex relationships when civil legislation was first recommended (Alberta Law Reform Institute, 1995), they have only been covered since 2003 (*Adult Interdependent Relationships Act*, 2002). Thus, the *Alberta PAFVA* did not apply to same-sex relationships in 2002. This difference may be another explanation for the low usage rate in Alberta, although in 2002, there were no applications involving same-sex relationships in Saskatchewan and only five in Manitoba.

The legislation is framed in gender neutral terms in all three jurisdictions. Nevertheless, most applications for emergency orders are made by women. In 2002, women made about 90% of the emergency applications in Alberta and 84.8% of the emergency applications in Winnipeg, and 93%

of the recipients of orders in Saskatchewan were women (Tutty et al., 2005; Tutty et al., forthcoming; Wiegers & Douglas, 2007). These figures are consistent with statistics on the rates of police-reported family violence, which show that women are the primary victims (Brzozowski, 2004; Federal-Provincial-Territorial Ministers Responsible for the Status of Women, 2002). Further, while the legislation can apply to all family relationships, it is used most often in spousal or intimate relationships. In 2002, 83.1% of applications in Winnipeg were made in the context of intimate relationships (Tutty et al., forthcoming), as were 90% of applications in Alberta (Tutty et al., 2005) and 94% of orders granted in Saskatchewan (Wiegers & Douglas, 2007). Again, this is consistent with statistics indicating that most incidents of reported intrafamily violence are perpetrated by a male partner against a female partner (Brzozowski, 2004).

It is notable that even though they are not expressly covered by the *PAFVA*, 13 applications (9.8% of all applications) in 2002 in Alberta were made in dating relationship situations (Tutty et al., 2005). Of these, 10 (76.9%) were granted, a lower proportion but not statistically significantly different from the 87.9% grant rate of emergency orders for all other relationships. Studies show that 16% of women have experienced violence in a dating context and that young women are at a particularly high risk of intimate violence; because of their age, young women are more likely to be in dating relationships (Federal-Provincial-Territorial Ministers Responsible for the Status of Women, 2002; Brzozowski, 2004). The high number of dating relationship applications as well as these studies support the need for protection against violence in all intimate relationships and not just those where the parties have lived together. Elder abuse (for example, an aunt or an in-law) is also not covered unless the parties have lived together. This exclusion is problematic given the high vulnerability of older people to abuse by family members, even if they have not lived together (Manitoba Law Reform Commission, 1999).

In 2005, Manitoba repealed the cohabitation requirement, and the *Manitoba DVSA* now permits orders against respondents in current or former familial, spousal, intimate and dating relationships regardless of whether the parties have lived together. Alberta repealed the cohabitation requirement for family members in 2006 when the amendments to its legislation took effect. As a result, elder abuse and other family abuse are now included even if the parties never lived together, but dating relationships are still not expressly included. It would be preferable to expressly include dating relationships if the civil legislation is to be as broadly protective of family and intimate relationships as possible.

What Legal Remedies Are Available?

The legislation in all three provinces provides for both emergency and non-emergency protection orders, as well as other legal remedies. Emergency orders typically prohibit communications between the parties, removal of the respondent from the family home and supervised removal of his personal belongings. Emergency orders in Alberta and Manitoba can also restrain the respondent from attending at places like the family home, the applicant's workplace and the children's schools, and allow the seizure of weapons. Manitoba orders can prohibit the respondent from following the applicant or others and can permit a peace office to enter a place and seize items that the respondent fails to deliver up as ordered. Alberta and Saskatchewan also permit any other orders that provide for the applicant's immediate protection.

Exclusive possession of the family home can be granted by an emergency order in Saskatchewan and Alberta, but such orders can only be granted in Manitoba by a non-emergency order. In 2002, exclusive possession was granted in 93% of the orders made in Saskatchewan and 57% of the orders made in Alberta. This condition provides a significant benefit to applicants who seek to remain in the family home. It might be expected that the availability of exclusive possession would increase the attractiveness of the civil legislation in Saskatchewan and Alberta and result in higher usage rates, but this has not been the case. It may be that the other conditions in Manitoba emergency orders (such as no-contact and restrained physical proximity) effectively give applicants exclusive possession of their homes in many cases.

Victims of family or domestic violence (and, in Manitoba, stalking) can apply for non-emergency orders from the Courts of Queen's Bench on notice to the respondent in situations where the danger posed is not "immediate" (or, in Manitoba, "imminent") or where they want conditions that are more extensive than those permitted for emergency orders. These orders are called "Queen's Bench Protection Orders" in Alberta, "victim assistance orders" in Saskatchewan and "prevention orders" in Manitoba. In this chapter, they are referred to as "non-emergency orders." In addition to the same conditions that can be made on emergency orders, non-emergency orders allow for additional remedies such as protection against dealing with property, recommending or requiring the respondent to obtain counselling, compensation to victims for monetary losses sustained as a result of violence and, in Manitoba, loss of a driver's licence. However, non-emergency orders are rarely applied for in Saskatchewan and Alberta, perhaps because they are so similar to civil restraining orders, with the same difficulties in terms of accessibility (Howard Research, 2000; Prairie Research Associates, 1999). While exact figures are not available, in 2002 non-emergency orders appear to have been more commonly sought in Manitoba than Alberta and Saskatchewan, but still less often than emergency protection orders. The number of non-emergency orders in Manitoba has likely increased following *Shaw* v. *Shaw* (2000), in which the court held that if proceedings have already commenced in family court an applicant should apply for a non-emergency order and have the application heard in the context of the rest of the family proceedings. Emergency protection orders were by far the most widely used remedy in all three jurisdictions in 2002 and will be our primary focus for the remainder of this chapter.

Who Can Make the Applications?

Emergency orders are available 24 hours a day, although the application procedures differ. In Alberta, applications must be made in person by the applicant or a representative during the working hours of the Provincial Court or justice of the peace office. Peace officers (including First Nations police officers) and child welfare workers can apply by telecommunication and therefore can make applications 24 hours a day (*[Alberta] Protection Against Family Violence Regulation*). Saskatchewan allows applications to be made by telecommunication at any time by victims' services coordinators and crisis workers as well as by the police (*[Saskatchewan] Victims of Domestic Violence Regulation*). While the legislation permits applications by First Nations caseworkers and in-person applications before justices of the peace, in practice they are unavailable. The Manitoba legislation permits telecommunication applications for emergency orders to be made by both the police and lawyers. An amendment in 2005 also permits telecommunication applications by "designated persons." Designates include shelter, crisis and social workers. Emergency applications may be made in person before a magistrate 24 hours a day in Manitoba.

Data from 2002 show that the police make almost all telecommunication applications for emergency orders in Alberta, especially outside of the major urban centres (Tutty et al., 2005, p. 48) and about 75% of such applications in Saskatchewan (Wiegers & Douglas, 2007). In Manitoba, only data for Winnipeg were available, and in this city, all applications in 2002 were made in person; none were made by telecommunication, even though this mode of application is authorized under the *Manitoba DVSA*. Ninety-five percent of the Winnipeg applications were made by the applicants themselves, with the remaining 5% by police, lawyers or others on behalf of the applicant (Tutty et al., forthcoming). Given that the legislation in all three provinces permits both in-person applications and assisted telecommunications applications, it is notable that such different practices developed. Possible explanations for these differences may include an emphasis on the part-time use of justices of the peace with specialized training in domestic violence in Saskatchewan; hours of operation and the ability of the public to access magistrates and justices of the peace in Manitoba; and, in general, the expectations or understandings of the legislation following training for police, judicial officers and victims' advocates when the legislation first came into force.

In light of mandatory charging directives, police involvement in emergency order applications (especially in Alberta and Saskatchewan) could trigger criminal charges. Even if claimants themselves, lawyers or other designates apply for emergency orders, the police may also become involved when, for example, the order is served or a breach of the order is reported. Police involvement with the applications can be problematic for women, particularly those who are marginalized and who do not want to engage with the criminal system (Martin & Mosher, 1995; Koshan, 1998; McGillivray & Comaskey, 1999). While the civil legislation was never intended to displace the criminal justice system, it might nevertheless provide a useful alternative to women seeking to avoid the criminal process. To the extent that the application process under the legislation relies on the police, this potential advantage is diminished.

The relatively low number of emergency applications in Alberta, the decline in emergency applications in Saskatchewan and the disparate urban-rural rates in Manitoba could, in part, be explained by the practical necessity of police involvement. As well, the marked difference in the number of emergency order applications in Calgary (30) and Edmonton (187) in 2002 may be partly attributable to regional differences in police training and culture that could affect their willingness and ability to use the legislation (Tutty et al., 2005). Interviews with stakeholders in Alberta indicate that some police may be frustrated with the response of justices of the peace to emergency applications, and have stopped applying for emergency orders as a result (Tutty et al., 2005). This concern may also explain regional differences in Alberta, even in the face of an increasing application rate and a high grant rate overall.

In Alberta, emergency order applications are heard by Provincial Court judges or designated justices of the peace. Emergency order applications are heard in Saskatchewan by justices of the peace who are specifically selected and trained to hear the applications (Ad Hoc Federal-Provincial-Territorial Working Group, 2003). In Manitoba, emergency order applications were heard by designated justices of the peace and magistrates until an amendment to *The Provincial Court Act* in 2006 limited the applications to justices of the peace only.

The Duration of Emergency Orders

The *Alberta PAFVA* specifies that protection orders (including both emergency and non-emergency orders) cannot be granted for more than one year unless extended by further order. When enacted, neither the *Saskatchewan VDVA* nor the *Manitoba DVSA* specified a maximum duration for emergency orders. Yet the duration of orders varies quite significantly between the provinces in practice. In Saskatchewan, emergency orders are typically granted for only 30 days. In Alberta, emergency orders are subject to automatic review by the Court of Queen's Bench, as we will discuss in more detail in the next section. When emergency orders are confirmed in Alberta, they are for periods that typically range between 90 days and one year. In stark contrast, in 2002, Manitoba emergency orders did not contain an expiry date and therefore were indefinite. In 2005, the *Manitoba DVSA* was amended to provide that orders expire in three years unless the order specified a longer duration period. The short duration of the Saskatchewan and Alberta orders, especially when contrasted to the indefinite Manitoba orders (or even the now-standard three-year order), could significantly impact an applicant's view of the usefulness of obtaining an order and is therefore likely a significant factor in explaining the differences in usage rates among the three provinces.

Judicial Review of the Orders

The legislation varies between the three provinces on higher court review of the orders. Emergency orders are automatically reviewed by the Saskatchewan Court of Queen's Bench within three days and by the Alberta Court of Queen's Bench within seven days. This review period was extended to nine days when amendments to the *Alberta PAFVA* came into force in 2006. In Alberta, the review is to be based upon affidavit and other sworn evidence in addition to the transcript from the emergency hearing, and hearings are standard practice on review. This means that claimants must appear themselves or by counsel at the review hearing if they want their order to be confirmed. In Saskatchewan, the review is based upon the order and its supporting documentation, and a hearing is only required if the reviewing judge is not satisfied with the evidence or if the respondent or victim apply to set the order aside. On review, emergency orders may be confirmed, varied or set aside. In contrast, Manitoba does not have an automatic review of emergency orders; such a review only occurs if the respondent applies to have the order set aside.

The different judicial review requirements may offer another explanation for the lower rates of usage of the civil legislation in Alberta and, to a lesser extent, Saskatchewan. Applicants must engage more fully in order to maintain their emergency orders, and will likely need a lawyer's assistance with the review process. The cost and potential complexity of the judicial review process is particularly problematic outside of the larger urban centres, where legal services are more difficult to obtain.

Threshold Criteria: Establishing Seriousness or Urgency

In addition to meeting the statutory requirements described above, applicants for emergency orders in Saskatchewan must show that by reason of seriousness or urgency an order should be made without waiting for the next available sitting of a judge of the court in order to ensure the immediate protection of the applicant. The *Alberta PAFVA* similarly requires that the applicant demonstrate that "by reason of seriousness or urgency, the order should be granted to ensure immediate protection." Under the *Manitoba DVSA* provisions in force in 2002, the applicant was required to establish that the specific relief claimed was necessary or advisable for his/her immediate protection but there was no explicit requirement to establish urgency or seriousness. The interpretation and constitutionality of these provisions is at issue in the *Baril* v. *Obelnicki* case, which is currently on reserve by the Manitoba Court of Appeal. The Manitoba act was amended in 2005 to require an applicant to demonstrate that the order was necessary for her "immediate or imminent protection." In Alberta and Saskatchewan, judges and justices of the peace are required to consider other factors, including the nature and history of the violence, the existence of immediate danger to persons or property and the best interests of the applicant and any children in her care.

Insufficient Evidence of an Emergency

Insufficient evidence of an emergency appears to be the most common reason in all three jurisdictions for failing to issue, refusing to confirm or reversing orders (Prairie Research Associates, 1999; Tutty et al., 2005). In the few cases where reasons were given for the decision, judges have generally interpreted the legislation as requiring the applicant to clearly establish a high level of seriousness or urgency (Wiegers & Douglas, 2007). This heavy burden is placed on applicants because of the coercive impact of orders on respondents and because relief is sought without notice and without allowing respondents an opportunity to be heard.

Incident-based Assessments of Risk

In interpreting whether an emergency exists, judges on review applications have tended to focus on discrete, isolated acts or threats of physical violence instead of assessing risk in a more contextual way, taking account of the cumulative trauma of past violence or the ongoing controlling conduct and the cyclical nature of violence that is typical of battering relationships. In *Dyck* v. *Dyck* (2005), in denying an application for leave to appeal, the Saskatchewan Court of Appeal effectively limited the basis for an emergency order on the evidence of a single incident rather than on evidence related to the relationship as a whole, including the respondent's difficulties with anger management. Closer examination of a leading Saskatchewan case demonstrates how this interpretation can be problematic.

In *Bella* v. *Bella* (1995), the applicant sought an emergency order five days after a violent incident during which the respondent, after the applicant had refused his sexual advances, "shouted profanities," grabbed her by the arm, shook her, told her to get out of the house and dragged her off the sofa. He stopped when the eldest child entered the room. In revoking an emergency order issued by a justice of the peace, Mr. Justice Gerein of the Saskatchewan Court of Queen's Bench, stated:

> When I look at the conduct itself, I have real reservations whether it was serious enough to warrant intervention. No blows were struck; the incident was brief; remorse was expressed in the form of an apology; calm returned to the household and there was no suggestion of a real likelihood of repetition. In these circumstances I would hold that there was no emergency to warrant intervention.

However, the *Saskatchewan VDVA* does not require the striking of blows, only a reasonable fear of bodily harm. Moreover, acts of violence are often followed by an apology and a period of calm, particularly where the violence is cyclical (Walker, 1979). Justice Gerein also appears to examine the last incident as a discrete event, disconnected from prior events, including a statement made six months earlier that "a good beating was what the wife needed two years ago — in fact two good beatings and one bullet" (*Bella* v. *Bella*, 1995). The judge failed to note that the respondent's conduct was not isolated, the conduct appeared to be escalating in terms of its seriousness over time, and was apparently interrupted on the last occasion only by the child's entry into the room. Finally, to the extent that the history of the parties' relationship in *Bella* was mentioned in the judgement, only prior physical threats or force were identified. The risk of violence is thus also assessed without any reference to emotional or psychological abuse, even though such behaviour is a risk factor for violence in spousal relationships (Johnson, 1996; Pottie Bunge, 2000; Mihorean, 2005).

Controlling behaviour can include threats or damage to possessions or property, threats of harm to someone close to the victim, limiting access to the family income, put downs or insults, the monitoring of activities, limiting contact with family or friends and acts of jealousy. Kropp and Hart (2004) describe the association between negative attitudes such as male prerogative, possessiveness and misogyny and an increased risk of spousal assault. Emotional abuse or controlling behaviour should therefore be considered along with past incidents of violence in assessing immediate or imminent risk to applicants.

Leaving the Home

While the risk of further violence should be the dominant issue in determining urgency, judges have expressed concern with confirming emergency orders where the applicant was no longer in the family home when the application was made. In *Dolgopol* v. *Dolgopol* (1995) an emergency order was overturned by Mr. Justice Wimmer of the Saskatchewan Court of Queen's Bench because the applicant was "not at risk of immediate harm" at the time of application. On the facts, the wife applied for an emergency order four days after she fled the house to stay in a shelter with her child. From the judge's sparse reasons, it is not clear whether the wife was found to be not at immediate risk because of her presence in a shelter at the time of the application or because four days had passed since the violent incident.

Prairie Research Associates' 1999 impact study of Saskatchewan's legislation in 1997 identified a belief among shelter workers that an emergency order is no longer available once an applicant has left the home and entered a shelter. Resort to a place of refuge should not preclude a finding of urgency where the respondent's violence has made flight from the home necessary before an emergency application can be made. The effect of denying applications in such circumstances is to punish victims who may act reasonably in leaving their homes to secure their safety and to deny them and their children the benefits of remaining in their home. Although the *Saskatchewan VDVA* requires that the best interests of the child be considered in making an emergency order, the judge in *Dolgopol* did not allude to this factor in revoking the order.

Delay in Making the Application

Delays occurring between the violence and the date of application appear to raise even more significant concerns and barriers to a finding of an emergency. As already noted, a four-day delay appears to have been an important factor in the *Dolgopol* case. In *Bella*, the judge found that the applicant was not at immediate risk due to a time lapse of five days since the violent incident. In *T.P.* v. *J.P.* (2005), Madam Justice Veit of the Alberta Court of Queen's Bench found that injury had not been inflicted by the respondent because no injuries had been reported to social workers within a week. As well, there was a lack of urgency because the parties had slept in close proximity for three nights without incident following the alleged violence.

In Alberta and Saskatchewan, where emergency relief is intended or has been interpreted to be temporary, a delay in applying for an emergency order may be a relevant consideration in determining whether to grant an order. Nonetheless, there may be many reasons for a delay, including a lack of information about the application process, the emotional aftermath of the incidents such as confusion, depression, ambivalence about leaving the relationship, and a fear of retaliatory violence. Research has consistently shown that the risk of stalking, harassment, serious injury and death escalates in the immediate post-separation period (Kong, 1997; Wilson, Johnson & Daly, 1995) and therefore it is not surprising that applicants carefully weigh options before taking action. Whatever the reasons for delay, the most important concern should be whether the lapse of time has substantially reduced the risk of violence for the victim. A time lapse may reduce the risk in some cases by providing a cooling-off period; however, in many other cases, particularly where there are patterns of psychological abuse and the violence has been persistent or escalating in severity over time, the victim can remain at significant risk notwithstanding a subsequent period of calm. Moreover, where there has been a history of violence and control, decision-makers should be sensitive to other indicators of impending or imminent violence in the respondent's behaviour and to a heightened risk of assault in the event that notice were to be given of the applicant's desire to separate (Wiegers & Douglas, 2007; Mihorean, 2005).

The Impact of Victim Behaviour

Another area of potential concern in relation to findings of seriousness and urgency regards the impact of the applicant's behaviour. None of the reported cases deal in depth with this issue; however, in *MacDonald* v. *Kwok* (1997), Madam Justice Wilkinson of the Saskatchewan Court of Queen's Bench stated that:

> The use of the term "victim" with all that implies can be a potent weapon. It evokes strong images of helplessness and vulnerability on the one side, and violence and aggression on the other. Care must be taken not to diminish the value of this legislation by its indiscriminate application.

This approach endorses an image of helplessness and passivity, "one-dimensional images" that have "rarely matched the experiences of women who are abused," according to Linda MacLeod (1994, p. 10). Reliance on a stereotype of helplessness and passivity suggests that women who survive violence by leaving the home or who in other ways actively seek assistance will not be viewed as victims deserving of relief under the legislation. Conceptions of the ideal victim are particularly problematic for marginalized groups of women who may be more likely to be perceived as not meeting the stereotype (Snider, 2006).

The Absence of Police Involvement

A recent Alberta case, *T.L.O.* v. *K.J.S.* (2004), suggests that the failure of police to apply on the victim's behalf may be significant in determining whether to issue an emergency order. In this case, the emergency order was revoked in part because the Edmonton City Police Services failed to lay criminal charges or arrest the respondent and failed to apply for an emergency order on behalf of the applicant. Mr. Justice Lee of the Alberta Court of Queen's Bench held that "the failure then of the police to act in any manner is an indication that even on the civil standard, this extraordinary remedy should not be granted." In sharp contrast, Mr. Justice Martin (also of the Alberta Court of Queen's Bench) refused to follow the *T.L.O.* case in *K.K.O.* v. *O.K.O* (2005), noting that some potential reasons why police may not be involved include "police indifference, mistake in judgment or pre-occupation with other cases." Without a fuller evaluation of the context, police inaction alone should not be relied upon to refute the applicant's evidence.

In summary, judges, at least in reported cases, have narrowly inter-preted the statutory basis for issuance of emergency orders. Alberta has responded to some of the foregoing concerns with amendments.to the *PAFVA* explicitly providing that emergency orders should not be denied because, among other reasons, the applicant is temporarily residing in an emergency shelter or other safe place. These amendments also require that justices of the peace and judges consider controlling behaviour by the respondent, repetitive or escalating family violence and the applicant's need for a short-term safe environment as factors in making an order. In 2005, Manitoba expanded the language of "immediate protection" to include "imminent protection." It is unclear what this inclusion will mean in practical terms. However, it would be useful if all provinces directly addressed these issues through legislative change. This is a particular con-cern in Saskatchewan, where there is evidence that a restrictive judicial interpretation has influenced justices of the peace and crisis workers (Prairie Research Associates, 1999; Wiegers & Douglas, 2007) and may, thereby, have contributed over time to a decline in usage rates. A review of the cases also suggests that judges need more awareness of cycles of vio-lence and the stereotypes of victimhood and need to examine the best interests of children and the history of the relationship more closely, par-ticularly with reference to the dynamics of power and control.

Procedural Protections for Respondents

Applications for emergency orders are heard by justices of the peace or magistrates usually without any notice to the respondent of the hearing and without input from him. However, Manitoba courts have stated that notice of the applications should be given to respondents unless the danger is so immediate and imminent that notice cannot be given (see *Ballingal-Scotten* v. *Wayne*, 2005). The hearings are closed to the public and there is no requirement for any independent investigation. While there are good reasons for not giving notice in most cases (including the need to preserve safety and have an expeditious hearing), the absence of the respondent means that he is unable to present his own case in a situation in which he faces a significant loss of rights. In *Baril* v. *Obelnicki* (2004), a Manitoba judge held that emergency orders violate constitutional rights protected by the Charter, including free expression (who he can talk to), liberty (where he can go) and security (as the existence of an order can affect his reputation). It is obvious that the existence of an emergency order significantly impacts a respondent's life.

Rights protected by the Charter can be compromised for good reason, such as protecting a victim of violence. But even then, the respondent's constitutional rights must be affected as little as possible. For example, it was argued in the *Baril* case, which is currently before the Manitoba Court of Appeal, that the legislative provisions setting out when an emergency order is appropriate are too weak and that having emergency orders for an unspecified duration is not justified. As noted earlier, the act was changed by amendments first introduced before this case began, to clarify when an emergency order can be issued and to impose a three-year limit on orders unless a court rules otherwise.

Constitutional principles also require that a fair process must be used before the violation of rights can be justified. As the respondent will not be present at the emergency order hearing, particular attention needs to be given to ensuring procedural protections at the first hearing that help to compensate for his absence. Such protections include legislative requirements that the applicant's evidence be taken under oath, that telecommunication applications must be made by police officers, lawyers and others who can be trusted to respect the integrity of the legal system and that a higher court has the ability to conduct a timely and full review of the appropriateness of the order. There is also a general legal principle applicable to other "without notice" applications, which is that an applicant must disclose other proceedings involving the parties and make full disclosure of all evidence, including evidence that does not support the application. Even though this full disclosure rule is not expressly included in the *Manitoba DVSA*, the court held in *Baril* that it is applicable on emergency order applications.

In the *Baril* case, the Manitoba Court of Queen's Bench found that some procedural aspects of the *Manitoba DVSA* were unconstitutional. In particular, the court found that it was unfair for the respondent to show that the emergency order should be set aside, but rather determined that the applicant should have the obligation to demonstrate (again) that it should remain in place. More significantly, the court held that the evidence presented before the magistrate or justice of the peace could not be relied on at a judicial review hearing. Instead, the applicant must either appear in court to give oral evidence or swear an affidavit and then be subject to a cross-examination by the respondent on her evidence. As the Saskatchewan act contains both of the provisions successfully challenged in *Baril*, it is vulnerable to constitutional challenge. The validity of the Alberta act is less clear as it requires a review based on sworn evidence in addition to the transcript from the emergency hearing but does not clearly require the applicant to give evidence (and be subject to cross-examination) at the review hearing.

As the *Baril* case is on appeal, it is premature to consider the implications of the case in much detail. In particular, it is difficult to anticipate what the court might say about the constitutionality of the provisions on when an emergency order is appropriate and its duration. Regarding the question of whether the applicant should be subject to cross-examination on her evidence, it may be argued that many types of evidence are not subject to cross-examination and that the respondent has in any case a significant advantage where an applicant does not appear at the hearing (Bala & Ringseis, 2002, p. 35). Studies also suggest that applicants can experience anxiety and fear as a result of testifying before respondents in the context of intimate partner violence (e.g., Rigakos, 2002). However, there remains a strong chance that courts will affirm the requirement that the applicant make full disclosure at the emergency order hearing and that she be required to give evidence including a cross-examination if judicial review of the order is sought. In that event, applicants will need more information in advance of the original hearing about what evidence they must disclose and they will need to be aware that they are risking the possibility of a more complicated court review, including the potential to be cross-examined by the respondent.

The Application of Civil Legislation on First Nations Reserves

Another constitutional issue relates to the application of civil legislation on First Nations reserves. Section 91(24) of the *Constitution Act, 1867* gives exclusive legislative jurisdiction over "Indians and Lands reserved for the Indians" to the federal government. At the same time, the *Indian Act* allows provincial laws of general application to apply to First Nations unless the laws are inconsistent with the *Indian Act*.

Provincial legislation concerning the ownership and possession of family homes does not apply on First Nation reserves. In two 1986 cases, *Derrickson* v. *Derrickson* and *Paul* v. *Paul*, the Supreme Court of Canada held that provincial family law legislation on the division of family property and occupancy of a family residence following a separation did not apply to residences and property on reserve land. These cases suggest that the Alberta and Saskatchewan provisions allowing for an order of exclusive occupation of the family residence as part of an emergency order will not apply on First Nations reserves (see also Cornet & Lendor, 2002).

Due to the patriarchal underpinnings of the *Indian Act*, certificates of possession for the family home are usually issued in the name of the male partner (Cornet & Lendor, 2002; Eberts & Jacobs, 2004; Turpel, 1991). On relationship breakdown, or even during a temporary separation because of violence, the certificate holder retains the right to continue occupying the family home. Even where certificates are jointly held, the British Columbia Supreme Court found in *Darbyshire-Joseph* v. *Darbyshire-Joseph* (1998) that courts cannot require one partner to transfer an interest to property held on a reserve to the other partner.

Where the respondent is the holder of a certificate of possession, provisions of civil legislation permitting restraint of the respondent from attending the family residence and removal of the respondent from the residence may also be inapplicable on reserves, as these are aspects of possession. Bala and Ringseis (2002) argue that if the applicant is able to continue residing in the family home, a simple no-contact order may be a valid constraint and may effectively offer the same relief as an exclusive possession order. This argument suggests that the situation in Manitoba, where no-contact orders are effectively used to provide exclusive possession to applicants, is constitutionally permissible. This approach might also provide an alternative for First Nations women in Alberta and Saskatchewan. However, even if no-contact provisions in emergency orders are constitutionally permissible, police who are concerned about jurisdictional issues on reserves may not enforce them (Cornet & Lendor, 2002).

A First Nations victim of violence who flees the home will have no legal remedies to regain possession of the home and will often have few other options. Many reserve communities do not have shelters and face severe housing shortages (CERA, 2002; Cornet & Lendor, 2002; Eberts & Jacobs, 2004; FAFIA, 2003). First Nations women who are victims of violence must then choose between living with friends or relatives in overcrowded housing, leaving the reserve or remaining in a violent relationship. Leaving the reserve may not be an option for women in remote communities and, if they do leave, this entails separation from family, language and community, and often a life of urban poverty and racism (Cornet & Lendor, 2002; Eberts & Jacobs, 2004). Turpel (1991, p. 36) calls this situation "barbaric," particularly considering the traditional role of Aboriginal women in their communities and the place of land in First Nations culture.

There have been no constitutional challenges to the application of civil legislation on First Nations reserves to date, perhaps because the legislation and the exclusive possession remedy is being underutilized on reserves. In 2002, only four emergency protection orders were issued to applicants living on reserves in Saskatchewan; all awarded exclusive occupancy of the residence. Only one of the four listed additional conditions: respondent prohibited from contacting the victim or others; respondent prohibited from attending at or near victim's residence; peace officer to remove respondent from residence; and peace officer to accompany specified person to residence to remove personal belongings. While 25 orders were issued in 1997, only six of these gave the victim exclusive possession (Prairie Research Associates 1999, p. 10). Data are not available on the number of emergency order applications made by applicants living on reserves in Manitoba and Alberta. Interestingly, Alberta's *PAFVA* regulations specifically state that a First Nations police officer is empowered to make an application for an emergency order, but it is unclear whether this power is being used.

Many have critiqued First Nation women's lack of family property rights on reserves, arguing that this legislative gap violates the Charter, Aboriginal rights and international law (see for example CERA, 2002; FAFIA, 2003; Standing Senate Committee on Human Rights, 2003). Given the high rates of violence against Aboriginal women (Canadian Panel on Violence Against Women, 1993; Federal-Provincial-Territorial Ministers Responsible for the Status of Women, 2002; Lane, Bopp & Bopp, 2003), the lack of property rights, including the lack of civil remedies when applicants and children are being subject to abuse, is a critical issue.

Several recommendations have been made to alleviate this situation on an interim basis. Turpel (1991) has suggested that band bylaws could be developed to deal with family property issues; some bands have enacted such bylaws giving exclusive possession of family homes to violence victims (Ad Hoc Federal-Provincial-Territorial Working Group, 2003). Similarly, under the *First Nations Land Management Act* First Nations can adopt a land code and, once this code is established, the *Indian Act* no longer applies to land use on that reserve. It would appear that a First Nation has authority under this act to create rules regarding the possession of family homes in cases of marriage breakdown. However, to date few First Nations have adopted land codes. Another possibility is the inclusion of family property rights during the negotiation of self-government agreements, but this is recognized as a longer-term solution (Standing Senate Committee on Human Rights, 2003; Cornet & Lendor, 2002).

The Application of Section 96

Section 96 of the *Constitution Act, 1867* requires that superior, district or county court judges be appointed federally. The Supreme Court of Canada has interpreted this section to mean that provincially appointed decision-makers (Provincial Court judges, magistrates and justices of the peace) cannot normally exercise powers that were exclusively within the jurisdiction of federally appointed judges at the time of Confederation. They can only do so where these powers are administrative or legislative (not judicial) in nature, or are incidental to a broader administrative or policy function (*Residential Tenancies Act (N.S)*, 1996). In *Baril* (2004), Mr. Justice

Scurfield held that the power to make no contact orders under the *Manitoba DVSA* was a judicial function that was not incidental to a broader administrative or policy function. However, because injunction-like powers were within the powers of provincial magistrates and justices of the peace to maintain the peace and prevent criminal behaviour in 1867, and not within the *exclusive* jurisdiction of federally appointed judges at that time, the power to make no-contact orders did not violate section 96. This issue is currently before the Manitoba Court of Appeal in the *Baril* appeal.

The validity of the power to grant exclusive possession of the family home or personal property in emergency circumstances has not yet been considered in Alberta or Saskatchewan. However, these powers were upheld under the Prince Edward Island act in *A.L.G.C.* v. *Prince Edward Island* (1998), subject to the proviso that the orders issued by justices of the peace not "[intrude] more than necessary upon the proprietary rights of a respondent or extend for a longer duration than necessary." Section 96 is an important limit on both the scope of emergency orders and potential amendments to civil domestic violence legislation.

Conclusions

The disparate and declining application and grant rates for emergency orders are troubling. While the application rate has increased overall in Alberta over time, there are still marked disparities in the number of applications in different regions of the province. As discussed in this paper, changes to the legislative provisions setting out what is family or domestic violence, the seriousness and urgency requirements, the duration of the orders and the inclusion of all stalking situations as well as dating and non-cohabiting familial relationships could increase the likelihood that emergency orders would be granted in situations where they could provide protection to applicants. Ensuring that applicants can make in-person applications for emergency orders themselves without relying on an agent, such as the police, may also encourage applications. In order to ensure appropriate procedural protections for respondents and to better inform applicants of their obligations, consideration should be given to including provisions on the full disclosure requirements at the original hearing and evidentiary and burden of proof obligations on judicial review. The limited protection afforded to First Nations women by these provincial acts or other matrimonial property mechanisms remains a serious concern.

Postscript

The Manitoba Court of Appeal in *Baril* v. *Obelnicki* (April 2007) found that the *DVSA* did not overstep provincial powers and upheld the lower court's finding that section 96 of the *Constitution Act, 1867* permitted provincially appointed magistrates to grant no-contact orders. It also found that respondents' Charter rights to fair procedures were sufficiently protected by the *DVSA*. In particular, it held that "without-notice hearings are an important and integral part of the act and a balanced attempt to deal with the reality of a situation where certain individuals require emergency protection. The situation of the applicants justifies the use of without-notice hearings in that it is reasonable to fear that the respondents will act improperly if notice is given" (at para. 98). A judge reviewing a without-notice order could permit the respondent to cross-examine the applicant under appropriate circumstances. The court also held that the act should be interpreted so that respondents need only demonstrate on a review that it is just and equitable to set aside an order. For example, respondents could show that "full disclosure was not made or that the restraints on his liberty are unnecessary or too restrictive or that the stalking will not continue or based on the weight of the evidence at the review hearing the order should be set aside" (at para. 127).

Acknowledgements: The authors would like to acknowledge the research assistance contributed by then-law students Lisa Robbins, Meaghan Campbell, Victoria Coffin, Rebecca Beeny, Carolyn Wright, Amy Nixon and Gayle Hiscocks, and the support of the Legal Research Institute of the University of Manitoba. We are also grateful to Fiona Douglas, Cheryl Laurie, Leslie M. Tutty and Jane Ursel for answering many queries about the empirical data.

Appendix: Domestic Violence Protection Legislation in the Prairie Provinces

	Protection Against Family Violence Act (Alberta)	Victims of Domestic Violence Act (Saskatchewan)	The Domestic Violence and Stalking Prevention Protection and Compensation Act (Manitoba) (Renamed The Domestic Violence and Stalking Act in 2005)
Came into force	June 1, 1999. Amended 2006.	February 1, 1995	Sept. 30, 1999. Amended 2005.
Who may claim protection?	• current or former cohabitants • parents of a child • children in the care and custody of parents/cohabitants • persons residing together where one has care/custody over the other (s. 1) • 2006 amendments removed the cohabitation requirement for those related by blood, marriage, adoption, or an adult interdependent relationship	• current or former cohabitants and parents of a child (s. 2(a))	• current or former co-habitants and parents of a child (s. 1) • a person being stalked (ss. 1, 2) • amendments in 2005 expanded protection to non-cohabitating family members and dating relationships (s. 2 (1))
What conduct is covered?	• "family violence" definition is similar to Saskatchewan but includes the additional requirement that "the purpose" of the respondent's act "is to harm or intimidate a family member." (s. 1)	• "domestic violence" means "intentional or reckless act or omission that causes bodily harm or damage to property" • "threatened act" that causes a "reasonable fear of bodily harm or	• "domestic violence" definition is the same as Saskatchewan but also includes stalking (s. 2(2)) and "conduct that reasonably, in all the circumstances, constitutes psychological or

	emotional abuse". (s. 2(1)) (after 2005 s. 2(1.1))	• or damage to property • forced confinement • sexual abuse. (s. 2(d))	• The "purpose" requirement was repealed in 2006 • expressly does not include reasonable correction of children • stalking was added by amendment in 2006, but only as between family members (s. 1(1)(k))
Applicants for emergency orders	• applicant in person (s. 4(2)) • lawyer or peace officer in person or by telecommunications (amended in 2005 to include "person designated by the minister") (s. 4(2))	• victim in person • person on victim's behalf (with leave of the court) • peace officers • victim assistance or crisis workers as specified in the regulation (see s. 8 of the *VDVA* and *VDVA Regulation* s. 3)	• claimant in person • any other person on the claimant's behalf (with leave of the court) • police and child welfare officials (see s. 6 of the *PAFV* Act and the *PAFVA Regulations*)
When can orders be made?	• domestic violence or stalking has occurred and the applicant believes it will continue (s. 6(1)) (amended in 2005 to require that the applicant believe that [and that there is a reasonable likelihood] the domestic violence or stalking will continue or resume) • order is necessary or advisable to the applicant's immediate protection (s. 7(1)); amended in 2005 to "immediate or imminent protection" (s. 6(1))	• domestic violence has occurred • "by reason of seriousness or urgency, the order must be made without waiting for the next available sitting of a judge of a court to ensure the immediate protection of the victim" (s. 3(1))	• family violence has occurred • "by reason of seriousness or urgency, the order should be granted to ensure the immediate protection of the claimant" (s. 2(1)) • amendments added the requirement that the claimant has reason to believe that the respondent will continue or resume carrying out family violence (s. 2(a.1))

Appendix: Domestic Violence Protection Legislation in the Prairie Provinces (continued)

	Protection Against Family Violence Act (Alberta)	Victims of Domestic Violence Act (Saskatchewan)	The Domestic Violence and Stalking Prevention Protection and Compensation Act (Manitoba) (Renamed The Domestic Violence and Stalking Act in 2005)
Procedures on emergency order applications	• notice to the respondent is not required (s. 2(1)) • evidence must be given under oath (*PAFVA Regulation* s. 5)	• notice to the respondent is not required (s. 3(1)) • under oath or promise to tell the truth (*VDPA Regulation* s. 7)	• notice to respondent is not required (s. 6(1)) • evidence must be given under oath (s.4 (3))
Factors the designated justice of the peace or Provincial Court judge shall consider	• same as Saskatchewan (s. 2(2)) • amendments added several factors, including controlling behaviour by the respondent, whether the violence is repetitive or escalating, the vulnerability of elderly claimants and the claimant's need for a short-term safe environment (s. 2(2))	• nature of domestic violence; history of domestic violence; existence of immediate danger to persons or property; best interests of victim and any child of victim (s. 3(2))	• no factors stated in the legislation
Provisions that can be included in an emergency order	• called an "emergency protection order" • same provisions as Saskatchewan and, additionally, restraining respondent from attending specific places attended regularly by	• called an "emergency intervention order" • granting victim and other family members exclusive occupation of residence • directing peace officer to remove	• called a "protection order" (s. 6(1)) • same provisions as Saskatchewan (except that there is no "any other necessary order" clause and no exclusive possession clause)

	• and additionally, prohibiting respondent from following a person; prohibiting a respondent from attending at or near or entering any place a person attends regularly, including work, home, business; directing respondent to surrender firearms; authorizing a peace officer to enter a place to seize items. (s. 7(1))	the respondent from residence • directing a peace officer to accompany a person to residence to supervise removal of personal belongings • restraining respondent from communicating with or contacting victim and other persons • any other provision necessary for immediate protection. (s. 3(3))	applicant and other family members • directing seizure and storage of weapons where they have been used or threatened to be used to commit family violence (s. 4)
Duration of emergency orders	• original act was silent but amended in 2005 to specify that orders expire three years after being granted unless a longer time period is specified (s. 8.1(1))	• act is silent	• "for such specified duration as a judge considers appropriate" but cannot exceed one year unless extended by further order (s. 7)
Review of emergency orders	• respondent may apply to set aside within 20 days (s. 11) or "at any time" (s. 19(1)) • no provision for automatic review • onus is on the respondent to demonstrate that the order should be set aside (s. 12(2)) • evidence before the DJP shall be considered and the original applicant may present additional evidence (s. 12(3))	• a Queen's Bench judge shall review the order (and review supporting documents including the JP's notes) within three days of receiving it • confirm the order if the evidence supports granting the order (s. 5(1)) or call for a rehearing, on notice to the respondent, if the evidence does not support the order; onus is on the respondent to demonstrate that the order should be set aside and the victim/applicant may	• order must be reviewed within seven working days (increased to nine by amendment in 2006 by a Queen's Bench judge, on affidavit and other sworn evidence • evidence from the original hearing can also be considered (ss. 2(6), 3(2)). • the judge can confirm or revoke the order or direct that an oral hearing be held

Appendix: Domestic Violence Protection Legislation in the Prairie Provinces (continued)

	Protection Against Family Violence Act (Alberta)	Victims of Domestic Violence Act (Saskatchewan)	The Domestic Violence and Stalking Prevention Protection and Compensation Act (Manitoba) (Renamed The Domestic Violence and Stalking Act in 2005)
		(but is not required) to participate (s. 5(5)) • at any time, the respondent or the applicant can apply to vary or revoke the order (s. 6(1))	

Provisions of non-emergency orders
 	
•
	• called a "Queen's Bench protection order" (s. 4(1)) and it can be granted if a judge determines that the applicant has been subject to family violence
	• same conditions as are available for an emergency protection order very similar conditions as are available in Saskatchewan for a victims assistance order (s. 4(1))
		• called a "victims assistance order" and it can be granted if a judge determines that the applicant has been subject to domestic violence
		• same provisions as are available for emergency orders, plus the following:
		  • restraining respondent from making any communication likely to cause annoyance or alarm to victim
		  • temporary possession of personal possessions
			• called a "prevention order" (s. 14(1)) and it can be granted if a judge determines that the applicant has been subject to domestic violence or stalking
			• same conditions as are available for emergency orders
			• very similar conditions as are available in Saskatchewan for a victims assistance order and, additionally:
			  • temporary exclusive possession of the residence

• payment of compensation for lost income, expenses (such as living, medical, security-related) and legal fees • restraining respondent from dealing with property that victim may have interest in • recommending that respondent receive counselling • posting security • any other provision (s. 7(1))	• suspension of driver's licence (s. 15(1))

CHAPTER TEN

Seeking Protection for Victims of Stalking: *The Domestic Violence and Stalking Act of Manitoba*

Cheryl Laurie

The Domestic Violence and Stalking Act (DVSA) of Manitoba was implemented on September 30, 1999, and was designed to offer victims[1] of domestic violence and stalking relief in the form of protective orders under civil law. In the period leading up to its implementation, key stakeholders working in the area of violence against women in Manitoba heralded the act as a powerful tool that would offer victims a means of protection that was available quickly and easily. In its seven-year history, the legislation has been heavily utilized. However, it also came to be widely criticized as not being implemented in the way its proponents had originally envisioned. Protection orders under the *DVSA* became increasingly difficult to obtain, as the criteria for issuing them became more stringent year after year. In 2005, amendments were made to the legislation that were designed to address the primary concerns raised by key players over the implementation of the act.

This chapter describes the development and features of the *DVSA*, the nature, prevalence and consequences of stalking, factors which influence whether or not protection orders under the *DVSA* are granted in cases of stalking and implications of the recent legislative amendments. A focus on stalking is important because of the pivotal role it played in the development of the *DVSA*. The data used in this analysis are drawn from a

RESOLVE research project (forthcoming) entitled "Evaluating the Justice and Community Response to Family Violence in the Canadian Prairie Provinces." The larger RESOLVE study involved an in-depth quantitative study of the 775 protection order applications made in Winnipeg in 2002, 483 of which included evidence of stalking (for a comprehensive analysis of the applications made on the basis of stalking, see Laurie, 2006). For our present purposes, the stalking sample will be limited to only those applicants who were seeking protection from former intimate partners ($N = 389$, 80.6% of the total stalking-related applications). In addition to the quantitative data, the larger RESOLVE study included qualitative interviews with female victims of domestic abuse and stalking, 17 of whom applied for protection orders. Selected narratives of those women who applied on the basis of stalking will also be presented in order to further illustrate key concepts identified throughout this chapter.

Development and Features of the DVSA

In the 1990s, several Manitoba women were stalked and then murdered despite their repeated requests for police protection. Two reports released in 1997, the Manitoba Law Reform Commission's *Stalking* report and the *Commission of Inquiry into the deaths of Rhonda and Roy Lavoie* (the Lavoie Inquiry, see Schulman, 1997), identified limitations in both the criminal and civil laws in existence at that time. Previous remedies under the civil law were vaguely worded and were only available to individuals who were married or were cohabitants, and intervention through the criminal justice system was seen to be slow and uncertain. For example, the *Stalking* report (Manitoba Law Reform Commission, 1997) reviewed the offence of criminal harassment and found it to be ineffective in many instances. "Concerns include prosecutors' willingness to accept plea bargains, the unwillingness of judges to impose jail terms on convicted stalkers and the lack of mandatory minimum sentences for criminal harassment" (1997, p. 16). The commission believed that the best remedy to this situation was to enact provincial legislation so that victims of stalking would have an opportunity to proceed with civil action rather than relying only on the federal law of criminal harassment as it is set out in section 264 of the Criminal Code. The primary purpose of "anti-stalking" legislation is to stop threatening and harassing conduct before it escalates into violence. The commission believed that the new act would empower victims of stalking by providing a means of protection without having to rely on the police and the Crown for protection.

The Lavoie Inquiry (Schulman, 1997) recommended sweeping changes to enhance the protection of victims of domestic violence and stalking. The report found that the justice system had failed in providing adequate protection to Rhonda Lavoie, even though the couple had several encounters with "restraining" orders, under both criminal and civil law. Many problems were identified with the existing civil remedies, including unclear language, difficulty with obtaining orders in some rural and remote areas, insufficient enforcement of orders and inadequate penalties for breaching the orders.[2] As a result of similar recommendations made in both the Lavoie Inquiry and the *Stalking* report, the *DVSA* was born. The legislation was designed to provide people at risk with more comprehensive protection and to address the shortcomings of other civil remedies.

Under the *DVSA*, remedies for victims are available by applying for a protection order or prevention order. A protection order is intended to be used in emergency situations where there is imminent danger that abuse will occur, and therefore the act provides for immediate relief. Protection orders are granted *ex-parte* (without the respondent[3] being present) and without notice to the respondent that a hearing is taking place. During business hours, a person may apply before a designated justice of the peace (JP), either on his/her own or with the assistance of a police officer or lawyer. Immediate relief is also available on a 24-hour basis via telecommunication. This method requires the assistance of a lawyer or police officer, who telephones a JP on the victim's behalf. If the order is granted, the necessary documents are faxed for service upon the respondent. Depending on the method used, the application process can take anywhere from one hour to several hours to complete. There are no court fees associated with protection order applications. Once the JP issues the order, it is then filed as an order of the Court of Queen's Bench.

Unlike the previous non-molestation order, the wording in a protection order is very clear. Provisions can be applied that prohibit the offender from following the applicant or a specified person, from communicating with or contacting the applicant or a specified person and from attending at or near places the applicant attends regularly. It can also direct police to remove the respondent from the residence, can grant temporary possession of necessary personal effects to the applicant and can direct police to accompany the applicant to the residence to supervise the removal of necessary personal effects. Finally, a protection order may require the offender to turn over any weapons and firearms certificates to the police, and the police may search the residence for any weapons they have reason to believe are there. A respondent has 20 days to apply to have the order set aside, although the order remains in effect during this process (Legislative Assembly of Manitoba, 1998).

While the focus of this chapter is on protection orders, it is important to note that the *DVSA* also contains prevention orders. A prevention order is appropriate in more complicated situations where the victim requires additional remedies. These orders generally take longer to obtain (typically several weeks)[4] and require that a motion and affidavit be filed with the Court of Queen's Bench in order for an application to be heard. Although it is possible to proceed through this process without counsel, it is recommended that an applicant have the assistance of a lawyer. Prevention orders are heard in the Court of Queen's Bench and can therefore impose more stringent conditions on the respondent than those available in a protection order.

Table 10.1 outlines the protection order applications heard in Winnipeg from the first full year the *DVSA* was implemented to the end of 2005. The number of applications fell steadily from 2000 to 2004, and then rose again in 2005. There are two reasons for the decline in applications. First, the JPs reviewing the applications at the first point of contact with the victims became more adept at screening them. That is, individuals who are not eligible to apply or those who would be served more appropriately by a different type of remedy were more often being redirected to a different type of remedy as time went on. The second reason is related to the decreased likelihood of orders being granted over time, also shown in Table 10.1. The percentage of orders being issued showed a general decline over time, from 65% when the act was first implemented, with a low of 36% in 2003. With the odds of successfully receiving an order dropping, many of the service providers who had been referring their clients to seek protection orders were increasingly reluctant to do so. The reduction in successful applications came about as the JPs began interpreting the legislation more narrowly after learning of orders they had issued being set aside by the Court of Queen's Bench. The decline in orders being granted was met with frustration on the part of many stakeholders, who argued that the legislation was not being implemented as intended.

Table 10.1: Winnipeg Protection Order Hearings, 2000–05

Year	Number of Applications	Orders Granted		Applications Dismissed	
2000	1,208	790	65%	418	35%
2001	992	533	54%	459	46%
2002	775*	388	50%	387	50%
2003	640	228	36%	412	64%
2004	496	211	43%	285	57%
2005	621	277	45%	344	55%

SOURCE: Manitoba Justice-Judicial Services, 2006

* Note: The number of applications listed for 2002 is slightly higher than that provided by Manitoba Justice. In its detailed review of the files, RESOLVE (forthcoming) uncovered 775 applications, whereas the court data identified 772 files (this discrepancy has to do with files being transferred from one court location to another). All other years in this table reflect the Manitoba Justice statistics.

The effect of a narrow interpretation of the need for emergency protection is particularly troubling in cases of stalking. Stalking is composed of a totality of events and cannot be broken down into isolated incidents without stripping it of its fundamental meaning. When an applicant is asked to focus on a discrete incident that has occurred recently that gives rise to the need for immediate protection, it becomes difficult for that applicant to properly articulate the nature of the problem. Jeffrey Schnoor of Manitoba Justice authored the 1997 Manitoba Law Reform Commission's *Stalking* report and was therefore instrumental in the development of the act. He explained (personal communication, October 19, 2001) that the drafters of the legislation intended that a somewhat more liberal interpretation would be applied given the urgency of these situations. At the same time, there is pressure from the opposite direction that the constitutional rights of the respondent may be compromised if the interpretation of the act is too liberal (see chapter 9 in this volume).

Manitoba's Minister of Justice formed a multidisciplinary working group to review the implementation of the *DVSA* and to identify steps that could be taken to ensure the goals of the legislation could be met. As a result of this group's recommendations, amendments to the act were made under Bill 17 (Legislative Assembly of Manitoba, 2005a). These changes took effect on October 31, 2005, and addressed many of the concerns raised by key players working in the field of violence against women. The rise in applications in 2005 came in part as a result of these amendments, which opened up the type of relationships eligible under the application, relaxed some of the criteria the JPs were to use in their rulings and allowed designated individuals from a number of service provider agencies to assist victims in making their applications. As a senior official of Manitoba Justice explained (personal communication, April 11, 2006), at the time these changes were about to go into effect, Manitoba Justice conducted information sessions and distributed a booklet about the amended legislation to various service providers dealing with violence issues. This created an increased awareness of the amendments and prompted a surge in applications in the last two months of the year.

The Nature, Prevalence and Consequences of Stalking

While the extent, seriousness and pervasiveness of the problem of domestic violence has been known for several decades (Johnson, 1996; Statistics Canada, 2005a), the nature and prevalence of stalking as it relates to domestic violence has only received attention in the past fifteen years or so. Therefore it is not as well understood, compared to domestic violence, in terms of being a serious social problem. The prevalence of stalking in Canada was assessed in the 2004 General Social Survey (GSS). The GSS is an anonymous telephone survey conducted annually by Statistics Canada. In 2004, surveyors asked 24,000 randomly chosen adults (over the age of 15) a number of questions about victimization, including a special module on stalking. Questions in this module conform to the definition of criminal harassment as outlined in section 264 of the Criminal Code, which includes such behaviours as repeatedly following a person from place to place, repeatedly communicating with or contacting that person, watching a place where the other person works, lives or happens to be and engaging in threatening contact directed at the other person or someone known to that person. The GSS found that 1.4 million females over the age of 15 (11% of the population) and 882,000 males over the age of 15 (7% of the population) had been stalked in the five years preceding the survey (Statistics Canada, 2005a).

Using data from the 2004 GSS, Johnson (2006) found that 80% of stalkers were male in cases involving female stalking victims, and stalkers were also predominantly male (73%) in cases of male victims. Females stalked males in only 5% of all cases. Women were stalked by current or former intimate partners in 21% of cases, compared to 10% of males. In cases of male victims, stalkers were more likely to be other people known to them, such as neighbours, friends, co-workers and people known by sight only.

Stalking is a distinctive form of criminal activity because it is composed of a series of acts rather than a single event. These behaviours may seem innocent in isolation, but taken together form a pattern of conduct that is very threatening to the subject of the stalker's actions. According to Coleman (1997), defining the characteristics of the offender is difficult, as stalkers come from all backgrounds and frequently have no prior criminal record. They can exhibit a variety of psychological syndromes from minor emotional difficulties to severe sociopathic tendencies.

Numerous stalker typologies exist in the literature, and all contain similar classifications based on the motivations of the stalker. A commonly cited one developed by Kropp, Hart and Lyon (2002) identifies four categories of stalkers. These authors claim that the "ex-intimate partner" stalker is the most common form. These individuals frequently have a history of abusive relationships and refuse to accept the rejection of their former partner. "Love obsessionals" comprise the second category. These are people who have intense emotional feelings for a person whom they have come to know through a casual acquaintanceship or work relationship. Love obsessionals believe that those whom they have feelings for will come to love them if given a chance to get to know them. The third category in this typology is made up of "delusional stalkers" who falsely believe that the subject of their attention is in love with them, and continue to make attempts to establish a relationship with them (this is usually the case when celebrities are stalked). The final category is comprised of "grudge stalkers" who harbour resentment for their victims. Rather than desiring a relationship with the people they are stalking, this type of stalker is acting out of revenge.

In domestic situations, stalking typically occurs after the woman has attempted to terminate the relationship. Leaving an abusive partner does not necessarily mark the end of the violence. Statistics Canada data show that in 1999, 40% of women and 32% of men with a former violent marriage or common-law relationship reported that violence occurred after the couple separated (Hotton, 2001). In fact, this is often the most volatile time in a relationship that has been characterized by violence (Johnson, 1996). Unable to come to terms with the rejection, the man is unwilling to let the woman leave the relationship and begins to engage in stalking behaviours such as following, threatening or assaulting her (National Institute of Justice, 1996). As Brewster (2000) explains, abusive men tend to experience a loss of control in situations where their partner has attempted to end the relationship, and therefore one would expect an already volatile situation to worsen under these circumstances. Following separation, violence often escalates when the abusive partner discovers that their former partner has entered a new relationship. This is supported by Hotton (2001), who found that in estranged marriages, the victim's new partner was the most frequent third-party victim in cases of attacks involving multiple victims.

The U.S. National Violence Against Women Survey found a definite link between stalking and other forms of domestic violence. Eighty-one percent of the women who were stalked by a current or former intimate partner reported that that partner had also physically assaulted them (Tjaden & Thoennes, 1998). The 2004 GSS supports the premise that stalkers with a previous intimate relationship were more likely to be violent than in other stalking relationships, with 54% of female victims being stalked by an ex-spouse reporting being physically intimidated and verbally threatened (Statistics Canada, 2005a). Bernstein (1993) considers the link between stalking and former violent relationships to be so strong that she proposes that Lenore Walker's Cycle Theory of Violence (see Walker, 1979) be modified to include stalking as the fourth distinct phase in the cycle. Australian research conducted by Mullen, Pathe, Purcell and Stuart (1999) found that stalking by intimate partners (current or former) also tends to continue for longer periods of time relative to other types of stalking relationships. The GSS supports this theory, with 61% of Canadians stalked by a former spouse reporting stalking which lasted for more than a year. Conversely, non-intimate stalkers most commonly continued their activities for periods of between one and six months (Statistics Canada, 2005a). Stalking by former intimate partners has the potential of escalating to more serious crimes. In Canada, there were 12 homicides from 1997 to 2000 that involved criminal harassment as the precipitating crime. In each of these cases, the victim was a female who was being stalked by a former intimate partner (Hackett, 2000; Fedorowycz, 2001).

Victims of stalking are often reluctant to contact the police. U.S. figures (Tjaden & Thoennes, 1998) indicate that approximately half of all stalking victims report the harassing behaviour to the police, while Canadian figures show that stalking is only reported to the police in 37% of cases (Statistics Canada, 2005a). Research shows that stalking victims give similar reasons to victims of domestic violence for their reluctance to contact authorities. Reasons frequently cited are that the victims feared reprisal from their stalker or abuser, they did not believe the police would be able to do anything for them, that police would not take the matter seriously and that police might lay criminal charges in cases where the victim did not want charges laid against the stalker or abuser (Eisikovits & Buchbinder, 2000; Manitoba Association of Women and the Law, 1991; Statistics Canada, 2000; Tjaden & Thoennes, 1998).

Stalking has a profound impact on those subjected to it. Research by Mechanic, Uhlmansiek, Weaver and Resick (2001) reports that, as a result of living in constant fear, many victims experience severe psychological distress. Loss of appetite, lack of sleep and severe depression are among the symptoms reported. The psychological impact can be extreme, as evidenced in one study suggesting that 37% of stalking victims meet the clinical diagnostic requirements for post-traumatic stress disorder (Pathe & Mullen, 1997). The GSS found that 60% of women who were stalked by ex-partners feared for their lives (Johnson, 2006). That survey also found that many victims modify their daily activities in an effort to escape the stalking. For example, over half (52%) of all female victims avoid going to particular places or having contact with certain people as a result of being stalked. The negative effects of stalking on one's day-to-day life are evidenced in the narratives of participants in RESOLVE's (forthcoming) research. As one woman comments:

> He would phone my work ... and speak to my co-workers and tell
> them I was a junkie and a slut. He would phone any number if he
> thought [I was there], well one day it was 117 times. And he would
> leave threatening messages ... threatening me, threatening my life,
> threatening people around me, their children. [*What impact did
> that have on your life?*] Horrible ... I couldn't go anywhere. I was
> bringing [trouble] to my friends, people that I cared about. They
> don't want to hear threats to their children ... I felt he was still
> keeping me isolated, you know, he still had that control over me.
> He still used what he could.

Stalker-Victim Characteristics

The applicants in the Winnipeg sample are overwhelmingly female at
85.9%, while males comprise 86.1% of respondents. This is consistent with
the literature cited above that identifies stalking as an offence that is
primarily perpetrated by men against women. The stalkers in the Winnipeg
sample range from 15 to 68 years of age, with a mean age of 34 years. The
majority of applicants (292 cases, 60.5%) do not list children on their
application forms. It should be noted that this does not mean that these
individuals do not have children, only that they elect not to apply for
protection for their children.[5]

Nature of Abuse

As shown in Table 10.2, the victims experience a wide range of abusive
behaviours, with stalking behaviours making up the most common category of abuse in the sample (49.5%). Almost two-thirds of the victims
(65.3%) are subjected to stalking in the form of unwanted communication,
which includes phone calls, email and messages conveyed through third
parties. The second most frequently cited form of stalking is unwanted contact (52.4%), which includes direct personal contact or attempts to make
such contact (for example, going to the victim's home or workplace to seek
out the victim). Another common form of stalking is in the form of the

Table 10.2: Nature of the Abuse

Nature of the Abuse Total Cases N=389	Frequency	Percent	Percent of Total
Stalking behaviours			
Stalking — unwanted communication	254	65.3%	
Stalking — unwanted contact	204	52.4%	
Stalking — watching or following	196	50.4%	
Stalking — vandalism	27	6.9%	
Stalking — delivery of unwanted items	22	5.7%	
Stalking — monitoring activities	4	1.0%	
Total stalking behaviours	707		49.5%
Physical/other abusive behaviours			
Physical assault	161	41.4%	
Emotional/psychological abuse	128	32.9%	
Property damage	53	13.6%	
Forced confinement	20	5.1%	
Financial abuse	15	3.9%	
Sexual assault	11	2.8%	
Making false allegations about victim to authorities	7	1.8%	
Abuse of pet(s)	2	0.5%	
Total physical/other abusive behaviours	397		27.8%
Threatening behaviours			
Threat of physical assault	80	20.6%	
Threat to kill applicant or others named on application	78	20.1%	
Unspecified threats (e.g., "You're going to get it.")	49	12.6%	
Threat of respondent self-harm or suicide	41	10.5%	
Threat to kill relative or friend	18	4.6%	
Threat to take children	22	5.7%	
Threat of property damage	11	2.8%	
Threat of harm to pet(s)	4	1.0%	
Threat of sexual assault	4	1.0%	
Total threatening behaviours	307		21.5%
Miscellaneous (thefts, break-ins, dangerous driving, etc.)	17	4.4%	1.2%
TOTAL	1,428		100%

Note: More than one type of abuse was experienced by most applicants, therefore figures total more than the 389 cases included in the sample.

respondent watching or following the victim (50.4%), which includes activities such as repeatedly driving by the victim's home, watching the victim from a distance, or following the victim from place to place. Less commonly cited stalking behaviours are the vandalism of the victim's property (6.9%) and the delivery of unwanted items (5.7%). Finally, in a small number of cases (1.0%), victims had discovered that the respondents were monitoring their activities (by video- or audiotaping them, opening their mail, checking their voice mail, etc.).

The category of "physical/other abusive behaviours" represents 27.8% of the behaviours in evidence. In order of frequency, the types of abuse within this grouping include physical assault, emotional and psychological abuse, property damage, forced confinement, financial abuse, sexual assault, making false allegations about the victim to authorities and abuse of pet(s).

Victims also endure threats, with this category comprising 21.5% of the abuse cited by applicants. Threats come in many forms, including threats of physical assault, threats to kill the applicant or others named on the application, unspecified threats (e.g., "You're going to get it"), threats of the respondent harming him/herself or committing suicide, threats to take the children, threats to kill a relative or friend, threats of property damage, threats to harm pets and threats of sexual assault. Finally, various activities such as thefts, break-ins and dangerous driving comprise the remaining 1.2% of the abusive behaviours in evidence.

These findings are consistent with the literature stating that stalking is frequently associated with relationships characterized by violence. For example, Tjaden and Thoennes (1998) report that 81% of women stalked by an intimate partner have been physically assaulted by that person. Similarly, using 2004 GSS data, Johnson (2006) found that 75% of women who were stalked by an ex-partner within the previous five years had also been physically or sexually assaulted.

Seeking that "Piece of Paper": Factors Influencing Application Outcome

The vast majority of evaluations conducted with respect to civil protective relief are focused on outcomes rather than on process. That is, these studies tend to examine orders of this type in terms of how effective they are in making the offenders stop their problematic behaviour. By contrast, this research identifies the factors that are involved in obtaining a protection order in the first place. While I agree that the effectiveness of existing orders is of critical importance, taking this step backward fills a gap by answering the question, "What does it take to get this 'piece of paper?'" After all, the effectiveness of a protection order is moot in cases where an applicant cannot get one to begin with.

Protection orders were granted in slightly over half (53.7%) of the applications involving stalking by intimate partners in 2002, similar to the 50% likelihood of success in that year for all applications processed. I will now outline the factors that influence whether or not protection orders are granted when applications are made on the basis of stalking by former intimate partners.

Various logistic regression models were tested, with one revealing five variables that reach statistical significance in influencing outcomes of protection order applications while controlling for the effects of others in the model. Coding for these variables is shown in Table 10.3. As indicated in Table 10.4, the statistically significant predictors include victim sex, the "threatening behaviours" category of abuse, the magistrate conducting the hearing,[6] previous court orders issued between the parties and presence of weapons. Additional variables of victim age, racial background of the victim and respondent, and length of relationship could not be included in the model because they either contained too many missing cases or were too highly correlated.

An interesting picture emerged in terms of victim sex, with female applicants being almost two-and-a-half times more likely to have a protection order granted than males. Two factors help to make sense of this finding. First, men are far less likely than women to articulate feelings of fear when victimized by female stalkers (Davis, Coker & Sanderson, 2002; Kropp, Hart & Lyon, 2002), and fear is one of the criteria written into the *DVSA* that the JPs are to take into consideration when deciding on cases of stalking. Second, when examining the reasons for dismissal cited by magistrates, it became apparent that it is sometimes the case that people apply for protection orders because their former partners have obtained "no-contact orders" against them but are continuing to contact them in spite of

Table 10.3: Coding of Variables in Logistic Regression Model of Stalking by Intimate Partners

Variables	Coded
Respondent age	continuous
Victim sex	0 = male, 1 = female
Number of children named on application	continuous
History of abuse in relationship	0 = no, 1 = yes
Presence of weapons	0 = no, 1 = yes
Previous court orders issued	0 = no, 1 = yes
"Physical/other abusive behaviours" category of abuse[a]	0 = not present, 1 = present
"Threatening behaviours" category of abuse[b]	0 = not present, 1 = present
Degree of stalking activity[c]	continuous
Magistrate conducting hearing[d]	categorical

Notes:

a   Category includes physical assault, emotional/psychological abuse, property damage, forced confinement, financial abuse, making false allegations about victim to authorities, sexual assault and abuse of pet(s).

b   Category includes threat of physical assault, threat to kill applicant or others named on application, unspecified threats, threat of respondent harming self or committing suicide, threat to kill relative or friend, threat to take children, threat of property damage, threat of harm to pet(s) and threat of sexual assault.

c   Number of different types of stalking experienced by victim (from stalking in the forms of unwanted communication, unwanted contact, watching or following, delivery of unwanted items, vandalism and monitoring victim's activities).

d   Coded categorically to avoid risking identity disclosure of individual magistrates.

these orders. Therefore, the parties who have the restrictions placed on them (typically men) are afraid that they will be subject to criminal charges of breach even though they are not the ones initiating the contact with the people who have obtained the orders. Applications made under these circumstances were dismissed with an explanation that the fear being experienced needs to be for their personal safety, not for fear of criminal sanctions.

A second variable shown as having an influence in cases of intimate partners is the category of threatening behaviours. This result indicates that when cases include evidence of threatening behaviours, orders are more than one-and-a-half (1.7) times more likely to be granted than in cases where these behaviours are not present. It is unclear why this category of behaviours reaches statistical significance in the model while the two categories of stalking behaviours and physical/other abusive behaviours do not.

Table 10.4: Model of Stalking by Intimate Partners†

Variables in the Equation	Exponent (B)
Respondent age	1.010
Victim sex	2.498**
Number of children named on application	1.081
History of abuse in relationship	.750
Presence of weapons	.450**
Previous court orders issued	.576*
"Physical/other abusive behaviours" category of abuse	1.564
"Threatening behaviours" category of abuse	1.669*
Degree of stalking activity	1.098
Magistrate conducting hearing	.923**

Notes:
*   Significant at the p <.10 level.
** Significant at the p <.05 level.
†   Omnibus tests of model coefficients significant at the p <.05 level.

Another statistically significant variable influencing the outcome of applications is the magistrate who conducts the hearing. It is not possible to present this finding in detail without the risk of disclosing the identity of individual magistrates; however, the model does indicate that the particular magistrate has a slight influence (.92) on whether or not an order is granted. While these data cannot explain the reason behind the differences in rulings of various magistrates, it is possibly a combination of factors involving how each magistrate interprets the wording in the *DVSA* and his/her own personal biases about the utility of protection orders in addressing the issues of domestic violence and stalking. Applicants interviewed as part of the larger RESOLVE study (forthcoming) expressed widely varying opinions of the magistrates they encountered, with their views being based primarily on the demeanour of the magistrates they dealt with.

> She is the only person who made me believe there is some empathy in the court system. ... I said, "I've been reporting, but because there wasn't a restraining order, the cops said there was nothing they could do" ... So she stayed [to process the order]. She didn't

leave until seven-thirty on a Friday night ... That made me feel like maybe somebody does listen.

She just looked totally disinterested ... I felt as though I'd interrupted her lunch. I felt as though I was inconveniencing her. She only spoke when she had to speak ... She didn't explain to me what she was doing when she left [to make her decision]. I'm standing there thinking, Well where the hell is she going? Do I go, do I stay? That's how I felt.

The magistrate upstairs was great, she was wonderful, totally. [S]he was listening to me, she made it more obvious that she was listening ... And you could see some emotion on her face, she wasn't cold [as she found the first magistrate she dealt with had been].

She was very thorough and not condescending ... just very matter-of-fact, which is fine with me ... It was practical, logical advice' ... She put on the protection order for the police to get my passport, things that I needed. That made sense.

The last case illustrates the important point that the role of a magistrate is not to act as a counsellor. While this woman understood this distinction and in fact welcomed it, this fact was lost on many of the applicants, and likely contributed to the impression held by some applicants that the magistrates appeared to be uncaring.

A fourth influential variable in protection order outcomes is whether or not previous court orders exist between the parties. In cases where previous court orders have been issued, applicants are approximately half as likely (.58) to have the protection order granted as in cases where no previous orders exist. Further analysis revealed that in many cases, this is due to the tendency of magistrates to turn down applications for protection orders when other segments of the civil justice system have already been involved in the case, or where criminal remedies are a possibility.

The final statistically significant variable having an influence in the logistic regression model is the presence of weapons. Cases where weapons are involved are about half as likely (.45) to result in an order being granted than cases where there is no evidence of weapons. Again, where there is sufficient evidence to suggest that action might be taken in other segments of the justice system, magistrates tend to turn down protection order applications.

Reasons for Dismissal

In cases where orders are turned down, magistrates explain the reason for dismissal on the record. As shown in Table 10.5, the most common reason cited for dismissing applications is that the victim does not require immediate protection (57.2%). This is a particularly troublesome reason because it was sometimes the case that orders were turned down because the applicant had fled to a women's shelter or some other place deemed safe by the magistrate, and therefore it was determined that the woman was not in immediate need of protection at the time of the hearing. This reason was also commonly cited when the respondent was temporarily out of town or incarcerated, and therefore the magistrate determined that the victim was safe for the time being. The recent amendments to the *DVSA* address this problem by directing the JPs hearing the orders to take into consideration not only the *immediate* need for the victim's protection but also the *imminent* need, with the intent of expanding the criteria that the JPs are to follow when making their decisions. It will be interesting to see how the amended text is interpreted under the newly worded legislation.

The second most common reason cited for turning down an order in this sample is insufficient evidence that domestic violence or stalking has occurred (53.3%). It was not uncommon to hear magistrates explain on the record that, while they believed the applicant was experiencing domestic abuse or stalking, they could not issue the order without being presented with compelling evidence of particular incidents. Given the emotional state of many of the victims during the application process, they are unable to clearly articulate the nature of abuse that has occurred and most have no one to assist them in preparing their evidence in a manner in which the magistrates believe can justify issuing an order. Under the recent changes to the *DVSA*, designated individuals are now being made available through various organizations dealing with domestic abuse in an effort to provide assistance to victims in preparing their evidence prior to the hearing.

Table 10.5: Reasons for Dismissal Cited in Protection Order Applications Dismissed (*N* = 180)

Reasons Cited	N	%
No immediate protection required	103	57.2%
Insufficient evidence that domestic violence or stalking occurred	96	53.3%
Too much time elapsed since the domestic violence or stalking occurred	55	30.6%
Relief sought is outside the magistrates' jurisdiction	21	11.7%
Respondent arrested on criminal charges with orders not to contact or communicate with the victim	8	4.4%
Cohabitation requirement not met (for domestic violence)	3	1.7%
Other (includes insufficient fear, other civil orders in place, isolated incidents of stalking, criminal charges pending, etc.)	15	8.3%
TOTAL	301	167.2%

Note: More than one reason for dismissal was cited in many cases, therefore figures total more than the 180 cases in which protection orders were dismissed, and percentages total more than 100.

It is hoped that the availability of these Protection Order Designates (PODs) will provide the support victims need to present more effective applications.

Almost one-third (30.6%) of the applications in this sample are dismissed because the magistrates determine that too much time has elapsed since the domestic violence or stalking occurred. The amount of time considered to be "too much" is surprisingly short in some cases, as indicated in Table 10.6. By combining the first three timeframes (from "less than one week" to "over two weeks to one month"), we see that in one-third (32.7%) of the cases where it is determined that too much time has elapsed, the time considered to be excessive falls within one month or less of when the abuse had occurred. The reason this is particularly problematic is that victims frequently are not in a position to apply for these orders until after they flee the abusive situation (often moving into an emergency shelter), become settled in their new surroundings, obtain domestic violence counselling and/or legal advice and receive information on how to go about applying for this type of order. The time it takes for these things to occur is

Table 10.6: Amount of Time Elapsed Since the Abuse or Stalking Occurred in Cases Not Granted because Too Much Time Had Elapsed

Time frame	N	%
Less than one week	2	3.6%
One to two weeks	10	18.2%
Over two weeks to one month	6	10.9%
Over one month to six months	13	23.6%
Over six months to one year	3	5.5%
Over one year	6	10.9%
Time not specified	15	27.3%
TOTAL	55	100%

typically from one to several weeks following the most recent episode of abuse. In recognition of this problematic reason for dismissal, section 6(1) of the *DVSA* has been changed as part of the recent legislative amendments. These amendments are designed in part to address the restrictive wording that existed in the former version of the legislation. Again, it will be interesting to see the impact these legislative amendments have on the outcome of protection order applications in terms of broadening the criteria being considered by the JPs when conducting the hearings.

In a smaller percentage of cases resulting in dismissal, the relief being sought by victims is beyond the jurisdiction of the magistrate (11.7%). Examples of where this can occur are situations where there are custody orders already put in place by a higher court judge that allow the respondent to have contact and communication with the applicant for purposes of child access, or where the applicant is requesting that he or she be given sole occupancy of the home before such decisions have been considered by the proper higher authority.

Orders are turned down because the respondent has been arrested on criminal charges in 4.4% of dismissed applications. In these cases the magistrates are often reluctant to issue another order because they believe that if the respondent is unwilling to abide by one type of order, another one will not likely have any deterrent effect.[7]

A very small percentage of applications in this sample (1.7%) are dismissed partly because the cohabitation requirement is not met. This pertains to applications where there is evidence of both stalking and domestic violence, the order cannot be issued on the basis of stalking due to insufficient evidence *and* the magistrate cannot consider evidence of domestic violence because that type of abuse requires the parties to meet the definition of cohabitants as laid out in the *DVSA*. Now that the legislation has been opened up in that regard by including dating relationships as well as certain other relationships of non-cohabitation (such as a grandparent and grandchild who have never resided together), this reason for dismissal will no longer be as likely to occur under the revised act.[8]

In many cases where protection orders are denied, victims are being redirected to alternative remedies where those exist. Often, the alternative remedy is to seek relief through the Court of Queen's Bench. While this may indeed be the appropriate avenue for matters beyond the jurisdiction of a JP, there can be lengthy delays in securing legal representation and preparing the proper filing documents. Victims may be particularly vulnerable during this time, pointing to the value of having advocates work with them to help them safely negotiate through the various channels.

With respect to alternative remedies under the criminal law, there is an "either/or" mindset in some cases. That is, while the intent of civil legislation is that it can be used in a complementary fashion to the criminal law, there is pressure to seek criminal intervention where evidence exists that would support a charge. However, as evidenced in the qualitative interviews conducted with victims as part of the larger RESOLVE study (forthcoming), there are women who are reluctant to call police for a variety of reasons, such as being afraid of retaliation by the offender, revealing their own involvement in the gang or drug culture or having had previous negative experiences with police. Many of these women wanted to use the civil law system as a first step in attempting to curtail the activities, that is, as a measured response to the abuse they were experiencing. To clarify, they wanted to allow the abuser or stalker the opportunity to cease the offensive behaviour before resorting to criminal sanctions. Women who are advised by the magistrate to contact the police may simply return to an unsafe situation rather than bring the matter to the police. The spirit of the legislation is being usurped when there is resistance to using the civil law and criminal law in a complementary fashion. Perhaps complementary usage will occur more often with the newly worded act, in that the relaxed wording might be more likely to result in an order being granted even when other alternatives exist.

Service providers interviewed for the RESOLVE study (forthcoming) discussed the difficulty in obtaining orders on the basis of stalking and described the detrimental effects to their clients of being turned down. As one crisis shelter worker explained, "[T]hey're denied, and they say to us, 'I will never go through that process again, I don't care if he comes to try to kill me, I will never go through that process again.'" The stalking victims interviewed in that study confirmed this reaction, using terms such as "devastated," "powerless" and "very, very scared" when describing how they felt when their applications were dismissed.

The Value of Obtaining a Protection Order: Is it "Just a Piece of Paper"?

The findings presented here have illustrated that obtaining civil protective relief under the *DVSA* is not an easy task — the threshold for obtaining these orders is very high, indeed. An important question is: Even if orders are issued in greater numbers, how valuable are these "pieces of paper" in providing relief from domestic violence and stalking? The interviews conducted with women in the RESOLVE study (forthcoming) speak to this question. Of the 12 protection orders issued in that sample, three-quarters (75%) of them were breached. However, three (25%) of those breaches were not of a nature that caused the women to fear for their safety. Not surprisingly, the women for whom the orders had effectively curtailed the offenders' activities reported satisfaction with the orders. The women whose former partners had breached the orders, but not in a manner that caused them to fear for their safety, also found the orders to be effective to some degree, stating that at least the problematic behaviours that led to them seeking the orders had subsided. Interestingly, even the women who reported that breaches had occurred, and which made them fear for their safety, said that they found some degree of satisfaction with having obtained the protection orders. Some valued the fact that the problems they were experiencing were being validated by the magistrates issuing the orders. For others, it was simply that they believed these orders sent a strong message to the offenders that this type of behaviour was not acceptable. Therefore, it would appear from the qualitative findings that women who obtain these orders do indeed benefit from them, albeit to varying degrees. This knowledge contributes to the debate in the feminist literature over the appropriateness of using the justice system in dealing with violence against women (see chapters 1 and 4 in this volume). I contend that civil orders represent an important component in the overall response from the justice system in addressing stalking by former intimate partners.

Looking Ahead

As indicated throughout this chapter, a number of concerns identified with respect to the tight criteria used by magistrates have been addressed through the recent legislative amendments to the *DVSA* (for a complete description of these amendments, see Manitoba Justice, 2005a). These changes to the legislation are intended to provide victims with a greater likelihood of being successful in their protection order applications. An important finding previously identified had to do with the disparity among the various magistrates in their rulings. Along with the changes to the legislation came training sessions for the newly designated judicial justices of the peace (JJPs), which were designed, in part, to clarify the wording in the amended legislation. While those hired in the new positions came largely from the existing pool of magistrates, one would assume that all JJPs came away from the training sessions with a similar interpretation of the criteria to be used in their rulings. It is possible, therefore, that there will be less disparity as a result of the training.

The most common reason for dismissal identified in this sample was that the magistrates found no immediate need for protection. Now that the *imminent* need is to be considered in addition to the *immediate* need for the victim's protection, orders should be issued more often in cases where the applicant is safe for the time being, for reasons such as having fled to a women's shelter or some other place deemed safe by the magistrate, or when the respondent is temporarily unable to make contact with the victim.

A promising amendment was the one appointing PODs from victim services agencies to assist applicants in applying for protection. This should address another common reason for dismissal, that of insufficient evidence to support the granting of an order. Obtaining a protection order is a daunting task, and even the most articulate applicants have difficulty expressing themselves effectively when under the degree of stress that violence and stalking provoke. Having supportive individuals available to provide victims with suggestions on how to clearly convey their experiences in their applications will very likely result in more orders being granted. This advocacy will reap additional benefits as well. As explained in the training sessions being offered to PODs (Manitoba Justice, 2005b), successful applicants also need to be cautioned against adopting a false sense of security as a result of obtaining the orders, and to be given advice on safety planning in the event the order is breached. Even more importantly, however, is what this type of advocacy can contribute for those whose orders are dismissed. Victims need to be prepared for the possibility that the order will not be granted and have a backup plan in place. They need validation that even though they may not meet the criteria for having the order issued, the violence or stalking they are experiencing is a serious concern. Women who have suffered the effects of violence and stalking in their lives often have a myriad of problems to contend with, which requires a multi-faceted approach. The agencies offering the services of PODs are experienced in addressing problems such as poverty and inadequate housing that, for many applicants, cannot be disentangled from the abuse they experience.

The amended wording in the legislation should allow for situations where a period of time has elapsed since the most recent incident, as long as the applicant can demonstrate that the abuse or stalking has occurred and that there is a reasonable likelihood it will resume. This will hopefully address cases where previously the abuse or stalking had to have occurred within a very short period of time prior to when the application was made, sometimes within only one or two weeks.

This research can serve as a baseline from which to gauge the recent changes with respect to the outcome of applications, the utilization rates and the factors involved in making a successful application for victims who seek protective relief under the amended *DVSA*. Preliminary data on application outcomes since the changes to the act took effect are presented in the paragraph below; however, readers are cautioned that it is too soon to make definitive statements about these figures, for several reasons. First, these data reflect Winnipeg protection order applications overall rather than for a sample such as mine that was selected specifically on the basis of stalking. Secondly, at the time of this writing, the figures for applications granted and dismissed were only available for the first 12 months following the amendments. Given that it takes time for staff to learn new procedures and for interpretations of amended wording to be worked out by those hearing the orders, it will be difficult to identify the true effect of the changes for some time. Furthermore, even though the PODs received training about the legislation, they will need practical experience in assisting their clients through the process before they gain a complete understanding of how best to assist them. Moreover, many variables in addition to the raw outcome data need to be taken into consideration to accurately judge the true effects of the amendments and the experiences of the victims in the process of engaging with this segment of the justice system.

The figures for Winnipeg hearings conducted over the 12 months preceding the amendments (November 2004 through October 2005) are available to compare to the following 12 month period (November 2005 through October 2006) to gain a preliminary sense of the changes. The proportion of orders granted increased by only four percentage points between the two time frames (from 45% to 49% respectively). While that does not immediately appear to be a significant increase in orders being issued, this was accompanied by an 81% surge in the number of applications being made (from 545 over the earlier period to 986 in the 12 months following the amendments). In terms of real numbers, 488 protection orders were issued in the period following the amendments, twice as many as the 244 that were granted over the previous 12 months (personal communication, senior official of Manitoba Justice, December 15, 2006).

Again, only time and ongoing analysis will reveal the true effects of the legislative amendments and, therefore, future research is called for that can build on the present findings. Additional research can also delve into areas where there are gaps in this research. In particular, these findings only examine protection order applications made in Winnipeg. It is important to examine the experience of rural and northern women in applying for protection under the *DVSA*. In addition, data collection could be expanded to gather information on the extent to which PODs are utilized, to what extent they have a bearing on application outcomes and the degree to which they are providing other types of assistance to victims that they may not have accessed had they not contacted a POD for assistance in making a protection order application.

Conclusion

The conditions underlying whether or not protection orders are issued on the basis of stalking are very complex. Besides the potential physical risks to victims experiencing escalating acts of violence, we have also seen the devastating effects stalking can have on one's psychological well-being. Given the severity of the consequences of stalking, the lengths it takes for most victims to seek help and the value successful applicants ascribe to obtaining these orders, it is imperative that ongoing efforts are taken to monitor protection order utilization in Manitoba. Only through continued scrutiny will victims of this serious social problem be assured de jure and de facto accessibility to this important form of intervention.

Notes

1   The use of the word "victim" is controversial in domestic violence discourse because that terminology portrays women as passive recipients of legal intervention instead of as active agents negotiating among various options in dealing with their abusive partners (see Lewis et al., 2001). However, that term will be used throughout this chapter to remain consistent with the language used in much of the literature on stalking. The term "applicant" is also used interchangeably with the word "victim" in this chapter.

2   Prohibition orders could contain no-contact provisions and were obtained through the Court of Queen's Bench under the *Family Maintenance Act*. The assistance of a lawyer was recommended in applying for an order and to represent the victim in court. These orders were therefore difficult to obtain. Non-molestation orders were available through a magistrate and were available quickly and without cost. However, non-molestation orders only contained wording that prohibited the offender from "molesting, annoying or harassing" the victim, and could not prohibit the victim's partner from going to the victim's residence or any other premises. Non-molestation and prohibition orders were available only to individuals who had been married or had been cohabiting with the offender being named in the order. Therefore, many relationships were not included under

the former civil remedies. For example, a victim of stalking who knew the stalker only casually, and victims who had been involved in a dating relationship (but had never cohabitated with the offender) were unable to access these orders. The only available remedy in these cases was to obtain a peace bond under section 810 of the Criminal Code; however, these are difficult to obtain due to the requirement that the offender consents to enter into this no-contact agreement.

3   The respondent is the person who the applicant is seeking protection from. Throughout this chapter the terms respondent, offender, stalker and abuser will be used interchangeably.

4   In circumstances where speedy processing is warranted by an urgent need for protection, prevention orders may be heard on an expedited basis.

5   In some cases the parent making the application does not fear that the respondent poses a danger to the children. In other cases there may already be a higher court order awarding the other parent custody or visitation, and the applicant is advised that unless there is evidence of abuse by the respondent against the children, the protection order will not be issued for the children.

6   At the time of data collection for this project, magistrates were designated for this purpose. Therefore, the term "magistrate" is used in this chapter. However, it should be noted that amendments to *The Provincial Court Act* (Legislative Assembly of Manitoba, 2005b) took effect on May 29, 2006, and changed this designation from magistrates to judicial justices of the peace (JJPs).

7   This reason was a source of frustration with some of the key respondents working within the justice system who were interviewed in the qualitative portion of the larger RESOLVE study (forthcoming). These individuals believed the layering of various no-contact orders issued through both the criminal and civil courts provides the police with an opportunity to charge offenders with multiple counts of breach of court orders, and this in turn provides the Crown with additional leverage when negotiating plea agreements with defense counsel.

8   There may still be cases involving relationships that do not meet the definition (for example, violence occurring between a caregiver and a patient).

CHAPTER ELEVEN

Domestic Violence and Child Custody Disputes: *The Need for a New Framework for the Family Court*[1]

Peter G. Jaffe, Claire V. Crooks and Nick Bala

Over the past twenty years, domestic violence has been recognized as a crime in Canada, with police forces adopting policies for mandatory charging in any cases where a police officer believes domestic violence has occurred. Crown attorneys have special training and procedures to prosecute these cases. Across Canada, there are specialized services connected to the criminal courts that include victim and witness support programs and access to community services for abuse victims, perpetrators and children exposed to violence.

A growing body of social science research shows there is a wide range of violence in separating and divorced families. Some of it is severe and ongoing, perpetrated largely by males who should be identified as "batterers"; in many other cases, it can be attributed to poor conflict-resolution skills by the both partners, or the violence may be a response limited to the trauma and stress inherent in the separation, perpetrated by either or both males and females (Johnston & Campbell, 1993). In this chapter we focus on battering, which is characterized by an abuser engaging in an ongoing pattern of violence, intimidation and control that creates fear and helps the abuser maintain dominance over an intimate partner. While all domestic violence is a serious concern, the battering cases typically pose the greatest risks for victim spouses and children.

Despite improvements in the criminal court system for victims of domestic violence, victims may experience a less responsive system when they enter the Family Court to deal with disputes over child custody and access. Part of the problem lies in the philosophy of the Family Court, which encourages parents to resolve conflicts by putting the past behind them. Separating parents are rightfully being supported to move past their differences and focus on the best interests of their children as co-parents. While this approach is appropriate for the non-violent majority, it is often contraindicated for abuse victims, for whom the past may inform their safety planning and attempts to limit contact with the perpetrator. When domestic violence concerns are present, a different approach is required.

The growing support for co-parenting and the growing awareness of domestic violence are on a collision course when it is time for Family Court and when court-related professionals, such as lawyers and custody assessors who assist parents in settling their differences about post-separation parenting arrangements, become involved. While the majority of separating. parents may be able to work out a co-parenting (joint custody) plan, those parents with a history of domestic violence may need different resolutions. These resolutions could involve limited, supervised or no contact with children for the abusive parent, depending on the safety concerns for the children as well as the non-offending parent. Some advocates of co-parenting are concerned that many of the parents who raise concerns about domestic violence are making false or exaggerated claims of abuse to further their desire to not share their children with their ex-spouse or to gain a tactical advantage in the litigation of, for example, possession of the home. There are legitimate issues related to proof of claims of spousal abuse, but it should be appreciated that denial and minimization of abuse by genuine abusers are more common than false or exaggerated claims of spousal abuse by alleged victims (Shaffer & Bala, 2004; Johnston, et al., 2005). The need for proper assessment and investigation into all claims is essential to ensure that appropriate parenting arrangements are matched to each family's circumstances.

The search for ideal co-parenting arrangements after separation and the search for child and parent safety and accountability after domestic violence represent two solitudes. The purpose of this chapter is to bridge the gap between these two solitudes. We discuss a model of how to consider findings of domestic violence in child custody and access disputes as well as the critical role of court-related resources, training and collaboration amongst professionals in the field.

Why is Spousal Abuse Relevant to Post-Separation Parenting Arrangements?

A finding of child maltreatment has long been recognized as a critical factor to consider in determining post-separation parenting arrangements and possible child protection intervention. The child protection movement has a long history of debating the role and threshold for state intervention and for promoting safe contact with formerly abusive parents whenever possible. In contrast, it has largely been only within the last decade that legal and mental health professionals have acknowledged that spousal violence is relevant to the determination of child custody and access. Prior to this time, spousal violence was seen as an adult issue not relevant to the best interests of children. It was believed that a man could be a violent spouse but still be a "good father." Many groups have challenged this notion and encouraged legislative reform to recognize domestic violence as a critical factor to consider in these cases (e.g., National Council of Juvenile and Family Court Judges, 1994; American Psychological Association, 1998; Bala et al., 1998).

There have been significant legislative changes in the U.S., Australia and New Zealand to reflect domestic abuse concerns in post-separation parenting (and the accompanying challenges) (Jaffe & Crooks, 2004). Major program initiatives have been undertaken such as the U.S. Department of Justice's Safe Havens Project, which provides funding and technical assistance for supervised visitation in cases of domestic violence, and new guidelines for judges for using custody evaluations in cases that involve domestic violence (Dalton, Drozd & Wong, 2004). Although all provinces recognize domestic violence as a societal problem, only Ontario, Alberta, Newfoundland and Labrador, and the Northwest Territories have enacted legislation that require the courts to consider spousal violence when making custody and access decisions. Legislation in other provinces is more general, leaving it up to judges to use their discretion to determine the relevance of domestic violence in custody outcomes.

The rationale for legal and programmatic changes that include spousal violence as a relevant factor in determining the appropriate post-separation parenting arrangement include the following:

- *Spousal abuse often does not end with separation.* Research has shown that physical abuse, stalking and harassment continue at significant rates post-separation, and may become more severe, especially when the violence in the relationship is perpetrated by an abusive batterer (Hotton, 2001; Statistics Canada, 2001; Liss & Stahly, 1993). Promoting contact between children and a violent ex-spouse may create an opportunity for renewed domestic violence through visitation and exchanges of children (Sheeran & Hampton, 1999; Jaffe, Crooks & Poisson, 2003).

- *High overlap between spousal violence and child abuse.* The presence of domestic violence is a red flag for the co-existence of child maltreatment. In Edleson's (1999b) review of studies investigating this overlap, between 30% and 60% of children whose mothers had been assaulted by their male partners were themselves likely to be abused. Spousal violence in itself may be harmful to child development and may leave children with significant emotional and behavioural problems (Jaffe, Baker & Cunningham, 2004; Cunningham & Baker, 2004).

- *Batterers are poor role models.* Children's socialization with respect to relationships and conflict-resolution is negatively affected by exposure to a perpetrator of domestic violence. When children witness one parent assaulting the other or using threats of violence to maintain control within a relationship, their own expectations about relationships may come to parallel these observations (Bancroft & Silverman, 2002).

- *Victims of domestic violence may be undermined in their parenting role.* Perpetrators of spousal violence may undermine their (ex-)partner's parenting in a range of obvious and more insidious ways (Jaffe & Crooks, 2005). For example, male perpetrators may blame the children's mother for the dissolution of the family or even explicitly instruct the children not to listen to her directions (Bancroft & Silverman, 2002). Intervention with these fathers requires that this facet of their parenting be addressed; fathers need to both recognize the ways in which they undermine the mothers' authority and commit to stopping these behaviours (Scott & Crooks, 2004).

- *Perpetrators may use litigation as a form of ongoing control and harassment.* The Family Court litigation process can become a tool for batterers to continue their abusive behaviour in a new forum (Jaffe, Crooks & Poisson, 2003). Litigation exacts a high emotional and financial price for abused women already overwhelmed with the aftermath of a violent relationship. Several authors have suggested that some batterers have the social skills to present themselves positively in court and convince assessors and judges to award them custody (Bowermaster & Johnson, 1998; Zorza, 1995).

- *In extreme cases, spousal violence following separation is lethal.* Domestic violence and homicides are inextricably linked. National figures from the Canada and the U.S. suggest that women are at a greater risk of homicide from estranged partners with a prior history of domestic violence than when they remain in an intimate abusive relationship (Fox & Zawitz, 1999; Statistics Canada, 2001; Websdale, 2003). The growing literature linking domestic violence, separation and homicide has raised awareness of the need for prompt police reaction and careful investigation of post-separation violence and stalking. To assist with this work, risk assessment tools have been developed (Campbell, 1995; Campbell, Sharps & Glass, 2001). There have been many advances in Canadian research and practice in this area, including the work of Kropp and his colleagues in British Columbia, who developed the Spousal Assault Risk Assessment (SARA) (Kropp et al., 1994, 2000) and the Ontario Domestic Assault Risk Assessment (ODARA) developed by researchers in Ontario (Hilton et al., 2004). In these extreme cases, children may become involved as witnesses to homicides or become homicide victims themselves (Websdale, Town & Johnson, 1999; Ontario Domestic Violence Death Review Committee, 2004). Child abduction represents another traumatic outcome in these cases, illustrating a batterer's ultimate desire for control after separation and punishment of his ex-partner.

- *Domestic violence may negatively affect the victim's parenting capacity.* Victims of spousal abuse may experience depression, low self-esteem and substance use difficulties, all of which can compromise their parenting. However, for many of these parents, separation from the perpetrator of domestic violence may lead to improvement in both general functioning and parenting. During the court process, these parents may present more negatively than they will in the future, once the stress of the proceedings and life change has attenuated (see Jaffe & Crooks, 2005).

In summary, spousal violence is an important area of inquiry to address in making post-separation parenting arrangements. A history of spousal violence, especially one that involves a battering relationship, demands a different approach from that taken in most cases. Legal and mental health professionals need a paradigm shift, and when making determinations about the best interests of a child must consider information about spousal violence, even if this requires resolution of competing allegations about the nature of a relationship. In the face of a real threat, a mother who lives in fear of her abusive ex-partner is not paranoid. Rather, her seemingly suspicious and distrustful attitude is based on a history of abuse and violence, and attempts to closely monitor the relationship between her children and their father are appropriate safeguards.

The majority of separating parents make arrangements for the care of their children without the need to go to court or have an assessment by a mental health professional; but in cases where spousal violence is a concern, greater professional involvement and support is required. When parents express concerns about their safety and their children's safety, the issue must be closely examined.

Trying to understand the dynamics that lead to a marital breakdown can be a highly complex undertaking. When children are involved and their future care is at stake, intense emotions can cloud parents' portrayal of the marriage to an independent third party, such as a police officer, assessor or judge. There are strong psychological tendencies on the part of abusers to deny or minimize the abuse, as well as tendencies to colour one's perceptions of responsibility for the breakdown of the relationship.

The resolution of disagreements about post-separation arrangements for children may take a number of different pathways. Many parents are able to develop amicable co-parenting arrangements without court intervention, but in other cases, the nature of the conflict and the potential existence of domestic violence should be investigated by the court in order to ensure the safety of women and their children.

Even in domestic violence cases, there is a range of methods of resolving disagreements that need not include the formal court system. In some cases, abusers may leave the jurisdiction or move on to other relationships, showing no interest in maintaining an ongoing relationship with their former partner or children. In other cases, a spousal abuse victim may flee for her safety and the perpetrator takes no action to pursue her and their children. In some cases, the perpetrator may reappear years after separation when ordered to provide child support and try to re-establish a relationship with the children and some custodial rights in order to avoid this financial commitment. In one survey of abuse victims, some avoided any engagement with their perpetrator over financial- or child-related issues by ignoring their legal rights and entitlement (e.g., living in poverty was seen as preferable to living with ongoing violence and harassment) (Jaffe, Crooks & Poisson, 2003).

In some cases, there is police and criminal justice system involvement when there is ample evidence of a pattern of battering and child abuse. With the growing awareness of family violence issues, in cases where serious violence concerns are clearly documented, the criminal and Family Courts will generally terminate or suspend contact between the abuser and his children, though the protection of victims and their children by court orders can be very difficult to effect. Perhaps the cases that pose the most significant challenges to legal and mental health professionals in the Family Court system are ones in which the parties present diametrically opposed versions of their relationship, post-separation events and abuse issues.

Assessing Domestic Violence Allegations

The ultimate decision about what happens to disputes before the courts rests with a judge who hears the evidence and determines the validity of the allegations. Judges and lawyers may give significant weight to independent third-party mental health professionals who prepare custody assessments (or evaluations) based on interviews with all of the parties, collateral information from community professionals and psychological testing. All court-related professionals are involved in an assessment process, whether it is a formal or informal exercise, in gathering and weighing relevant information about the individual parents and children in the dispute.

To understand the context for these assessments, it is important to be cognizant of the current climate in Family Courts (Jaffe & Crooks, 2004). Family Court judges generally want cases settled in a cost-efficient and timely manner by pre-court interventions, such as mediation and settlement conferences. Judges and lawyers often encourage parents to co-operate with each other, often suggesting that this is synonymous with the promotion of their children's best interests. It is true that *in cases in which domestic violence is not at issue,* children generally benefit from having their parents resolve their differences in a co-operative and non-adversarial fashion. Common wisdom in the divorce field suggests that the "friendly parent," that is, the parent who is best able to promote a relationship between the child(ren) and the other parent, is more appropriate for a custodial role, and this is reflected in provisions like Canada's *Divorce Act,* section 16(10). Unfortunately, the friendly parent concept can be misleading in cases where the "lack of friendliness" is a response to abusive and violent behaviour (Jaffe, Crooks & Poisson, 2003).

Domestic violence allegations raised in the context of parental separation are often met with skepticism and a concern that the allegation is being utilized to limit the involvement of the other parent, especially if there has *not* been significant police and criminal justice system involvement. The making of abuse allegations can be a double-edged sword for abuse victims. If the allegations are proven in court, the victim and her children could find a degree of safety, with recent legal reforms and improvements in community resources providing a greater degree of safety than in the past. However, if the allegations appear unfounded and are considered by the judge to have been made "maliciously," an abuse victim could lose custody. In some of these cases, the response of a father to an allegation of spousal abuse is to claim that the mother is trying to "alienate" the children from him. In reality, it is often abusive men who attempt to alienate children from their mothers after separation by engaging in a campaign of denigration, which continues the pattern of verbal abuse that began prior to separation. Clearly a thorough assessment of abuse allegations is warranted as part of a Family Court decision-making process, given the high stakes of a finding of domestic violence.

A psychologist or social worker who is assessing a case involving allegations of domestic violence should identify whether there are patterns of behaviour as opposed to isolated incidents. Incidents of abuse that in isolation seem less severe, may give rise to greater concerns if they fit within a larger pattern of abuse and domination. A multi-method, multi-informant approach is required. Figure 11.1 identifies the additional elements of assessment for cases where either party has made allegations of violence. The first layer of the pyramid identifies the principal elements of a custody and access assessment in a typical case, including understanding the children's individual needs, the parents' skills, the ability of the parents to co-operate and the developmental considerations of any parenting plan. In a high-conflict case, these initial assessment domains are still pertinent; however, the second layer of the pyramid identifies additional concerns, such as the history of the parental conflict, children's coping strategies and the identification of the less toxic parent. In high-conflict cases involving domestic violence, the assessment challenges are significantly increased, as it is also necessary to consider such issues as the risk of recurrence of violence, including homicide risk assessment, and to understand the impact of the violence on the children.

To competently complete this final layer of assessment, practitioners must be aware of indicators pointing to the danger of homicide. These risk factors have emerged from research and domestic violence death review committees, which have identified characteristics most closely associated with lethal violence (see Campbell, 1995; Campbell, Sharp & Glass, 2001; Kropp et al., 1994; Kropp et al., 2000; Hilton et al., 2004). Commonly reported factors include separation in a relationship where there has been a history of battering; access to firearms; substance abuse; post-separation stalking; threats of homicide or suicide; and violations of previous court orders. The Ontario Domestic Violence Death Review Committee (2004) contains a more detailed review of this literature.

In conducting an assessment where domestic violence has been alleged, collecting all of the information is a complex process. Every assessment should include individual interviews with both parents on more than one occasion. While perpetrators can present themselves as very reasonable individuals on one or two occasions, interviewing them over time, and challenging their perspective on the basis of other information that has been gathered, can provide the assessor with the opportunity to see past the veneer. Another important element in an assessment is the giving of a

FIGURE 11.1: Child Custody — Specialized Assessment Needs in Spousal Violence Cases

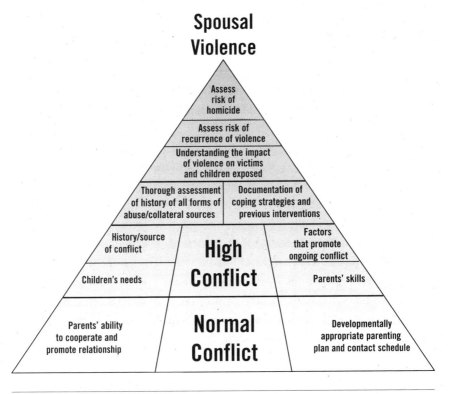

Adapted from Jaffe & Crooks (2006).

structured inventory instrument to each parent that records the frequency and severity of physical, sexual, verbal and psychological abusive behaviour experienced by each partner as well as the injuries suffered (e.g., Abusive Behaviour Observation Checklist in Dutton, 1992). A follow-up interview on the abuse inventory is helpful for ascertaining the context of the abuse. For example, assessors should gain an understanding of the impact of the abuse on the victim, his/her coping styles, disclosures to friends, family and professionals, and the effects of the violence on the children.

Given that the determination of the validity of claims, counterclaims and denials is an important element of the assessment process, obtaining collateral information to substantiate or refute the reports of the parents is critical. Therefore, the assessor should include interviews with professionals who may have been involved with the family, including a review of records (police, child protection, emergency room physicians, etc.). Emphasis on this documentation is not meant to imply that allegations of domestic violence are credible only if there is third-party evidence; indeed, many spousal abuse victims do not disclose to other professionals or involve the police. Rather, it is important to review this documentation in cases where it does exist, while remaining mindful that a lack of such evidence does not imply fabrication.

It is also important to keep the needs of the children foremost in the assessment. It is essential to include interviews with the children to ascertain their understandings and observations of events and how exposure to violence has affected them. Those individuals who come into contact with the children should also be interviewed (e.g., teachers, doctors, counsellors) in case the children disclosed what they witnessed or experienced to them. As with the reports of the parents and relatives, the reports of children need to be treated with caution; in some cases children, especially adolescents, will identify with an abusive parent and minimize the abuse or blame the victim.

Analyzing the information gathered requires an understanding of domestic violence. For example, although a prevailing belief of some professionals may be that women lie or exaggerate claims of abuse, research reveals that spousal abuse victims often minimize or are reluctant to disclose the extent of abuse that they endure. For example, in one study based on interviews with abused women, they reported that they rarely volunteered information about sexual abuse by their partner. Their reluctance stemmed from feelings of personal embarrassment, lack of trust or rapport with the professional and the concern that the professional could not handle the information (Jaffe, Crooks & Poisson, 2003). This finding supports the importance of asking direct questions about a range of abusive behaviours, as victims may be reluctant to volunteer sensitive information. Perpetrators of domestic violence often deny or minimize the abuse as part of their skill in avoiding responsibility for their behaviour and externalizing blame for any difficulties (Bancroft & Silverman, 2002).

Without a careful domestic violence analysis, these allegations may be misunderstood as more of "he said/she said" perspectives on a relationship often found in high-conflict divorce. Once domestic violence has been identified and understood, this analysis should provide the context for assessing other information, such as communication patterns between the partners. For example, a mother who avoids phone contact with an abusive ex-partner might be seen as neglecting her duties to inform him/her about the children's activities; however, within the context of domestic violence, this same behaviour can be understood as an attempt to protect herself and her children from further harassment and abuse.

Strategies for Intervention

Intervening in child-related disputes where there is a history of spousal violence is a complex undertaking. In dealing with abusive parents there may be a range of responses that may change over time, depending on the availability of appropriate services and documented changes in the abuser's behaviour.

Within the Family Court system, judges have to consider a range of options in dealing with a violent spouse. These options include no contact, supervised visitation, supervised exchanges, exchanges in a public place, unsupervised visitation, liberal and regular visitation, and joint custody/co-parenting. (Many jurisdictions have dropped the term "custody" in favour of "parenting arrangement" and "residential parent"; similar changes were proposed for the reform of Canada's *Divorce Act* [Bill C-22]. However, these changes have not been enacted to date by the federal government. Some provinces did proceed to amend provincial legislation consistent with the proposed federal changes. See, for example, the new Alberta *Family Law Act*.) Beyond the basic legal terminology, in spousal violence cases the court should make detailed orders that deal with a range of issues such as the length of a visit, advisability of overnight access, determination of suitable supervisors and safe locations for exchanges.

As noted, all of these options exist within a culture that promotes parental co-operation and shared parenting as much as possible. The number of separating parents who enter into some form of joint custody has been steadily increasing, with over 40% of parents who divorced in Canada having some type of shared parenting or joint custody (Statistics Canada, 2004). In our experience, most of these cases are a result of situations in which parents have chosen this arrangement in a process of negotiation or mediation, with only a relatively small number having been imposed by a court. Joint custody is often the best arrangement for children, but it can be very problematic in high-conflict cases, and will most likely be inappropriate (if not dangerous) in high-conflict cases where there are domestic violence concerns.

Figure 11.2 tries to capture this reality with the analogy of a highway leading to co-parenting in which domestic violence cases need an off-ramp to avoid being carried along with the traffic. It is a schematic diagram portraying the broad picture. A more fine-grained analysis of specific considerations within a history of domestic violence is discussed later in this chapter. At the broad level, a history of domestic violence contraindicates co-parenting. Whereas the majority of families can benefit from educational programs and mediation, in cases where there are domestic violence concerns, there is a need for specialized intervention, including supervised visitation, batterer's intervention and support services for children. Dispute resolution processes that require victims and perpetrators to be together in mediation or settlement conferences have the potential to endanger victims or intimidate them into accepting inappropriate parenting arrangements, such as co-parenting, which may pose a risk to their safety or the safety of their children.

High-conflict cases involving couples without a history of domestic violence also require specialized intervention. Even if there are no physical safety concerns, children's exposure to ongoing parental conflict is clearly emotionally harmful.

Parallel parenting may be an option in high-conflict cases without domestic violence issues, as well as for a limited number of domestic violence cases where the abuse is minor, historical and does not represent a pattern of behaviour. Parallel parenting arrangements give each parent responsibility for the child while in his/her care, and usually include specific directions to minimize contact and communication between the parents. Responsibility for major decisions, such as schooling, is given to one of the parents, with no expectation of joint decision-making. Parallel parenting is premised on each parent being capable of meeting their children's needs by themselves, but the parents are unable to co-operate. Each parent is accepted as being a beneficial influence for the child, but any expectation of collaboration between the parents is futile and potentially harmful for the children.

Some high-conflict couples can, with appropriate therapeutic intervention and the passage of time, be helped to achieve more amicable parenting arrangements. Thus, for some families, parallel parenting may be a transition phase to bridge the troubled waters of a high-conflict separation; for other families parallel parenting may be all that is possible on a long-term basis.

FIGURE 11.2: Differentiated Custody Interventions in Spousal Violence Cases

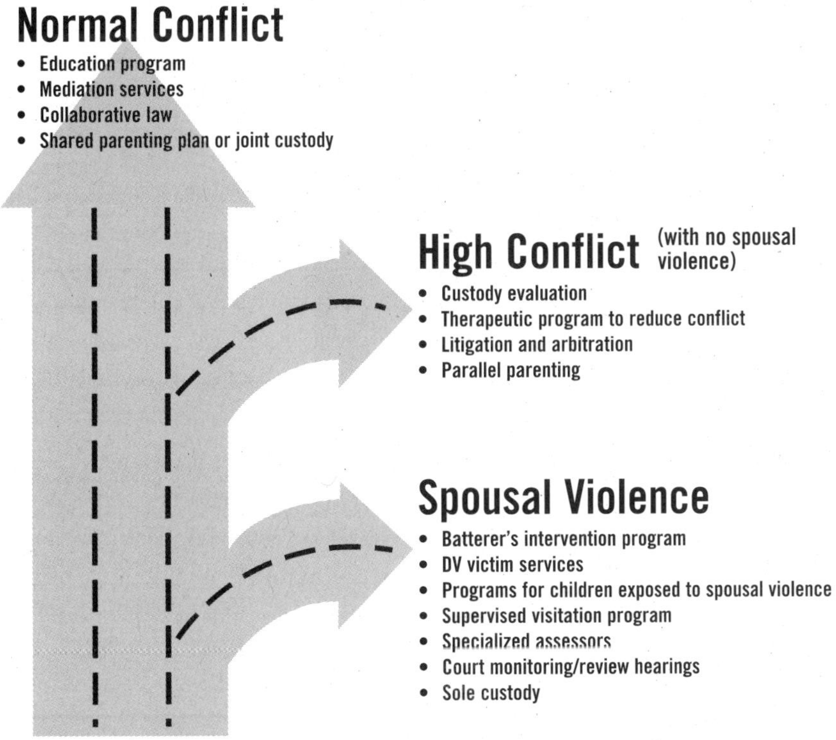

Normal Conflict
- Education program
- Mediation services
- Collaborative law
- Shared parenting plan or joint custody

High Conflict (with no spousal violence)
- Custody evaluation
- Therapeutic program to reduce conflict
- Litigation and arbitration
- Parallel parenting

Spousal Violence
- Batterer's intervention program
- DV victim services
- Programs for children exposed to spousal violence
- Supervised visitation program
- Specialized assessors
- Court monitoring/review hearings
- Sole custody

Adapted from Jaffe & Crooks (2006).

The Gap Between Theory and Practice

There has been an increase in awareness and training programs to assist various professionals in becoming more sensitive to the dynamics of domestic violence and more skilled in intervention strategies, but there is significant variation in the extent to which professionals in different locations have actually changed their attitudes and practices. It is clear that, until relatively recently, most professionals working in the justice system did not adequately appreciate the effects of spousal abuse on children who witnessed violence or lived in homes where it occurred; but over the past decade there has been more research and education about this issue. Nonetheless, there seems to be a gap between theory and practice, and evidence of widespread systemic change remains inconclusive at best.

In a study of family law cases in New Brunswick between 1998 and 2001, Neilson (2004) found that many mediators, family lawyers and judges still did not appreciate the effects of spousal abuse on children. In the absence of clear evidence of physical abuse of children, mothers who were victims of spousal abuse were regularly pressured by mediators, lawyers and judges at settlement conferences to accept arrangements that gave their abusive former partners significant contact with their children and to accept joint custody. Concerns about the safety of mothers were given relatively little attention in the resolution of family proceedings, even if there was a clear history of spousal abuse.

In the field of child custody and access assessments, two recent studies present very different pictures of the extent to which practices have changed. Bow and Boxer (2003) surveyed custody assessors across the U.S. and found the vast majority reported that they now recognize domestic violence as a critical factor in their work. Practitioners in this study of attitudes indicated that they considered using specialized assessment resources and made differential custody and visitation recommendations when domestic violence was identified. In contrast, studies of actual practices in the Family Courts in Louisville, Kentucky, found that domestic violence was often ignored. Analysis of custody assessment reports revealed that domestic violence was generally not a factor in recommendations, even when it was mentioned in the report as being present (Horvath, Logan & Walker, 2002). Furthermore, an analysis of court records found that court settlement methods (e.g., mediation, adjudication) did not vary for families with or without domestic violence histories. Parents with a domestic violence history were as likely to be steered to mediation as those without such a history, despite the inappropriateness of mediation in these cases. Further, custody outcomes did not differ between families with and without this history (Logan, Walker, Horvath & Leukefeld, 2003).

Another example of this posited gap between theory and practice is revealed in a recent California study. It found that mediators held joint sessions for both parents in nearly half of the cases in which an independent screening interview had identified allegations of domestic violence, in direct violation of state regulations for separate sessions in these cases (Hirst, 2002). Further, other research has indicated that mediators were more likely to effect settlements in which batterers received custody compared with men who did not abuse their partners (Johnson & Saccuzzo, 2005). The extent to which these findings can be generalized is not clear; nonetheless, we would hypothesize that similar audits in many other courts would result in similar findings.

Implications

It is apparent that there continues to be a need for policy change and resource development. There needs to be *legislation* that establishes the necessary balance between promoting co-parenting arrangements and recognizing domestic violence cases where more limited or no access to the perpetrator may be appropriate. Other countries have struggled with finding this balance (Jaffe & Crooks, 2004; Bala et al., 1998). In some countries it is apparent that reforms intended to increase levels of shared parenting has resulted in a decrease in levels of safety for abused women and their children; there is the potential for negative and unintended consequences from legislative reform, highlighting the importance of careful planning and systemic readiness before the adoption of any new legislation (Jaffe, Crooks & Wolfe, 2003).

There is also a need for *resource and policy development* to support a more sophisticated analysis and response to domestic violence cases. A special challenge for the justice system and for community social services is the overlap between family law and child protection proceedings. Specific protocols are required to guide practitioners in managing cases with domestic violence allegations that fall into the area between public safety for children (i.e., triggering criminal or child protection process) and private family law matters. In addition, Family Courts rarely have access to the resources that they require to handle the more complex cases that go beyond the mandate of parent education and mediation services. The needed resources include timely access to specially trained child custody and access assessors with expertise in domestic violence, supervised access centres and treatment resources for individual family members (including perpetrators, victims, and children). Further, the different components of a full spectrum of services need to be well coordinated in order to monitor family members' progress and make revisions to parenting arrangements as needed.

It is not sufficient to assume that no news is good news in domestic violence cases. Ongoing court monitoring may be indicated in child custody disputes with histories of domestic violence. Building systemic capacity also includes the need for *education and training for* the professionals who work in the Family Court system, including judges and lawyers. Education programs have to be available to help court-related professionals recognize domestic violence in all its forms and to give them the skills to provide differential service responses to meet the level of need for a family. When domestic violence is recognized, there still needs to be a distinction made between cases where there have been relatively minor, isolated acts versus those cases where the violence occurs as part of a pattern of abuse, which engenders fear and harm for victims and children exposed to this behaviour. When the most intensive domestic violence interventions are misapplied to families who may be better characterized as experiencing transitory high conflict, there is the potential to harm parents' reputations, impede their problem-solving abilities and undermine parent-child relationships. Furthermore, it is an inefficient use of scarce resources. Conversely, a battering husband who engages community members and the court system in a dialogue about his wife, making false allegations about her being an unfit parent, has to be identified early in the process. Failure to identify these cases allows the batterer to use the justice system to revictimize his ex-partner. In some jurisdictions (e.g., California), mandatory training in domestic violence is a prerequisite for being a court-appointed child custody assessor.

Finally, there are significant *gaps in the existing research* that limit our ability to understand cases and identify best practices. Specifically, there is a lack of long-term follow-up studies to match children's adjustment with specific post-separation parenting arrangements in cases involving domestic violence. In addition, most research has been conducted with families in the formal judicial system, and less is known about the long-term experiences of those who choose not to engage in this system. Research in the divorce area has been criticized for looking at the outcome of biased samples. For example, the promotion of joint custody as a good outcome is largely based on retrospective studies of co-operative couples. In addition, the outcome may be linked to a simple factor when the reality is more complex; for example, negative outcomes associated with parental relocation may overlook the risk factors of domestic violence and poverty that triggered the move. There has been little attention to understanding the process of perpetrators changing their behaviour and appropriately healing the relationship with children in a respectful and safe manner. When it comes to individual cases, it is often hard to predict whether terminating contact promotes child healing or, conversely, triggers idealization of the perpetrator and anger toward the victim parent. We know little about the restoration process, and the circumstances under which healing the parent-child relationship is possible.

A starting point for an enhanced understanding is a better integration of the divorce literature and the domestic violence literature, which have largely developed independently of each other (Jaffe, Poisson & Cunningham, 2001). Leading experts in the field have pointed out that high-conflict cases involving domestic violence are often misguided by a divorce literature focusing on parents who were never involved in litigation (Johnston, 1994). Our goal in this chapter has been to assist policy-makers and practitioners by bridging the domestic violence and divorce literatures and by outlining a framework for examining situations where these issues may be present.

Notes

1   This chapter is based on a discussion paper entitled "Making Appropriate Parenting Arrangements in Domestic Violence Cases: Applying the Literature to Promising Practices," funded by Justice Canada and available at http://canada.justice.gc.ca/en/ps/pad/reports/2005-FCY-3/index. html.

CHAPTER TWELVE

The Verdict on Specialized Justice Responses to Domestic Violence

Leslie M. Tutty, Jane Ursel and Janice leMaistre

This book has provided an overview of a number of important issues with respect to intimate partner violence and new or specialized justice approaches whose purpose is to address domestic abuse in ways that better ensure the safety of victims and children. The literature cited throughout reminds us of the serious nature of domestic violence and the significant impacts it has, not only on victims and children but also on society as a whole.

That so many jurisdictions have developed and adopted specialized approaches to address the problem speaks for itself. Canadian society in general and the justice system in particular abhor the existence of such violence and the deaths that routinely result from it. That even one child like four-year-old Alex Fekete in Alberta is murdered by a father intent on exacting revenge from his estranged wife is beyond tragedy. The fact that it recurs numerous times across Canada each year is shameful.

The justice response to domestic violence has long been criticized since the early days when police officers often treated partner violence as a private matter. Today, the emergence of dual charging in cases of spousal assault is of significant concern but also highlights the difficult job of police officers in identifying the primary offender. Nevertheless, the extent to which dual charging occurs in some American states, with rates of up to almost 50%, seems more a police reaction to having been instructed to charge than a valid action. Essentially, rather than making their own determination as to who is the perpetrator and charging accordingly, the police officers decide to "let the courts sort it out." That similar dual charging rates were not reported in any of the jurisdictions covered by the researchers in this book suggests a higher level of co-operation with existing charge policies within Canadian police services.

Criticisms have also been made of prosecutors and the court for revictimizing the victims who recanted their testimony, either because of reconciling with partners or being threatened by them. The justice system has been hard pressed to understand the dynamics of couples in which violence and abuse regularly occurs. It makes sense that representatives of the legal system are more comfortable when victims do not have an intimate relationship with their abusers. The volatile nature of some of these relationships results in victims dramatically shifting their wishes with respect to both the police and the courts, sometimes back and forth. That some relationships survive chronic physical abuse in which the police are repeatedly called to intervene is understandably hard to believe. Yet, in such cases, it is even more important to understand the immediate safety that the police offer, whether or not it translates into a victim who is willing to provide evidence against her partner in court.

Concrete research evidence about the efficacy of specialized justice approaches to intimate partner violence has been elusive. Part of the excitement of editing this volume has been discovering that considerable research has already been conducted in Canada and that new partnerships are being developed in order to continue more collaborative research in the future.

The Chapters Revisited

The chapter authors describe a number of legal and court approaches to both intimate partner violence and custody and access issues when domestic violence has been a central feature of a divorcing couple's relationship. Five chapters present different models of specialized courts designed to more adequately address assaults and other criminal behaviours against an intimate partner. Two chapters describe the impact of civil legislation, specifically protection orders, in dealing with both domestic violence and stalking. With this overview, what now can we conclude about whether such approaches work?

The chapters on the specialized domestic violence courts are intriguing, if only for the differences that are highlighted. Each court arose in response to the unique needs in their communities. The overview in chapter 4 by Tutty, Ursel and Douglas provides a comparison of courts in four Canadian Prairie cities and identifies as many differences between the specialized courts and their outcomes as the differences between Regina's non-specialized court and those that have specialized.

Rekha Malaviya's focus in chapter 3 on the inside world of becoming a Crown prosecutor in Winnipeg — Canada's oldest specialized Domestic Violence Court — provides a compelling and rarely told narrative about the inner workings of the justice system. She articulates a unique perspective that Crown attorneys may adopt when working with victims of intimate partner violence. Similarly, in chapter 2, Tutty, George, Nixon and Gill provide the seldom heard voices of women speaking about their experiences when their abusive partners have been criminally charged for these assaults and dealt with by the justice system, specialized or not.

Busby, Koshan and Wiegers, three professors of law from the Prairie provinces, describe the civil legislations developed in each of these jurisdictions, comparing and contrasting the major constructs and identifying strengths and challenges in chapter 9. As with the specialized courts, each law is somewhat different and the practical procedures to both apply for emergency protection orders and ratify the court orders vary substantially. In chapter 10, Cheryl Laurie looks at the impact of Manitoba's civil legislation on the problem of stalking that is a relatively common occurrence in the lives of abused women, particularly after the breakup of a relationship. The criminalization of stalking behaviours has been questionably successful, so adding emergency protection orders as another potential tool to address harassment seems sensible. Other provinces, such as Alberta, have followed Manitoba's lead in including stalking in their civil legislations, but the efficacy of this provision needs continued monitoring.

Chapter 11 by Jaffe, Crooks and Bala examines another way that courts are commonly involved in addressing intimate partner violence: custody and access. This focus is critical because the mechanisms entailed in custodial visits of children can easily be used to extend the power and control issues inherent in a violent relationship. At worst, access to the children can be used to continue emotional and sometimes physical violence.

What of the Future?

Clearly, the jury is still out on what justice approaches best address intimate partner violence. Each of the programs and specialized court models offers solid ideas that could be considered by jurisdictions wishing to develop their own specialized approaches to domestic violence. We expect that there is no single best model but that different communities with different needs and capacities will design a model that best responds to those needs and that makes best use of their capacities.

The move to more specialized courts across the country indicates that the justice system itself has become more open to a change that was vigorously resisted when the first specialized court was introduced in Winnipeg in 1990. At that time, lawyers and judges alike criticized the concept of specialization, which was largely promoted by people outside the system, specifically women's and victims' organizations. Further, it was seven years before the second province, Ontario, introduced specialized courts. The justice system is an old and powerful system that has historically been resistant to change, particularly change suggested from the "outside." However, what the above chapters indicate is that change is occurring and that considerable creativity is being revealed in these changes.

What is most remarkable today is that often it is the judges themselves who are the agents of change, bringing the concept of specialization into their jurisdictions. At annual judicial meetings, judges across Canada hear their colleagues from provinces with established specialized courts talk about the benefits, progress and challenges they encounter in their courts. A recent interview with justice officials in Saskatchewan about changes in those courts indicated that it was the judges who brought the idea of specialization back to their communities.[1]

More encouraging still was that, in each Saskatchewan community in which a specialized court was introduced, the judges and the justice department convened a community committee to discuss and design their specialization process. In addition to justice representatives, each committee included service providers who work with victims and those who work with perpetrators. This openness to community involvement, unheard of in the 1990s, is a process that suggests a new trend in collaboration between the social services system and the justice system, as exemplified by the Home-Front Project in Calgary. Given the complex nature of domestic violence such collaboration between these two systems is a hopeful development.

Many of the chapters in this book document improvements within the justice system. While acknowledging change is important, we must not lose sight of the significant challenges within our courts. Specialization can result in competing pressures and expectations. On the one hand, there is the expectation that a specialized court will handle cases more rapidly; on the other hand, there is the reality that specialization is associated with substantial increases in the number of cases coming to court. Balancing these competing demands is a continual challenge.

Another challenge lies in the fact that as the system becomes better at tracking offenders, researchers are identifying a small percentage of chronic reoffenders (Gondolf, 2002; Ursel & Hagyard, chapter 5 in this volume). Identifying these chronic reoffenders is important; however, the system faces serious challenges in designing effective interventions for these perpetrators. At this point, the best the criminal justice system can do is put them in prison. However, incarceration is a temporary solution because not only are jail terms typically short, but also these offenders will eventually return to former partners or find new intimate partners and continue their abusive behaviour.

An ongoing challenge in our courts is how to make an adversarial legal system that requires proof "beyond a reasonable doubt" less intimidating to victims. The neccessity of standing up in court and telling the story of your abuse by the person who was supposed to love you is painful and humiliating. Such shame is particularly evident when sexual assault is involved or when children are witnesses. The Canadian Evidence Act (Criminal Code of Canada section 486.2) allows prosecutors to apply to have a vulnerable witness give his/her testimony via closed-circuit television, affording the victim/witness a higher level of privacy and protection. Unfortunately, prosecutors rarely invoke this option for child abuse victim/witnesses much less adult victim/witnesses. Canada has much to learn from legisla-tion in Australia, which asserts the vulnerable victim's right to testify by closed-circuit television without a special application by the prosecutor.

Vulnerable victims in Australia, typically children and victims of sexual assault, will give their testimony via closed-circuit television unless they choose to testify in court.

In Canada, service providers report and some studies reveal that victims of domestic violence are also frequently sexually assaulted. For example, Tutty and Rothery (2002) reported that over half of the 98 women residents in an emergency shelter in Calgary reported sexual abuse and/or harassment by their partners. However, our criminal court data indicates that 2% or less of the woman abuse cases heard in court include charges of sexual assault. Researchers have long suspected that women do not report their sexual violation because of the pain and humiliation involved in testifying in these cases. We wonder if the process of testifying were made less public and less humiliating, would more women feel safe enough to tell the whole story?

A final challenge facing our Family Courts is how best to provide safe custody and access in cases where domestic violence is part of the separating couples history. Until very recently this concern has been overwhelmed by the literature advocating joint custodial and co-operative parenting ideals. In chapter 11, Jaffe, Crooks and Bala, identify the risks of our past Family Court practices and call for a new protocol in justice that is not blind to the very real threats of post-separation violence in some relationships. Research on this topic is an important first step, and the experience of greater collaboration between the social service system and the justice system associated with the development of specialized domestic violence courts may perhaps provide a model for introducing change within the Family Court system.

To conclude, in our opinion the justice system has made significant progress over the past two decades in addressing intimate partner violence. The improvements include court processes that are less likely to revictimize the victim when their partners are prosecuted. More justice personnel from police to judges are learning about the dynamics of these unique relationships. This knowledge can improve their sensitivity to and understanding of how to proceed with the joint goals of keeping victims safe and holding offenders accountable.

The chapters in this book present diverse models of specialized justice responses to domestic violence. While limited research on specialized courts has been published to date, to our knowledge this book is one of the first attempts to conceptualize the differences between models and to research how well the variations work. While we do not present any definitive "best practices," on reflection, the most effective court models emerge from the needs of the community in combination with a strong understanding of the serious nature of intimate partner violence and the contradictions and challenges that it presents to the criminal and civil justice system.

Notes

1   Interviews were conducted with Rod McKendrick, manager of victim services, and Frankie Jordan, senior policy analyst, Policy and Evaluation Branch Saskatchewan Department of Justice, in the fall of 2007.

References

Ad Hoc Federal-Provincial-Territorial Working Group (2003). *Spousal abuse policies and legislation: Final report*. Final Report of The Ad Hoc FPT Working Group Reviewing Spousal Abuse Policies and Legislation.

Alberta Law Reform Institute (1995). *Domestic abuse: Toward an effective legal response report for discussion*. Edmonton: Alberta Law Reform Institute.

Alberta Law Reform Institute (1997). *Protection against domestic abuse*. Edmonton: author.

American Psychological Association (1998). *Potential problems for psychologists working with the area of interpersonal violence*. Available online at www.apa.org/pi/potential.html.

Amnesty International (2004). Stolen Sisters website, available online at www.amnesty.ca/resource_centre/reports/view.php?load=arcview&article=1895&c=Resource+Centre+Reports.

Aston, C. & Pottie-Bunge, V. (2005). Family homicide-suicides. In Statistics Canada, *Family violence in Canada: A statistical profile 2005* (pp. 60–67). Ottawa: Minister of Industry.

AuCoin, K. (2005). Stalking — criminal harassment. In Statistics Canada, *Family violence in Canada: A statistical profile 2005* (pp. 33–47). Ottawa: Minister of Industry.

Augusta-Scott, T. & Dankwort, J. (2002). Partner abuse group intervention: Lessons from education and narrative therapy approaches. *Journal of Interpersonal Violence, 17*, 783–805.

Babcock, J.C. & Steiner, R. (1999). The relationship between treatment, incarceration and recidivism of battering. A program evaluation of Seattle's coordinated community response to domestic violence. *Journal of Family Psychology, 13*, 46–59.

Babcock, J.C., Green, C. & Robie, C. (2004). Does batterers' treatment work? A meta-analytic review of domestic violence treatment. *Clinical Psychology Review, 23*, 1023–1053.

Bala, N. (2004). Spousal abuse and children: Family law issues. National Family Law Program of the Federation of Law Societies of Canada, La Malbaie, Quebec, July 2004. Available online at law.queensu.ca/faculty/bala/papers/spouseabuse&familylaw2004.htm.

Bala, N.C. & Ringseis, E.L. (2002). *Review of Yukon's Family Violence Prevention Act.* Whitehorse, YK: Victim Services Office, Department of Justice.

Bala, N.C., Bertrand, L.D., Paetsch, J.J., Knoppers, B.M., Hornick, J.P., Noel, J., Boudreau. L. & Miklas, S.W. (1998). *Spousal violence in custody and access disputes: Recommendations for reform.* Ottawa: Status of Women Canada.

Bancroft, L. & Silverman, J.G. (2002). The batterer as parent: The impact of domestic violence on family dynamics. Thousand Oaks, CA: Sage.

Barasch, A.P. & Lutz, V.L. (2002). Innovations in the legal system's response to domestic violence: Thinking outside the box for the silent majority of battered women. In A.R. Robert (Ed.), *Handbook of domestic violence: Policies, programs and legal remedies* (pp. 173–201). New York: Oxford University Press.

Barrera, M., Palmer, S., Brown, R. & Kalaher, S. (1994). Characteristics of court-involved men and non-court-involved men who abuse their wives. *Journal of Family Violence, 9*, 333–345.

Beattie, K. (2005). Spousal homicides. In Statistics Canada, *Family violence in Canada: A statistical profile 2005* (pp. 48–50). Ottawa: Minister of Industry.

Beattie, S. (2003). Criminal harassment. In *Family violence in Canada 2003: A statistical profile.* Ottawa: National Clearinghouse on Family Violence. Available online at www.phac-aspc.gc.ca/ncfv-cnivf/familyviolence.html.

Bennett, L. & Williams, O. (2001). Controversies and recent studies on batterer intervention program effectiveness. Available online at www.vawnet.org.

Bennett, L., Goodman, L. & Dutton, M. A. (1999). Systemic obstacles to the criminal prosecution of a battering partner: A victim perspective. *Journal-of-Interpersonal-Violence, 14*, 761–772.

Bergen, R.K. (2004). Studying wife rape: Reflections on the past, present, and future. *Violence Against Women, 10*, 1407–1416.

Bernstein, S.E. (1993). Living under siege: Do stalking laws protect domestic violence victims? *Cordozo Law Review, 15*, 525–567.

Bonnycastle, K.D. & Rigakos, G.S. (1998). *Unsettling truths: Battered women, policy, politics and contemporary Canadian research*. Vancouver: Vancouver Collective Press.

Bow, J.N. & Boxer, P. (2003). Assessing allegations of domestic violence in child custody evaluations. *Journal of Interpersonal Violence, 18*, 1394–1410.

Bowermaster, J. & Johnson, D. (October 1998). *The role of domestic violence in family court child custody determinations: An interdisciplinary investigation*. Paper presented at the Fourth International Conference on Children Exposed to Domestic Violence, San Diego, CA.

Bowlus, A., McKenna, K., Day, T. & Wright, D. (2003). *The economic costs and consequences of child abuse*. Ottawa: The Law Commission of Canada.

Brewster, M.P. (2000). Stalking by former intimates: Verbal threats and other predictors of physical violence. *Violence and Victims, 15*, 41–54.

Brown, T. (2001). *Charging and prosecution policies in cases of spousal assault: A synthesis of research, academic and judicial responses*. Department of Justice Canada. Retrieved August 4, 2005 from canada.justice.gc.ca/en/ps/rs/rep/2001-rr01-5a.pdf

Brzozowski, J.A. (2004). Spousal Violence. *Family Violence in Canada: A Statistical Profile 2004*. Ottawa: Canadian Centre for Justice Statistics.

Burch, R.L. & Gallup, G.G. (2004). Pregnancy as a stimulus for domestic violence. *Journal of Family Violence, 19*, 243–247.

Buzawa, E.S. & Buzawa, C.G. (1996). *Domestic violence: The criminal justice response*. Newbury Park, CA: Sage.

Buzawa, E.S. & Buzawa, C.G. (2003). *Domestic violence. The criminal justice response* (3rd ed.). Thousand Oaks, CA: Sage.

Cairns, K. (2005). The domestic violence treatment effectiveness study: Highlights of the final report. In *Family Violence: Community Resource Guide* (pp. 58–59). Edmonton: Ministry of Children's Services. Available online at www.child.gov.ab.ca/whatwedo/familyviolence/pdf/FVPMguidelinks.pdf.

Campbell, J.C. (1995). *Assessing dangerousness: Violence by sexual offenders, batterers, and child abusers*. Thousand Oaks, CA: Sage.

Campbell, J.C. (2001) Safety planning based on lethality assessment for batterers in intervention programs. *Journal of Aggression, Maltreatment and Trama, 5(2)*, 129–143.

Campbell, J.C. & Soeken, K.L. (1999). Forced sex and intimate partner violence: Effects on women's risk and women's health. *Violence Against Women, 5*, 1017–1035.

Campbell, J.C., Sharps, P. & Glass, N. (2001). Risk assessment for intimate partner homicide. In G.F. Pinard & L. Pagani (Eds.), *Clinical assessment of dangerousness: Empirical contributions* (pp. 136–157). New York: Cambridge University Press.

Canadian Broadcasting Corporation: CBC News (September 29, 2003). Man kills wife, son, turns gun on self, say police. Available online at www.cbc.ca/canada/story/2003/09/29/calgary_reddeer030929.html.

Canadian Panel on Violence Against Women (1993). *Changing the landscape: Ending violence ~ achieving equality*. Ottawa: Minister of Supply and Services Canada.

Cannavale, F.J. (1976). *Witness cooperation*. New York: Lexington Press.

Carlson, J., Harris, S. & Holden, G. (1999). Protective orders and domestic violence: Risk factors for re-abuse. *Journal of Family Violence, 14*, 205–206.

Centre for Equality Rights in Accommodation (CERA) (2002). *Women and housing in Canada: Barriers to equality*. Toronto: author.

Chang, J.C., Cluss, P.A., Ranieri, L., Hawker, L., Buranosky, R., Dado, D., McNeil, M. & Scholle, S.H. (2005). Health care interventions for intimate partner violence: What women want. *Women's Health Issues, 15*, 21–31.

Clarke, M. (2003). *Best practices review*. Calgary: Synergy Research Group. Retrieved April 30, 2004, from www.homefrontcalgary.com/newsletter.

Coleman, F.L. (1997). Stalking behavior and the cycle of domestic violence. *Journal of Interpersonal Violence, 12*, 420–432.

Comack, E. & Balfour, G. (2004). *The power to criminalize: Violence, inequality and the law*. Halifax: Fernwood.

Comack, E., Chopyk, V. & Wood, L. (2000). *Mean streets? The social locations, gender dynamics and patterns of violent crime in Winnipeg*. Winnipeg: Canadian Centre for Policy Alternatives.

Conti, C.T., Sr. (1998). Emergency departments and abuse: Policy issues, practice barriers, and recommendations. *Journal of the Association for Academic Minority Physicians; 9*, 35-39.

Cornet, W. & Lendor, A. (2002). *Discussion paper: Matrimonial real property on reserves*. Ottawa: Ministry of Indian Affairs and Northern Development.

Crocker, D. (2005). Regulating intimacy: Judicial discourse in cases of wife assault (1970 to 2000). *Violence Against Women, 11*, 197-226.

Cunningham, A. & Baker, L. (2004). What about me! Seeking to understand the child's view of violence in the family. Available online at www.lfcc. on.ca/what_about_me.pdf.

Currie, D. (1990). Battered women and the state: From the failure of theory to a theory of failure. *Journal of Human Justice, 1*, 77-96.

Dalton, C., Drozd, L.M. & Wong, F.Q. (2004). *Navigating custody and visitation evaluations in cases with domestic violence: A judge's guide*. Reno, NV: National Council of Juvenile and Family Court Judges.

Daly, K. (1987). Structure and practice of familial-based justice in a criminal court. *Law & Society Review, 21*, 267-290.

Daly, K. (1989). Rethinking judicial paternalism: Gender, work-family relations, and sentencing. *Gender & Society, 3*, 9-36.

Davis, K.E., Coker, A.L. & Sanderson, M. (2002). Physical and mental health effects of being stalked for men and women. *Violence and Victims, 17*, 429-443.

Davis, R.C., Lurigio, A.J. & Skogan, W.G. (1997). *Victims of crime* (2nd ed.). Thousand Oaks, CA: Sage.

Dawson, M. & Dinovitzer, R. (2001). Victim cooperation and the prosecution of domestic violence in a specialized court. *Justice Quarterly, 15*, 593-622.

Demaris, A. (1992). *Logit modeling: Practical applications*. London: Sage.

Department of Justice Canada (1996). *A review of Section 264 (Criminal Harassment) of the Criminal Code of Canada: Working document* (WD1996-7e). Ottawa: Research and Statistics Division, Policy Sector.

Dobash, R.E., Dobash, R.P., Cavanagh, K. & Lewis, R. (2000). *Changing violent men*. Newbury Park, CA: Sage.

Dutton, MA (1992). *Empowering and healing the battered woman: a model for assessment and intervention*. New York: Springer.

Dutton, M.A. & Goodman, L. (2005). Coercion in intimate partner violence: Toward a new conceptualization. *Sex Roles, 11/12*, 743-756.

Eberts, M. & Jacobs, B. (2004). Matrimonial property on reserve. In M. MacDonald & M. Owen (Eds.), *On building solutions for women's equality:*

Matrimonial property on reserve (pp. 7–39). Ottawa: Canadian Research Institute for the Advancement of Women.

Edleson, J.L. (1999a). *Problems associated with children's witnessing of domestic violence*. VAWnet. Available online at www.vaw.umn.edu/documents/vawnet/witness/witness.html.

Edleson, J.L. (1999b). The overlap between child maltreatment and woman battering. *Violence Against Women, 5*, 134–154.

Edleson, J.L. (1999c). Children's witnessing of adult domestic violence. *Journal of Interpersonal Violence, 14*, 839–870.

Edleson, J.L. (2004). Should childhood exposure to adult domestic violence be defined as child maltreatment under the law? In P.G. Jaffe, L.L. Baker & A. Cunningham. (Eds.), *Protecting children from domestic violence: Strategies for community intervention* (pp. 8–29). New York: Guilford Press.

Edleson, J. & Syers, M. (1991). The effects of group treatment for men who batter: An 18-month follow-up study. *Research on Social Work Practice, 1*, 227–243.

Eisikovits, Z. & Buchbinder, E. (2000). *Locked in a violent embrace: Understanding and intervening in domestic violence*. Thousand Oaks, CA: Sage.

Ellis, D. (1992) Woman abuse among separated and divorced women: The relevance of social support. In E.C. Viano (Ed.) *Intimate violence: Interdisciplinary perspectives* (pp. 177–189). Washington DC: Hemisphere.

Ellis, J.W. (1984). Prosecutorial discretion to charge in cases of spousal assault: A dialogue. *Journal of Criminal Law and Criminology, 75*, 56–102.

Eraz, E. & Belknap, J. (1998). In their own words: Battered women's assessment of the criminal justice system's responses. *Violence Against Women, 13*, 251–268.

Fagan, J. (1995). *The criminalization of domestic violence*. Washington, DC: National Institute of Justice.

Federal-Provincial-Territorial Ministers Responsible for the Status of Women (2002). *Assessing violence against women: A statistical profile*. Ottawa: Status of Women.

Fedorowycz, O. (2001). Homicide in Canada — 2000. *Juristat, 21*. Ottawa: Canadian Centre for Justice Statistics, Statistics Canada.

Feminist Alliance for International Action (FAFIA) (2003). *Canada's failure to act: Women's inequality deepens*. Submission of the Canadian Feminist Alliance for International Action to the United Nations Committee on the Elimination of Discrimination Against Women on the Occasion Of the Committee's Review of Canada's 5th Report. Ottawa: author.

Ford, D.A. (1991). Prosecution as a victim power resource: A note empowering women in violent conjugal relationships. *Law & Society Review, 25,* 313–334.

Ford, D.A. & Regoli, M.J. (1993). The criminal prosecution of wife assaulters. In N.Z. Hilton (Ed.), *Legal responses to wife assault* (pp. 127–164). Newbury Park, CA: Sage.

Ford, D.A. & Regoli, M.J. (1993). *The Indianapolis domestic violence prosecution experiment, Final report.* NIJ Grant no. 86-1j-CX-0012. Indianapolis: Indiana University and Washington, DC: U.S. Department of Justice, National Institute of Justice and U.S. Department of Health and Human Services, National Institute of Mental Health.

Fox, A.J. & Zawitz, M.W. (1999). *Homicide trends in the United States.* Washington, DC: U.S. Department of Justice, Bureau of Justice Statistics. Available online at www.ojp.usdoj.gov/bjs/homicide/homtrnd.htm.

Frederick, L. & Tilley, J. (2001). *Effective intervention in domestic violence cases: Context is everything.* Minneapolis, MN: Battered Women's Justice Project.

Friedman, L.N. & Tucker, S.B. (1997). Violence prevention through victim assistance: Helping people escape the web of violence. In R.C. Davis, A.J. Lurigio & W.G. Skogan (Eds.), *Victims of crime* (pp. 63–82). Thousand Oaks, CA: Sage.

Fusco, L.J. (1989). Integrating systems: Police, courts, and assaulted women. In B. Pressman, G. Cameron & M. Rothery (Eds.), *Intervening with assaulted women: Current theory, research and practice* (pp. 125–136). Hillsdale, NJ: Erlbaum.

Gazmararian, J.A., Lazorick, S., Spitz, A.M., Ballard, T.J. & Marks, J.S. (1996). Prevalence of violence against pregnant women. *Journal of the American Medical Association, 275,* 1915–1920.

Gondolf, E.W. (1997a). Expanding batterer program evaluation. In G. Kaufman Kantor & J. L. Jasinski (Eds.), *Out of the darkness: Contemporary perspectives in family violence* (pp. 208–218). Thousand Oaks, CA: Sage.

Gondolf, E.W. (1997b). Batterer programs: What we know and need to know. *Journal of Interpersonal Violence, 12,* 83–98.

Gondolf, E.W. (1999). A comparison of four batterer intervention systems: Do court referral, program length and service matter? *Journal of Interpersonal Violence, 14,* 41–61.

Gondolf, E.W. (2002). *Batterer intervention systems: Issues, outcomes, and recommendations*. Thousand Oaks, CA: Sage.

Gondolf, E. & Russell, D. (1986). The case against anger control treatment programs for batterers. *Response to the Victimization of Women and Children, 9,* 2–5.

Grasely, C., Stickney, J., Harris, R., Hutchinson, G., Greaves, L. & Boyd, T. (1999). *Assessing the integrated model of services for abused women: The consumers' perspective.* London, ON.

Gutmanis, I., Beynon, C., Tutty, L., Wathen, C.N. & MacMillan, H.L. (2007). Factors influencing identification of and response to intimate partner violence: A survey of physicians and nurses. *Biomed Central: Public Health, 7,* 12. Available online at www.biomedcentral.com/1471-2458/7/12.

Hackett, K. (2000). Criminal harassment. *Juristat, 20.* Ottawa: Canadian Centre for Justice Statistics, Statistics Canada.

Hankivsky, O. & Greaves, L. (1995). The costs of violence: Another piece of the puzzle. *Vis-à-vis, 13,* 4.

Harrell, A. (1998). The impact of court-ordered treatment for domestic violence offenders. In American Bar Association (Eds.), *Legal interventions in family violence: research findings and policy implications.* Washington, DC: U.S. Department of Justice. Available online at www.ncjrs.org/pdffiles/171666.pdf.

Healey, K.M., Smith, C. & O'Sullivan, C. (1998). *Batterer intervention: Program approaches and criminal justice strategies.* National Criminal Justice Reference Service. Available online at ojp.usdoj.gov/nij.

Hedderman, C. & Gelsthorpe, L. (1997). *Understanding the sentencing of women.* London: Home Office.

Hilton, N.Z., Harris, G.T., Rice, M.E., Lang, C., Cormier, C.A. & Lines, K.J. (2004). A brief actuarial assessment for the prediction of wife assault recidivism: The Ontario Domestic Assault Risk Assessment. *Psychological Assessment, 16,* 300–312.

Hirst, A. (2002) *Domestic violence in court-based child custody mediation in California.* Publication of the Centre for Families, Children & the Courts. San Francisco: Administrative Office of the Courts.

Hoffart, I. & Clarke, M. (2004). *HomeFront evaluation: Final report.* Calgary, AB: HomeFront Evaluation Committee. Available online at www.homefront calgary.com/statistics/index.htm.

Holder, R. & Mayo, N. (2003). What do women want? Prosecuting family violence at the ACT. *Current Issues in Criminal Justice, 15*, 5–25.

Holt, V., Kernic, M., Lumley, T., Wolf, M. & Rivara, F. (2002). Civil protection orders and risk of subsequent police-reported violence. *Journal of the American Medical Association, 288*, 589–594.

Holt, V. Kernic, M., Lumley, T., Wolf, M. & Rivara, F. (2003). Do protection orders affect the likelihood of future partner violence and injury? *American Journal of Preventative Medicine, 24*, 16–21.

Hornick, J., Boyes, M., Tutty, L. & White, L. (October, 2005). *The Domestic Violence Treatment Option in the Yukon.* World Conference on Family Violence. Banff, Alberta, Canada.

Hornick, J., Boyes, M., Tutty, L. & White, L. (in preparation). *The effectiveness of batterer treatment in the Yukon Domestic Violence Treatment Option.*

Hornick, J., Boyes, M., Tutty, L., Bertrand, L. & Paetsch, J. (2004). *Evaluation of the Domestic Violence Treatment Option, Whitehorse, Yukon.* Calgary: Canadian Research Institute on Law and the Family.

Horvath, L.S., Logan, T.K. & Walker, R. (2002). Child custody cases: A content analysis of evaluations in practice. *Professional Psychology: Research and Practice, 33*, 557–565.

Hotton, T. (2001). Domestic violence after marital separation. *Juristat, 21*, 7. Ottawa: Canadian Centre for Justice Statistics, Statistics Canada.

Howard Research (2000). *Implementation and impact of the Protection Against Family Violence Act: Final report.* Edmonton: Government of Alberta.

Hoyle, C. & Sanders, A. (2000). Police response to domestic violence: From victim choice to victim empowerment? *British Journal of Criminology, 40*, 14–36.

Jackson, S., Feder, L., Forde, D.R., Davis, R.C., Maxwell, C.D. & Taylor, B.G. (2003). Batterer intervention programs: Where do we go from here? *Report to the National Institute of Justice.* Washington, DC. Available online at www.ojp.usdoj.gov.nij.

Jaffe, P.G. & Crooks, C.V. (2004). The relevance of domestic violence in child custody determinations: A cross-national comparison. *Violence Against Women, 10*, 917–934.

Jaffe, P.G. & Crooks, C.V. (2005). *Understanding women's experiences parenting in the context of domestic violence: Implications for community and court-related service providers.* Washington, DC: Violence Against Women Online Resources.

Jaffe, P.G. & Crooks, C.V. (2006). Visitation and custody in cases of domestic violence. In J.L. Edleson & O.J. Williams (Eds.), *Parenting by men who batter women: New directions for assessment and intervention.* New York: Oxford University Press.

Jaffe, P.G., Baker, L.L. & Cunningham, A.J. (Eds.). (2004). *Protecting children from domestic violence: Strategies for community intervention.* New York: Guilford Press.

Jaffe, P.G., Crooks, C.V. & Poisson, S.E. (2003). Common misconceptions and addressing domestic violence in child custody disputes. *Juvenile and Family Court Journal, 54,* 57–67.

Jaffe, P.G., Crooks, C.V. & Wolfe, D.A. (2003). Legal and policy responses to children exposed to domestic violence: The need to evaluate intended and unintended consequences. *Clinical Child and Family Psychology Review, 6,* 205–213.

Jaffe, P.G., Poisson, S.E. & Cunningham, A. (2001). Domestic violence and high-conflict divorce: Developing a new generation of research for children. In S.A. Graham-Bermann & J.L. Edleson (Eds.), *Domestic violence in the lives of children: The future of research, intervention, and social policy* (pp. 189–202). Washington, DC: American Psychological Association.

Jennings, J. (1990). Preventing relapse versus "stopping" domestic violence: Do we expect too much too soon from battering men? *Journal of Family Violence, 5,* 43–60.

Johnson, H. (1996). *Dangerous domains: Violence against women in Canada.* Canadian Centre for Justice Statistics, Statistics Canada. Scarborough, ON: Nelson.

Johnson, H. (2006). *Measuring violence against women: Statistical trends 2006.* Ottawa: Minister of Industry. Available online at www.statcan.ca/Daily/English/061002/d061002a.htm.

Johnson, M.P. (1995). Patriarchal terrorism and common couple violence: Two forms of violence against women. *Journal of Marriage and the Family, 57,* 283–294.

Johnson, M.P. & Ferraro, K. (2000). Research on domestic violence in the 1990s: Making distinctions. *Journal of Marriage and the Family, 62,* 948–963.

Johnson, N.E. & Saccuzzo, D.P. (2005). Child custody mediation in cases of domestic violence: Empirical evidence of a failure to protect. *Violence Against Women, 11,* 1022–1053.

Johnson, R.M., Kotch, J.B., Catellier, D.J., Winsor, J.R. et al. (2002). Adverse behavioral and emotional outcomes from child abuse and witnessed violence. *Child Maltreatment, 7*, 179–186.

Johnston, J.R. (1994). High-conflict divorce. *Future of Children, 4*, 165–182.

Johnston, J.R. & Campbell, L.E. (1993). A clinical typology of interparental violence in disputed-custody divorces. *American Journal of Orthopsychiatry, 63*, 190-199.

Johnston, J.R., Lee, S., Olesen, N.W. & Walters, M.G. (2005). Allegations and substantiations of abuse in custody disputing families. *Family Court Review, 43*, 283–294.

Jordan, C.A. (2003). Intimate partner violence and the justice system: An examination of the interface. *Journal of Interpersonal Violence, 19*, 1412–1434.

Kaci, J.H. (1994). Aftermath of seeking domestic violence protection orders: The victim's perspective. *Journal of Contemporary Criminal Justice, 10*, 201–219.

Keilitz, S., Hannaford, P. & Efkeman, H. (1997). *Civil protection orders: The benefits and limitations for victims of domestic violence.* Williamsburg, VA: National Centre for State Courts.

Kimmel, M.S. (2002). "Gender symmetry" in domestic violence: A substantive and methodological research review. *Violence Against Women [Special Issue: Women's use of violence in intimate partner relationships], 8*, 1332–1363.

Kingsnorth, R., MacIntosh, R. & Sutherland, S. (2002). Criminal charge or probation violation? Prosecutorial discretion and implications for research in criminal court processing. *Criminology, 40*, 553–577.

Klein, A. (1996). Re-abuse in a population of court restrained male batterers: Why restraining orders don't work. In E. Buzawa, & C. Buzawa, (Eds.), *Do arrests and restraining orders work?* (pp. 192-213). Thousand Oaks, CA: Sage.

Kong, R. (1997) Stalking: Criminal harassment in Canada. *Canadian Social Trends, 46*, 29.

Koshan, J. (1998). Aboriginal women, justice and the Charter: Bridging the divide? *University of British Columbia Law Review, 32*, 23–54.

Kropp, P.R. & Hart, S.D. (2004). *The development of the Brief Spousal Assault Form for the Evaluation of Risk (B-Safer): A tool for criminal justice professionals.* Ottawa: Department of Justice Canada.

Kropp, R.P., Hart, S.D. & Lyon, D.R. (2002). Risk assessment of stalkers: Some problems and possible solutions. *Criminal Justice and Behaviour, 29,* 590–616.

Kropp, P.R., Hart, S.D., Webster, C.D. & Eaves, D. (1994). *Manual of the Spousal Assault Risk Assessment Guide* (2nd ed.). Vancouver: British Columbia Institute on Domestic Violence.

Kropp, P.R., Hart, S.D., Webster, C. D. & Eaves, D. (2000). The Spousal Assault Risk Assessment Guide (SARA): Reliability and validity in adult male offenders. *Law and Human Behaviour, 24,* 101–118.

Lane, P., Bopp, J. & Bopp, M. (2003). *Aboriginal domestic violence in Canada.* Ottawa: Aboriginal Healing Foundation.

Laurie, C. (2006). *Seeking that "piece of paper": An examination of protection orders under "The Domestic Violence and Stalking Act" of Manitoba.* Unpublished M.A. Thesis. University of Manitoba.

LaViolette, A. (2005). *Assessing dangerousness in domestic violence cases.* San Jose, CA: California Statewide Dispute Resolution Institute.

Lavoie Inquiry Implementation Committee (1998). *Final Report* (Manitoba). Winnipeg, MB: author.

Legislative Assembly of Manitoba (1998). *The Domestic Violence and Stalking Act,* c.D93.

Legislative Assembly of Manitoba (2005a). Bill 17: *The Domestic Violence and Stalking Prevention, Protection and Compensation Amendment Act.* Retrieved July 15, 2005 from web2.gov.mb.ca/bills/38-2/b017e.php.

Legislative Assembly of Manitoba (2005b). Bill 11: *The Provincial Court Amendment Act (Justices of the Peace).* Retrieved July 29, 2006, from web2. gov .mb.ca/bills/sess/b011e.php.

Lewis, R., Dobash, R.E., Dobash R.P. & Cavanagh, K. (2001). Law's progressive potential: The value of engagement with the law for domestic violence. *Social & Legal Studies. 10, 1,* 105–130.

Lewis, R., Dobash, R.P., Dobash, R.E. & Cavanagh, K. (2000). Protection, prevention, rehabilitation or justice? Women's use of the law to challenge domestic violence. *Internation Review of Victimology, 7,* 179–205.

Liss, M.B. & Stahly, G.B. (1993). Domestic violence and child custody. In M. Hansen & M. Harway (Eds.), *Battering and family therapy: A feminist perspective* (pp. 175–187). Newbury Park, CA: Sage.

Locke, D. & Code, R. (2000). *Canada's shelters for abused women, 1999–2000,*

Juristat Statistics Canada. Ottawa: Minister of Industry.

Logan, T., Walker, R., Horvath, L. & Leukefeld, C. (2003). Divorce, custody, and spousal violence: A random sample of circuit court docket records. *Journal of Family Violence, 18* (5), 269–279.

MacDonald, B. (2001). The Domestic Violence and Stalking, Prevention, Protection and Compensation Act. *Manitoba Law Journal, 28,* 269–286.

MacLeod, L. (1987). *Battered but not beaten: Preventing wife battering in Canada.* Ottawa: Canadian Advisory Council on the Status of Women.

MacLeod, L. (1994). *Understanding and charting our progress toward the prevention of woman abuse: An exploration of the contribution to prevention made by projects on woman abuse.* Ottawa: Minister of Supply and Services Canada. Retrieved September 18, 2006, from www.phac-aspc.gc.ca/ncfv-cnivf/familyviolence/html/femprogres_e.html.

Manitoba Association of Women and the Law (1991). *Gender equity in the courts: Criminal Law.* Winnipeg: author.

Manitoba Justice (2005a). *The Domestic Violence and Stalking Act*: Training and information package. Winnipeg: Victim Services Branch.

Manitoba Justice (March, 2005b). Domestic Violence and Stalking Act Information Session. Seminar conducted by Manitoba Justice, Victim Services Branch. Winnipeg.

Manitoba Law Reform Commission (1997). *Stalking* (Report No. 98). Winnipeg: Government of Manitoba.

Manitoba Law Reform Commission (1999). *Adult protection and elder abuse* (Report No. 103). Winnipeg: author.

Martin, D.L., & Mosher, J.E. (1995). Unkept promises: Experiences of immigrant women with the neo-criminalization of wife abuse. *Canadian Journal of Women and the Law, 8,* 3–44.

Martin, S.L., Harris-Britt, A., Li, Y., Moracco, K.E., Kupper, L.L. & Campbell, J. (2004). Changes in intimate partner violence during pregnancy. *Journal of Family Violence, 19,* 201–210.

Maxwell, C.D., Garner, J.H. & Fagan, J.A. (July, 2001). The effects of arrest on intimate partner violence: New evidence from the Spouse Assault Replication Program. In National Institute of Justice, *Research in Brief.* Washington, DC: U.S. Department of Justice. Available online at www.ncjrs.org/txtfiles1/nij/188199.txt.

McGillivray, A. & Comaskey, B. (1999). *Black eyes all the time: Intimate violence,*

Aboriginal women, and the justice system. Toronto: University of Toronto Press.

McGregor, M., Tutty, L., Babins-Wagner, R., & Gill, M. (2002). The long term impact of group treatment for partner abuse. *Canadian Journal of Community Mental Health, 21*, 67–84.

Mechanic, M.B., Weaver, T.L. & Resick, P. (2000). Intimate partner violence and stalking behavior: Explorations of patterns and correlates in a sample of acutely battered women. *Violence and Victims, 15*, 55–72.

Mechanic, M.B., Uhlmansiek, M., Weaver, M. & Resick, P. (2001). The impact of severe stalking experienced by acutely battered women: An examination of violence, psychological symptoms and strategic responding. *Violence and Victims, 15*, 443–458.

Mihorean, K. (2005). Trends in self-reported spousal violence. In K. AuCoin (Ed.), *Family violence in Canada: A statistical profile, 2005*. Catalogue no. 85-224-XIE. Ottawa: Statistics Canada, Canadian Centre for Justice Statistics.

Minaker, J. (2001). Evaluating criminal justice responses to intimate abuse through the lens of women's needs. *Canadian Journal of Women and the Law, 13*, 74–106.

Ministry of the Attorney General. (2001). Implementing the Domestic Violence Court Program. Toronto: Ministry of the Attorney General.

Montminy, L., Roy, V., Lindsay, J. & Turcotte, D. (July, 2003). *Therapeutic factors in groups for abusive men: Quantitative results and qualitative description*. Paper presented at the 8th International Family Violence Research Conference, Portsmouth, NH.

Mullen, P.E., Pathe, M., Purcell, R. & Stuart, G.W. (1999). A study of stalkers. *American Journal of Psychiatry, 156*, 1244-1249.

National Council of Juvenile and Family Court Judges (1994). *Model code for domestic violence*. Reno, NV: author. Available online at www.ncjfcj.org/dept/fvd/publications/main.cfm?Action=PUBGET&Filename=new_mod elcode.pdf.

National Institute of Justice (1996). Domestic violence, stalking, and anti-stalking legislation. *An annual report to Congress under the Violence Against Women Act: Research report*. Washington, DC: author.

Neilson, L. (2004). Assessing mutual partner-abuse claims in child custody and access cases. *Family Court Review, 42*, 411–43.

Nixon, K., Tutty, L.M., Weaver-Dunlop, G. & Walsh, C. (2007). Do good intentions beget good policy? A review of child protection policies to address intimate partner violence. *Children and Youth Services Review, 29,* 1469–1486.

Ogrodnik, L. (2006). Spousal violence and repeat police contact. In L. Ogrodnik (Ed.), *Family violence in Canada: A statistical profile 2006* (pp. 11–19). Ottawa: Ministry of Industry.

Ontario Domestic Violence Death Review Committee (2004). *Annual report to the Chief Coroner.* Toronto: Office of the Chief Coroner.

Ontario Ministry of the Attorney General (1993). *Crown policy manual.* Toronto: author.

Ontario Ministry of the Attorney General (2001). *Implementing the Domestic Violence Court Program.* Toronto: author.

Palmer, S., Brown, R. & Barrera, M. (1992). Group treatment program for abusive husbands: Long-term evaluation. *American Journal of Orthopsychiatry, 62,* 276–283.

Pathe, M. & Mullen, P.E. (1997). The impact of stalkers on their victims. *British Journal of Psychiatry, 170,* 12–17.

Pedlar, D. (1991). *The domestic violence review into the administration of justice in Manitoba.* Winnipeg: Manitoba Justice.

Pottie Bunge, V. (2000). Spousal violence. In Pottie Bunge V. & D. Locke, (Eds.), *Family violence in Canada: A statistical profile, 2000* (pp. 11–26). Ottawa: Canadian Centre for Justice Statistics. Catalogue no. 85-224-XIE.

Pottie Bunge, V. & Levett, A. (1998). *Family violence in Canada: A statistical profile.* Ottawa: Statistics Canada.

Prairie Research Associates (1996). *Review of the Saskatchewan Victims of Domestic Violence Act.* Ottawa: Department of Justice Canada.

Prairie Research Associates (1999). *A further review of the Saskatchewan Victims of Domestic Violence Act.* Ottawa: Department of Justice Canada.

Ptacek, J. (1999). *Battered women in the courtroom: The power of judicial responses.* Boston: Northeastern University Press.

Ramsden, C. & Bonner, M. (2002). A realistic view of domestic violence screening in an emergency department. *Accident and Emergency Nursing, 10,* 31–39.

Rigakos, G.S. (2002). *Peace bonds and violence against women: A three-site study of the effect of Bill C-42 on process, application and enforcement.* Ottawa: Department of Justice Canada.

Roberts, A.R. & Everly, G.S. (2006). A meta-analysis of 36 crisis intervention studies. *Brief Treatment & Crisis Intervention, 6,* 10–21.

Roberts, T. (1996). *Spousal assault and mandatory charging in the Yukon: Experiences, perspectives and alternatives.* Ottawa: Department of Justice Canada, Research and Statistics Division.

Rosenbaum, A., Gearan, P.J. & Ondovic, C. (2001). Completion and recidivism among court referred and self-referred batterers in a psychoeducational group treatment program: Implications for intervention and public policy. *Journal of Aggression, Maltreatment and Trauma, 5,* 199–220.

Russell, M. (2002). *Measures of empowerment for women who are victims of violence and who use the justice system.* Prepared for Victim Services Division, Ministry of Public Safety and Solicitor General, government of British Columbia

Schmidt, J. & Hochstedler Steury, E. (1989). Prosecutorial discretion in filing charges in domestic violence cases. *Criminology, 27,* 487–510.

Schuldberg, D. & Guisinger, S. (2001). Divorced fathers describe their former wives: Devaluation and contrast. In S. Volgy (Ed.), *Women and divorce/ Men and divorce: Differences in separation, divorce, and remarriage* (pp. 61–87). New York: Haworth Press.

Schulman, P.W. (1997). Commission of inquiry into the deaths of Rhonda Lavoie and Roy Lavoie: A study of domestic violence and the justice system in Manitoba. Winnipeg: Queen's Printer.

Scott, K.L. & Crooks, C.V. (2004). Effecting change in maltreating fathers: Critical principles in intervention. *Clinical Psychology: Science and Practice, 11,* 95–111.

Scott, K.L. & Wolfe, D.A. (2000). Change among batterers: Examining men's stories. *Journal of Interpersonal Violence, 15,* 827–842.

Sebba, L. (1996). *Third parties: Victims and the criminal justice system.* Columbus, OH: Ohio State University Press.

Shaffer, M. & Bala, N. (2004). The role of family courts in domestic violence: The Canadian experience. In L. Baker, P. Jaffe, & A. Cunningham (Eds.), *Ending domestic violence in the lives of children and parents: Promising practices for safety, healing, and prevention* (pp. 171–187). New York: Guilford Press.

Sheeran, M. & Hampton, S. (1999). Supervised visitation in cases of domestic violence. *Juvenile and Family Court Journal, 50*, 13–25.

Shepard, M.F. (1999). Evaluating coordinated community response. In M.F. Shepard & E. Pence (Eds.), *Coordinating community responses to domestic violence: Lessons from Duluth and beyond* (pp. 169-191). Thousand Oaks, CA: Sage.

Sherman, L. (1992). The influence of criminology on criminal law: Evaluating for misdemeanor domestic violence. *Journal of Criminal Law and Criminology, 85*, 901–945.

Snider, L. (1998). Struggles for justice: Criminalization and alternatives. In K.D. Bonnycastle & G.S. Rigakos (Eds.), *Unsettling truths: Battered women, policy politics and contemporary Canadian research.* (pp.145–155). Vancouver: Vancouver Collective Press.

Snider, L. (2006). Making change in neo-liberal times. In G. Balfour & E. Comack (Eds.), *Criminalizing women* (pp. 323–342). Halifax, NS: Fernwood Publishing.

Standing Senate Committee on Human Rights (2003). *A hard bed to lie in: Matrimonial real property on reserve. Interim Report of the Standing Senate Committee on Human Rights.* Ottawa: author.

Stark, E. (2007). *Coercive control: How men entrap women in personal life.* New York: Oxford University Press.

Statistics Canada (1999). *Violence Against Women Survey: A statistical profile.* Ottawa: Minister of Industry.

Statistics Canada (2000). *Family violence in Canada: A statistical profile 2000.* Ottawa: Canadian Centre for Justice Statistics. Catalogue no. 85-224-XIE.

Statistics Canada (2001). *Domestic violence in Canada: A statistical profile 2001.* Ottawa: Minister of Industry.

Statistics Canada (2002). *Family violence in Canada: A statistical profile.* Ottawa: Minister of Industry.

Statistics Canada (2004a). *Crime Statistics in Canada, 2004.* Ottawa: Minister of Industry.

Statistics Canada (2004b). *Domestic violence in Canada: A statistical profile 2001.* Ottawa: Minister of Industry.

Statistics Canada (2005a). *Family violence in Canada: A statistical profile 2005.* Ottawa: Canadian Centre for Justice Statistics. Catalogue no. 85-224-XIE.

Statistics Canada (June 15, 2005b). Shelters for abused women 2003/2004.

The Daily. Ottawa: Statistics Canada Catalogue no. 11-001-XIE.

Strack, G. (n.d.). She hit me too: Identifying the primary aggressor: A prosecutor's perspective. National Centre on Domestic and Sexual Violence. Retrieved July 14, 2005, from www.ncdsv.org/images/She_hit_me.pdf.

Strange, C. (1995). "Historical Perspectives on Wife Assault" in M. Valverde, L. MacLeod & K. Johnson (Eds.), *Wife assault and the canadian criminal justice system*, (pp. 293–304). Toronto: University of Toronto Press.

Taylor-Butts, A. (2007). Canada's shelters for abused women, 2005–2006. *Juristat: Canadian Centre for Justice Statistics, 27*, 1–20. Available online at www.statcan.ca/english/freepub/85-002-XIE/85-002-XIE2007004.pdf.

Thistlewaite, A., Wooldredge, J. & Gibbs, D. (1998). Severity of dispositions and domestic violence recidivism. *Crime & Delinquency, 44*, 388–398.

Thurston, W.E., Tutty, L.M., Eisener, A., Lalonde, L., Belenky, C. & Osborne, B. (in press). Implementation of universal screening for domestic violence in an urgent care community health centre. *Health Promotion Practice*.

Tjaden, P. & Thoennes, N. (1998). *Stalking in America: Findings from the National Violence Against Women Survey*. Research report of the National Institute of Justice and Centers for Disease Control and Prevention. Washington, DC: Center for Policy Research, U.S. Department of Justice.

Tjaden, P. & Thoennes, N. (2000). *Extent, nature and consequences of intimate partner violence*. Washington, DC: National Institutes of Justice.

Tolman, R.M. & Weisz, A. (1995). Coordinated community intervention for domestic violence: The effects of arrest and prosecution on recidivism of woman abuse perpetrators. *Crime & Delinquency, 41*, 481–495.

Tomz, J.E. & McGillis, D. (1997). *Serving crime victims and witnesses* (2nd ed.). Washington, DC: U.S. Department of Justice.

Trobert, J.F. (2001). *The Victims of Domestic Violence Act* revisited: A practitioner's guide. *The Saskatchewan Advocate, 3*, 24–26.

Trocmé, N., Fallon, B., MacLaurin, B., Daciuk, J., Felstiner, C., Black, T., Tonmyr, L., Blackstock, C., Barter, K., Turcotte, D. & Cloutier, R. (2005). *Canadian incidence study of reported child abuse and neglect — 2003: Major findings*. Ottawa: Minister of Public Works and Government Services Canada.

Tsai, B. (2000). The trend toward specialized domestic violence court: Improvements on an effective innovation. *The Fordham Review, 68*, 1285–1327.

Turner, J. (1995). Saskatchewan responds to family violence: *The Victims of*

Domestic Violence Act, 1995. In M. Valverde, L. MacLeod & K. Johnson (Eds.), *Wife assault and the criminal justice system* (pp. 183–197). Toronto: University of Toronto.

Turpel, M.E. (1991). Home/land. *Canadian Journal of Family Law, 10*, 17–40.

Tutty, L. (1999). *Domestic violence involving firearms in Alberta: Case studies of women and children*. Final report to The Canadian Firearms Centre. Ottawa: Department of Justice Canada.

Tutty, L. (2006). *Effective practices in sheltering women leaving violence in intimate relationships: Phase II*. Final report to the YWCA Canada. Available online at www.ywca.ca/public_eng/advocacy/Shelter/YWCA_Shelter Report_EN.pdf.

Tutty, L., & Goard, C. (Eds.) (2002). *Reclaiming self: Issues and resources for women abused by intimate partners*. Halifax: Fernwood.

Tutty, L. & Rothery, M. (2002). How well do emergency shelters assist women and their children? In L. Tutty & C. Goard (Eds.), *Reclaiming self: Issues and resources for women abused by intimate partners* (pp.25–42). Halifax: Fernwood.

Tutty, L., Babins-Wagner, R. & Rothery, M. (2006). Group treatment for aggressive women: An initial evaluation. *Journal of Family Violence, 21*, 341–349.

Tutty, L., Bidgood, B., Rothery, M. & Bidgood, P. (2001). An evaluation of men's batterer treatment groups: A component of a co-ordinated community response. Research on Social Work Practice, 11, 645–670.

Tutty, L., Koshan, J., Jesso, D. & Nixon, K. (May, 2005). *Alberta's Protection Against Family Violence Act: A summative evaluation*. Alberta's Office for the Prevention of Family Violence. Calgary: RESOLVE Alberta.

Tutty, L., Ursel, J. et al. (forthcoming). *Evaluating the justice and community responses to family violence in the Canadian prairie provinces*. Calgary: RESOLVE Alberta.

Tutty, L.M. & Nixon, K. (2004). *How domestic assault victims perceive Calgary's HomeFront Court*. Final report to the HomeFront Evaluation Committee. Available online at www.homefrontcalgary.com/statistics/index.htm.

Tutty, L.M., Barlow, A. & Weaver-Dunlop, J. (2007). Supervised access and exchange programs: Safety for parents and children in the context of domestic violence. In K. Kendall-Tackett & S. Giacomoni (Eds.), *Intimate partner violence*. (pp. 25-1–25-19). Kingston, NJ: Civic Research Institute.

Ursel, E.J. (2006). "Over policed and under protected." A question of justice for Aboriginal women. In M. Hampton & N. Gerrard (Eds.) *Intimate partner violence: Reflections on experience, theory, and policy.* (pp. 80, 99). Toronto: Cormorant Books.

Ursel, J. (1991). Considering the impact of the battered women's movement on the state: The example of Manitoba. In E. Comack & S. Brickey (Eds.), *The social basis of Law* (pp. 261–288). Halifax: Garamond Press.

Ursel, J. (1992). A progress report on the Family Violence Court in Winnipeg. *Manitoba Law Journal, 21,* 100–130.

Ursel, J. (1998a). Eliminating violence against women: Reform or co-optation in state institutions. In L. Samuelson & W. Antony (Eds.), *Social problems: Thinking critically.* (pp. 73, 81). Halifax: Garamond Press.

Ursel, J. (1998b). "Mandatory charging policy: The Manitoba model." In K. Bonnycastle & G. Rigakos (Eds.), *Unsettling truths: Battered women, policy, politics, and contemporary research in Canada.* Vancouver: Vancouver Collective Press.

Ursel, J. (2000). Winnipeg Family Violence Court report. In *Family violence in Canada: A statistical profile 2000.* Ottawa: Canadian Centre for Justice Statistics, Statistics Canada.

Ursel, J. (2002). "His sentence is my freedom": Processing domestic violence cases in the Winnipeg Family Violence Court. In L. Tutty & C. Goard (Eds.), *Reclaiming self: Issues and resources for women abused by intimate partners* (pp. 43–63). Halifax: Fernwood.

Ursel, J., Gorkoff, K. (1996) *The Impact of Manitoba Corrections Partner Abuse Treatment Program on recidivism.* Prepared for Manitoba Department of Justice, Winnipeg. RESOLVE Manitoba.

U.S. Department of Justice (1998). *New directions from the field: Victims' rights and services for the 21st century.* Washington, DC: author.

U.S. Department of Justice (2004). *Stalking.* Washington: National Centre for Victims of Crime, Stalking Resource Center.

Van de Veen, S.L. (September, 2003). *Some Canadian problem solving court processes.* Canadian Association of Provincial Court Judges Pre-Institute Conference Held September 2003. St. John's, Newfoundland: National Judicial Institute.

Varcoe, C. (2001). Abuse obscured: An ethnographic account of emergency nursing in relation to violence against women. *Canadian Journal of Nursing Research, 32,* 95–115.

Ventura, L.A. & Davis, G. (2005). Domestic violence: Court case conviction and recidivism. *Violence Against Women, 11*, 255–277.

Walker, L.E. (1979). *The battered woman.* New York: Harper and Row.

Weaver-Dunlop, J., Nixon, K., Tutty, L., Walsh, C. & Ogden, C. (2006). *A review of policies to address children/youth exposed to domestic violence.* Background paper prepared for the International Policy Forum on Family Violence.

Websdale, N. (2003). Reviewing domestic violence deaths. *National Institute of Justice Journal, 250*, 26–31.

Websdale, N., Town, M. & Johnson, B. (1999). Domestic violence fatality reviews: From a culture of blame to a culture of safety. *Juvenile and Family Court Journal, 50*, 61–74.

Weisz, A.N., Tolman, R.M. & Bennett, L. (1998). An ecological study of non-residential battered women within a comprehensive community protocol for domestic violence. *Journal of Family Violence, 13*, 395–415.

Whittemore, K.E. & Kropp, P.R. (2002). Spousal Assault Risk Assessment: A guide for clinicians. *Journal of Forensic Psychology Practice, 2*, 53–64.

Wiegers, W. & Douglas, F. (2007). *Civil domestic violence legislation in Saskatchewan: An assessment of the first decade.* Saskatoon, SK: Canadian Plains Research Centre

Wilson, M., Johnson, H. & Daly, M. (1995). Lethal and nonlethal violence against wives. *Canadian Journal of Criminology, 37*, 331–361.

Worden, A.P. (2000). The changing boundaries of the criminal justice system: Redefining the problem and the response in domestic violence, *Criminal Justice 2000* (pp. 215–266). Washington: U.S. Department of Justice. Available online at www.ncjrs.gov/criminal_justice2000/vol_2/02g2.pdf.

Yukon Department of Justice. (1993). *Final report of the committee to assess the responsiveness of Yukon Justice to family violence.* Yukon Department of Justice.

Zorza, J. (1995). How abused women can use the law to help protect their children. In E. Peled, P.G Jaffe & J.L. Edleson (Eds.), *Ending the cycle of violence: Community responses to children of battered women* (pp. 147–169). Thousand Oaks, CA: Sage.

Legislation

Adult Interdependent Relationships Act, S.A. 2002, c. A-4.5.

The Constitution Act, 1867 (U.K.), 30 & 31 Victoria, c. 3.

The Constitution Act, 1982, being Schedule B to the Canada Act 1982 (U.K.), 1982, c. 11.

Criminal Code, R.S.C., 1985, c. C-46.

The Domestic Violence and Stalking, Prevention, Protection and Compensation Act S.M. 1998. c. 41, C.C.S.M. c.D93 (renamed as The Domestic Violence and Stalking Act in S.M. 2004 c.13).

The Family Maintenance Act, C.C.S.M. c. F20.

First Nations Land Management Act, S.C. 1999, c.24.

Indian Act, R.S.C. 1985, c. I-5.

The Provincial Court Act, R.S.M. 1987, c. C275.

Protection Against Family Violence Act, R.S.A. 2000, c. P-27.

Protection Against Family Violence Amendment Act, S.A. 2006, c. 8.

Protection Against Family Violence Regulation, Alta. Reg. 80/99.

Victims of Domestic Violence Act, S.S. 1994, c. V-6.02.

Victims of Domestic Violence Regulation, R.R.S. c. V-6.02 Reg. 1.

Case Law

A.L.G.C. v. Prince Edward Island (Government of) (1998), CanLII 5189 (PEISCTD).

Ballingal-Scotten v. Wayne 2005 MBQB 12 (Manitoba Queen's Bench).

Baril v. Obelnicki 2004 MBQB 92 (Manitoba Queen's Bench).

Baril v. Obelnicki 2004 MBQB 92 (Manitoba Queen's Bench); 2007 MBCA 40 (Manitoba Court of Appeal).

Bella v. Bella, 1995 CanLII 5659 (Saskatchewan Queen's Bench).

Darbyshire-Joseph v. Darbyshire-Joseph, 1998 CanLII 3522 (British Columbia Superior Court).

Derrickson v. Derrickson, 1986 CanLII 56 (Supreme Court of Canada).

Dolgopol v. Dolgopol, 1995 CanLII 5717 (Saskatchewan Queen's Bench).

Dumlao v. Simon, [2005] A.J. No. 548 (Alberta Queen's Bench) (Quicklaw).

Dunstan v. Dunstan 2002 BCSC 335 (CanLII) (British Columbia Superior Court).

Dyck v. Dyck, 2005 SKQB 247 (CanLII). (Saskatchewan Queen's Bench).

K.K.O. v. O.K.O. , [2005] A.J. No. 72. (Alberta Queen's Bench) (Quicklaw).

MacDonald v. Kwok (1997), 159 Saskatchewan Reports 238 (Saskatchewan Queen's Bench).

Nichol v. Hawes (1997), 31 Reports on Family Law (4th) 399 (Saskatchewan Queen's Bench).

Paul v. *Paul*, 1986 CanLII 57 (Supreme Court of Canada).

Residential Tenancies Act (Nova Scotia) 1996 Can LII 259 (Supreme Court of Canada).

Shaw v. *Shaw*, [2000] M.J. 115 (Manitoba Queen's Bench) (Quicklaw).

Siwiec v. *Hlewka*, [2005] A.J. No.1182 (Alberta Queen's Bench) (Quicklaw).

T.L.O. v. *K.J.S.*, [2004] A.J. No. 1040 (Alberta Queen's Bench) (Quicklaw).

T.P. v. *J.P.*, [2005] A.J. No. 874 (Alberta Queen's Bench) (Quicklaw).

About the Authors

NICHOLAS BALA (law.queensu.ca//facultyAndStaff/facultyProfiles/bala.html) has been a professor at the Faculty of Law at Queen's University in Kingston since 1980, and has been a visiting professor at McGill University, Duke Law School and the University of Calgary. He has law degrees from Queen's (LL.B. 1977) and Harvard (LL.M. 1980). Professor Bala's primary area of teaching and research interest is family and children's law, focusing on such issues as juvenile justice; child abuse and child witnesses; the best interests of children; parental rights and responsibilities after divorce; support obligations; the legal definition of the family, including same-sex marriage; the Canadian Charter of Rights and family law; and the applicability in Canada of the United Nations Convention on the Rights of the Child.

MIKE BOYES is an associate professor in the psychology department at the University of Calgary. In addition to his scholarly activities he does program evaluation work with family violence, early intervention and parenting programs. Mike and his wife, fellow psychologist Nancy Ogden, share their lives with six children, two dogs and two cats.

KAREN BUSBY (Law, Manitoba) is a lawyer, teacher, researcher and activist concerned with various issues touching on law, violence, sex and sexuality.

JANIE CHRISTENSEN is a social worker born and raised in the Calgary area. Janie has worked in the field of family violence for over 10 years, including shelter work, research and extensive group counselling with men and women. Janie is currently the supervisor of adult programs at the YWCA Sheriff King Home in Calgary.

CLAIRE CROOKS is currently the associate director of the CAMH Centre for Prevention Science. She is also a research associate at the Centre for Research in Violence Against Women and Children of the University of Western Ontario (www.uwo.ca/violence). Her main research emphasis revolves around the development, implementation and evaluation of the Fourth R, a relationship-based curriculum aimed at preventing other risk behaviours in adolescents. The Fourth R is currently being piloted in 22 schools (11 demonstration and 11 control) in the Thames Valley District School Board (www.tvdsb.on.ca).

MYRNA DAWSON is an associate professor at the Department of Sociology and Anthropology, University of Guelph, Ontario. Her research focuses on trends and patterns in violence as well as social and legal responses to violent victimization, specifically intimate partner violence. Her publications appear in *Law & Society Review, The British Journal of Criminology, Social Problems, Justice Quarterly, Homicide Studies* and *Resources for Feminist Research.*

RONIT DINOVITZER is an assistant professor of sociology at the University of Toronto. Her collaborative research with Myrna Dawson on specialized domestic violence courts has been published in *British Journal of Criminology* and in *Justice Quarterly*. Her current research focuses on the social organization of the legal profession and a panel study of Toronto youth. She is the author of "Lawyer Satisfaction in the Process of Structuring Legal Careers" (with Bryant Garth), which was recently published in *Law & Society Review.*

FIONA DOUGLAS manages the Social Policy Research Unit (SPR), Faculty of Social Work, at the University of Regina. She was a founding member of RESOLVE Saskatchewan and a representative on the RESOLVE board. She is author of *Emergency Intervention Orders in Saskatchewan* (2006), available through SPR.

DEB GEORGE is proud of her rural Prairie roots. Deb has lived in Saskatch-ewan all her life and is a graduate of the University of Regina's Human Justice Program. She discovered her life's passion when she began working at a crisis shelter for women and children fleeing abuse and violence; today, she is the coordinator of Family Service Regina's Domestic Violence Programs. Deb and her partner Ken have a blended family of three sons, two daughters, two daughters-in-law and two granddaughters.

CARMEN GILL, Ph.D., is currently the director of the Muriel McQueen Fergusson Centre for Family Violence Research at the University of New Brunswick and is cross-appointed as an associate professor of sociology. She is leading *The Canadian Observatory on the Justice System's Response to Intimate Partner Violence* funded by the Social Sciences and Humanities Research Council of Canada.

CHRISTINE HAGYARD is a graduate student at the University of Toronto in the Department of Criminology. She worked as the coordinator of the Winnipeg Family Violence Court study for four years while studying at the University of Manitoba. Her areas of interest are woman abuse and child abuse and the justice system response.

JOSEPH P. HORNICK is executive director of the Canadian Research Institute for Law and the Family (CRILF), an independent institute affiliated with the University of Calgary. Dr. Hornick has conducted numerous studies related to law and the family and most recently published a report entitled *The Domestic Violence Treatment Option (DVTO), Whitehorse, Yukon: Final Evaluation Report*, which contained the results of a four-year evaluation of a special domestic violence treatment court in the Yukon.

PETER G. JAFFE, Ph.D., is a professor in the Faculty of Education at the University of Western Ontario and the Academic Director of the Centre for Research on Violence Against Women & Children. He is the Director Emeritus for the Centre for Children and Families in the Justice System, which is a chil-dren's mental health centre specializing in issues that bring children and families into the justice system in London, Ontario. He has co-authored nine books, 24 chapters and over 70 articles related to children, families and the justice system, including *Children of Battered Women* and *Working Together to End Domestic Violence*.

JENNIFER KOSHAN is an associate professor at the University of Calgary, Faculty of Law. Her research and teaching interests are in the areas of constitutional law, human rights, violence against women, feminist legal theory and public interest advocacy.

CHERYL LAURIE is a policy analyst at the Manitoba Women's Directorate, working in the areas of violence against women, Aboriginal women's experiences of violence and women's access to justice. Her main research focus has been domestic violence, particularly stalking by former intimate partners.

JANICE LEMAISTRE is a judge for the provincial court of Manitoba. She was appointed a judge of the provincial court in November 2006. Judge leMaistre worked for Manitoba Justice as a Crown attorney prior to her appointment and specialized for 12 years in the area of domestic violence prosecutions. She supervised the Domestic Violence Unit, Prosecutions, for seven years and had the opportunity to participate in the development of a number of initiatives involving domestic violence issues in the criminal justice system.

REKHA MALAVIYA is a Crown attorney for Manitoba Justice in Winnipeg. She began her legal career in June 2001 as a prosecutor in the Domestic Violence Unit (DVU). She was the Acting Supervising Senior Crown Attorney of the DVU from November 2006 to May 2008. Previous to her legal career, she was the coordinator of various programs at a local shelter for abused women for almost 11 years and currently chairs on the board of this shelter. In addition, she has worked as a counsellor for street-involved individuals and IV drug users.

KEVIN MCNICHOL, M.Sc. Counselling Psychology (University of Calgary), has worked for 12 years as a counsellor in domestic violence programs in Calgary and is currently the executive director of HomeFront, the society for the prevention of domestic violence, which brings together law enforcement, justice and community-based domestic violence serving agencies forming a coordinated community response to domestic violence. Kevin is the proud and exhausted father of two young children and married to a wonderfully supportive wife, Joanna.

KENDRA NIXON is a doctoral candidate in the Faculty of Social Work at the University of Calgary, Alberta. Kendra's research interests include child exposure to intimate partner violence, mothering in the context of intimate partner violence, violence against women, family and social policy and qualitative research methodology. Kendra is a research associate with RESOLVE Alberta.

LESLIE M. TUTTY is a full professor with the Faculty of Social Work at the University of Calgary. Over the past 20 years, her research has focused on services for family violence, including a number of evaluations of shelter and post-shelter programs for abused women, support groups for abused women, treatment for adult and child victims of sexual abuse and groups for men who abuse their partners. Since 1999, Leslie has served as the Academic Research Coordinator of RESOLVE Alberta, a tri-provincial research institute on family violence.

JANE URSEL is the Director of RESOLVE, a tri-provincial research network on intimate partner violence and associate professor in the Department of Sociology at the University of Manitoba. She is the principal investigator of the Winnipeg Family Violence Court study, which has collected data for 17 years. She is also the principal investigator of a longitudinal study of women's experience of intimate partner violence, "The Healing Journey," funded by SSHRC through the CURA program.

LEAH WHITE has worked for the past six and a half years at Victims Services/ Family Violence Prevention Unit in Whitehorse, Yukon, as a counsellor for men and women who choose to use violence in their intimate relationships. She worked as a research assistant for the DVTO evaluation. She has worked for 17 years as a front-line social worker with marginalized persons in the areas of domestic violence, women's issues and organizations, HIV/AIDS, child protection and grief work.

WANDA WIEGERS is an associate professor in the College of Law at the University of Saskatchewan. Her teaching and research interests focus on feminist and critical legal theory, family law, violence against women, children and the law, income security policy and poverty and the law.

Acknowledgements

This collaboration is a result of our ongoing work at RESOLVE, a tri-provincial Prairie research network that coordinates and conducts research aimed at ending intimate partner and interpersonal violence and abuse. Our ability to conduct our research and collaborate across the three Prairie provinces is due to the substantial operational support we receive from the Prairie Action Foundation (PAF). Not only do PAF members fund RESOLVE, they are also very active promoters and customers of our books. The editors and Cormorant Books appreciate their enthusiasm and interest in our publications.

This is the seventh book in our publication series and we are very pleased to have chapters from our colleagues associated with the Alliance of Family Violence Research Centres across Canada. We have a number of authors from Ontario and a contributor from New Brunswick. We are grateful to all of the authors who put such effort into the writing and editing process as well as to the service agencies that provided support and encouragement for this work.

This is our first book to focus exclusively on the law and its role in addressing the issues of family violence. The work could not have been done without the substantial contribution from a number of courts and court personnel across Canada. The access our authors were provided to court documents was critical to our ability to collect the data we present in this book. The introduction of specialized courts has generated an interest in evaluation of these courts within the justice system. We appreciate the co-operation we have received from justice officials in Ontario, Manitoba, Saskatchewan, Alberta and the Yukon. We especially want to acknowledge the 72 women who shared their stories about their encounters with the justice system. They have provided a critical perspective on the impact of the law on women's lives.

A special thank you to Holly Johnson, an expert in the field who found time in her busy schedule to comment on early drafts of the chapters. We appreciate her sharp eye, helpful comments and the excellent foreword she has written for this book.

A substantial portion of our research reported in this book was made possible by the Social Sciences and Humanities Research Council of Canada, which funded the Community University Research Alliance project "Evaluating the Justice and Community Response to Domestic Violence in The Prairie Provinces" (Leslie Tutty and Jane Ursel, co-principle investigators). The Alberta Law Foundation also supported the project financially; to both organizations, we extend our sincere appreciation.

The list of co-investigators for this project is long but deserves mention; without the team of academics and community members the research would not have been possible. Thanks to Karen Busby (Faculty of Law, U of Manitoba); Fiona Douglas (U of Regina); David Este (U of Calgary); Carmen Gill (U of R); Jennifer Koshan (Faculty of Law, U of C); Sarla Sethi (Faculty of Nursing, U of C); Wilfreda (Billie) Thurston (Community Health Sciences, U of C); Elizabeth Thomlinson (Faculty of Nursing, U of C); Lee Tunstall (U of C); Wanda Wiegers (Faculty of Law, U of S) and Stephen Wormith (U of S).

Access to the provincial justice data was facilitated by Deputy Minister Bruce McFarland (Manitoba), Francis Remedios (Alberta Justice) and Ms. Frankie Jordan (Saskatchewan Justice). The community agency collaborators included Rod McKendrick (Saskatchewan Justice); Robbie Babins-Wagner (Calgary Counselling); Karen Walroth (Action Committee Against Violence); and Irene Hoffart and Michele Clarke (Synergy Research). Lastly, although numerous research assistants assisted with this project, Christine Hagyard and Cheryl Laurie of the University of Manitoba and Kendra Nixon of the University of Calgary took leadership in several key aspects of the project.

We appreciate and admire the creativity of the artist, Teri Posyniak, who produced the artwork for the cover of this book. A number of individuals at Cormorant Books were essential to the final product: Marc Côté, publisher; and Tannice Goddard and Bryan Jay Ibeas for their book design and layout. We'd also like to thank Beth McAuley, copyeditor for the volume.

Finally, assembling a book involves many hours of editing and formatting that is done first at RESOLVE and later by the publishers. We owe a special thank you to our dear friend and former office manager, Dianne Bulback, for her sharp eye, formatting finesse and great generosity with her time. She was the midwife of this book, which had a rather long gestation.